Quest for Examined Beliefs

A Thematic Introduction to Religious Studies

REVISED EDITION

Edited by Hemchand Gossai

Georgia Southern University

cognella™
San Diego, CA

Bassim Hamadeh, CEO and Publisher
Christopher Foster, General Vice President
Michael Simpson, Vice President of Acquisitions
Jessica Knott, Managing Editor
Kevin Fahey, Cognella Marketing Manager
Jess Busch, Senior Graphic Designer
Zina Craft, Acquisitions Editor
Jamie Giganti, Project Editor
Brian Fahey, Licensing Associate

Printed in the United States of America

ISBN: 978-1-62131-378-6 (pbk)

www.cognella.com 800.200.3908

For
Annika Elizabeth and
Maren Ann

Contents

Introduction

Religion plays a key role in the modern world despite the fact that its relevance might not be immediately apparent to some. Whether or not one considers oneself to be religious; whether or not one sees religion as a positive or negative institution; whether one believes in God or not, the reality is that religion, its practice and effects are inextricably woven into the fabric of modern life. Throughout history, religion has been an inextricable part of life, whether or not the ideas or actions were classified as religious. That the root of the word *religion* (from the Latin *religare*) intimates a *binding to* means that, at some level, whatever one binds oneself to, whatever provides guidance and answers to life's questions, could be deemed as religious. Many of these questions are not altogether different from those that our ancestors posed thousands of years ago. Where did we come from? Where are we going? What is our purpose? Why is there suffering, pain, and evil in the world? Is there an afterlife? While the answers to these questions vary among different religions, it is significant that each religious system has confronted and continues to confront the same questions in one form or another. In response to some of these very questions, the poet Rainer Maria Rilke wrote , "…be patient toward all that is unsolved in your heart and try to love the *questions themselves* like locked rooms and like books that are written in a very foreign tongue. Do not now seek the answers, which cannot be given you because you will not be able to live them. And the point is, to live everything. *Live* the questions now." (*Letters to a Young Poet,* p. 35) Two of the related benefits in exploring religion are the discovery and understanding of other perspectives ("how such questions are asked") and to measure one's own beliefs (the "answers to the questions") against the beliefs of others.

Religion is so deeply a part of everyday life, with all of its vagaries and challenges, that it is commonly understood that polite conversation avoids mention of the topic, in order to avoid arguments that have more heat than light. In fact, religion is so pervasive that any attempt to navigate around or through it, howsoever careful, will likely result in conflict. Yet, can one truly avoid the topic of religion and all of its intricate connections and still have a substantive understanding of the world in which we live? Ultimately, it seems that this would only create substantial gaps in awareness and conversation topics!

For many, religion plays an essential role in making sense of the meaning of human existence, both in this life and what might be waiting in the hereafter. These individuals turn to religion to help contend with issues and questions that are simply beyond the scope and purview of human intellect and capacity for explanation, either logically or emotionally. Many individuals throughout history have exploited this all too human wish for comfort and clarity to satisfy their own agendas. They have abused religious thought and belief in the name of individual gain, political expediency and dominance, maintaining of power and perpetuation of social structure. Over the years, terrorism, slavery, ethnic cleansing, and genocide have all been justified in the name of religion. As a result, religion has that unique quality of being simultaneously a distinctly positive worldview and the compelling force behind many of the more atrocious and painful moments in human history.

The vast majority of persons who claim a religious affiliation or identify themselves as religious do so on the basis of inherited beliefs. This is hardly surprising, given that the world is comprised of many nations and regions that are predominantly of one religion or religious denomination: Catholics, Anglicans, Lutherans, Hindus, Muslims, Buddhists, among others. Inherited beliefs certainly introduce much good in terms of the connections that they establish with our ancestors in the form of tradition and ceremony. Yet there are certainly challenges to inherited beliefs, particularly those inherited beliefs that have been embraced without critical thought. In the United States, the subservience of women, and the institution of slavery, to name two of the more pointed examples, were both grounded in biblical mandates or, at the very least, in biblical

interpretation. I believe that it is incumbent upon all who claim a religious affiliation to critically examine what they believe, to do so in a way that offers a true challenge to one's most cherished beliefs. T.S. Eliot in his *Four Quartets* captured this:

> We shall not cease from exploration
> And the end of all our exploring
> Will be to arrive at where we started
> And know the place for the first time.

Socrates' well-known maxim that the unexamined life is not worth living might very well be adapted here: "The unexamined belief is not worth having."

This text brings together thirty articles, essays, sacred texts, a letter, and an interview, all of which explore religion and various aspects of life. The categories of this volume have therefore been organized to help illuminate the relationship between religion and various aspects of life, community, and the world. In every instance I presuppose the essential intersection between the vertical (God, Ultimate Reality) and the horizontal (humanity), intimating that if one is religious, one must, by necessity, practice what it means to be religious. Given this scope, it is practically impossible to cover every aspect in this volume; the choices made reflect what I see as particular and immediate interest and relevance. With a multitude of methodologies available, the choice in these pieces is but a small representation, and the various perspectives expressed will, I believe, lay the foundation for an informed conversation about the respective topics. Of course not everyone will agree with the choices in this text, but these essays will assuredly benefit those who engage with the topics and the arguments. In addition to their examination of key existential questions, these pieces also have practical implications.

In reading these pieces you will come to appreciate the wide interconnectedness of religion: politics, science, gender, notions of justice, peace, war, nationhood, suffering, evil, all are intertwined with religion. At some point, almost everyone will contend with one or more of these issues, and invariably the role and/or the presence of God will be invoked or engaged. Moreover, this very interconnectedness by definition gives religion an interdisciplinary character, making it further worthy of critical study. We will therefore encounter in these pieces a breadth of perspectives that reflect a variety of methodologies and approaches, experiences, ideologies and backgrounds. While this text is heavily weighted by Western tradition, the range is still decidedly wide in perspective. No one religion is given a privileged position, or established as the center from which all others will be compared and judged. Instead, in our exploration and examination, every religion highlighted is studied on its own merit.

Section 1

Excerpts from Sacred Texts

Rig Veda: The Hymn of Man

Purusa, the Cosmic Person

Thousand-headed is Purusa, thousand-eyed, thousand-footed. Having covered the earth on all sides, he stood above it the width of ten fingers.

Only Purusa is all this, that which has been and that which is to be. He is the lord of the immortals, who grow by means of [ritual] food.

Such is his greatness, yet more than this is Purusa. One-quarter of him is all beings; three-quarters of him is the immortal in heaven.

Three-quarters of Purusa went upward, one-quarter of him remained here. From this [one-quarter] he spread in all directions into what eats and what does not eat.

From him the shining one was born, from the shining one was born Purusa. When born he extended beyond the earth, behind as well as in front.

When the gods performed a sacrifice with the offering Purusa, spring was its clarified butter, summer the kindling, autumn the oblation.

It was Purusa, born in the beginning, which they sprinkled on the sacred grass as a sacrifice.

With him the gods sacrificed, the demi-gods, and the seers.

From that sacrifice completely offered, the clotted butter was brought together. It made the beasts of the air, the forest and the village.

From that sacrifice completely offered, the mantras [Rig Veda] and the songs [Samaveda] were born. The meters were born from it. The sacrificial formulae [Yajurveda] were born from it.

From it the horses were born and all that have cutting teeth in both jaws. The cows were born from it, also. From it were born goats and sheep.

When they divided Purusa, how many ways did they apportion him? What was his mouth? What were his arms? What were his thighs, his feet declared to be?

His mouth was the Brahman [caste], his arms were the Rajanaya [Ksatriya, warrior caste], his thighs the Vaisya [artisan caste]; from his feet the Sudra [servant caste] was born.

The moon was born from his mind; from his eye the sun was born; from his mouth both Indra and Agni [fire]; from his breath Vayu [wind] was born.

From his navel arose the air; from his head the heaven evolved; from his feet the earth; the [four] directions from his ear. Thus, they fashioned the worlds.

Seven were his altar sticks, three times seven were the kindling bundles, when the gods, performing the sacrifice, bound the beast Purusa.

The gods sacrificed with the sacrifice to the sacrifice. These were the first rites. These powers reached the firmament, where the ancient demi-gods and the gods are.

The Nature of Man is Evil

Hsün Tzu

The nature of man is evil; his goodness is the result of his activity. Now, man's inborn nature is to seek for gain. If this tendency is followed, strife and rapacity result and deference and compliance disappear. By inborn nature one is envious and hates others. If these tendencies are followed, injury and destruction result and loyalty and faithfulness disappear. By inborn nature one possesses the desires of ear and eye and likes sound and beauty. If these tendencies are followed, lewdness and licentiousness result, and the pattern and order of propriety and righteousness disappear. Therefore to follow man's nature and his feelings will inevitably result in strife and rapacity, combine with rebellion and disorder, and end in violence. Therefore there must be the civilizing influence of teachers and laws and the guidance of propriety and righteousness, and then it will result in deference and compliance, combine with pattern and order, and end in discipline. From this point of view, it is clear that the nature of man is evil and that his goodness is the result of activity.

Crooked wood must be heated and bent before it becomes straight. Blunt metal must be ground and whetted before it becomes sharp. Now the nature of man is evil. It must depend on teachers and laws to become correct and achieve propriety and righteousness and then it becomes disciplined. Without teachers and laws, man is unbalanced, off the track, and incorrect. Without propriety and righteousness, there will be rebellion, disorder, and chaos. The sage-kings of antiquity, knowing that the nature of man is evil, and that it is unbalanced, off the track, incorrect, rebellious, disorderly, and undisciplined, created the rules of propriety and righteousness and instituted laws and systems in order to correct man's feelings, transform them, and direct them so that they all may become disciplined and conform with the Way (Tao). Now people who are influenced by teachers and laws, accumulate literature and knowledge, and follow propriety and righteousness are superior men, whereas those who give rein to their feelings, enjoy indulgence, and violate propriety and righteousness are inferior men. From this point of view, it is clear that the nature of man is evil and that his goodness is the result of activity.

Mencius said, "Man learns because his nature is good" (6A:1-8). This is not true. He did not know the nature of man and did not understand the distinction between man's nature and his effort. Man's nature is the product of Nature; it cannot be learned and cannot be worked for. Propriety and righteousness are produced by the sage. They can be learned by men and can be accomplished through work. What is in him and can be learned or accomplished through work is what can be achieved through activity. This is the difference between human nature and human activity. Now by nature man's eye can see and his ear can hear. But the clarity of vision is not outside his eye and the distinctness of hearing is not outside his ear. It is clear that clear vision and distinct hearing cannot be learned. Mencius said, "The nature of man is good; it [becomes evil] because man destroys his original nature." This is a mistake. By nature man departs from his primitive character and capacity as soon as he is born, and he is bound to destroy it. From this point of view, it is clear that man's nature is evil.

By the original goodness of human nature is meant that man does not depart from his primitive character but makes it beautiful, and does not depart from his original capacity but utilizes it, so that beauty being [inherent] in his primitive character and goodness being [inherent] in his will are like clear vision being inherent in the eye and distinct hearing being inherent in the ear. Hence we say that the eye is clear and the ear is sharp. Now by nature man desires repletion when hungry, desires warmth when cold, and desires rest when tired. This is man's natural feeling. But not when a man is hungry and sees some elders before him, he does not eat ahead of them but yields to them. When he is tired, he dares not seek rest because he wants to take over the work [of elders]. The son

yielding to or taking over the work of his older brother—these two lines of action are contrary to original nature and violate natural feeling. Nevertheless, the way of filial piety is the pattern and order of propriety and righteousness. If one follows his natural feeling, he will have no deference or compliance. Deference and compliance are opposed to his natural feelings. From this point of view, it is clear that man's nature is evil and that his goodness is the result of activity.

Someone may ask, "If man's nature is evil, whence come propriety and righteousness?" I answer that all propriety and righteousness are results of the activity of sages and not originally produced from man's nature. The potter pounds the clay and makes the vessel. This being the case, the vessel is the product of the artisan's activity and not the original product of man's nature. The artisan hews a piece of wood and makes a vessel. This being the case, the vessel is the product of the artisan's activity and not the original product of man's nature. The sages gathered together their ideas and thoughts and became familiar with activity, facts, and principles, and thus produced propriety and righteousness and instituted laws and systems. This being the case, propriety and righteousness and laws and systems are the products of the activity of the sages and not the original products of man's nature.

As to the eye desiring color, the ear desiring sound, the mouth desiring flavor, the heart desiring gain, and the body desiring pleasure and ease—all these are products of man's original nature and feelings. They are natural reactions to stimuli and do not require any work to be produced. But if the reaction is not naturally produced by the stimulus but requires work before it can be produced, then it is the result of activity. Here lies the evidence of the difference between what is produced by man's nature and what is produced by his effort. Therefore the sages transformed man's nature and aroused him to activity. As activity was aroused, propriety and righteousness were produced, and as propriety and righteousness were produced, laws and systems were instituted. This being the case, propriety and righteousness, laws, and systems are all products of the sages. In his nature, the sage is common with and not different from ordinary people. It is in his effort that he is different from and superior to them.

It is the original nature and feelings of man to love profit and seek gain. Suppose some brothers are to divide their property. If they follow their natural feelings, they will love profit and seek gain, and thus will do violence to each other and grab the property. But if they are transformed by the civilizing influence of the pattern and order of propriety and righteousness, they will even yield to outsiders. Therefore, brothers will quarrel if they follow their original nature and feeling but, if they are transformed by righteousness and propriety, they will yield to outsiders.

People desire to be good because their nature is evil. If one has little, he wants abundance. If he is ugly, he wants good looks. If his circumstances are narrow, he wants them to be broad. If poor, he wants to be rich. And if he is in a low position, he wants a high position. If he does not have it himself, he will seek it outside. If he is rich, he does not desire more wealth, and if he is in a high position, he does not desire more power. If he has it himself, he will not seek it outside. From this point of view, [it is clear that] people desire to be good because their nature is evil.

Now by nature a man does not originally possess propriety and righteousness; hence he makes strong effort to learn and seek to have them. By nature he does not know propriety and righteousness; hence he thinks and deliberates and seeks to know them. Therefore, by what is inborn alone, man will not have or know propriety and righteousness. There will be disorder if man is without propriety and righteousness. There will be violence if he does not know propriety and

righteousness. Consequently by what is inborn alone, disorder and violence are within man himself. From this point of view, it is clear that the nature of man is evil and that his goodness is the result of his activity.

Mencius said, "The nature of man is good." I say that this is not true. By goodness at any time in any place is meant true principles and peaceful order, and by evil is meant imbalance, violence, and disorder. This is the distinction between good and evil. Now do we honestly regard man's nature as characterized by true principles and peaceful order? If so, why are sages necessary and why are propriety and righteousness necessary? What possible improvement can sages make on true principles and peaceful order?

Now this is not the case. Man's nature is evil. Therefor the sages of antiquity, knowing that man's nature is evil, that it is unbalanced and incorrect, and that it is violent, disorderly, and undisciplined, established the authority of rulers to govern the people, set forth clearly propriety and righteousness to transform them, instituted laws and governmental measures to rule them, and made punishment severe to restrain them, so that all will result in good order and be in accord with goodness. Such is the government of sage-kings and the transforming influence of propriety and righteousness.

But suppose we try to remove the authority of the ruler, do away with the transforming influence of propriety and righteousness, discard the rule of lases and governmental measure, do away with the restraint of punishment, and stand and see how people of the world deal with one another. In this situation, the strong would injure the weak and rob them, and the many would do violence to the few and shout them down. The whole world would be in violence and disorder and all would perish in an instant. From this point of view, it is clear that man's nature is evil and that his goodness is the result of activity.

Job Chapters 1-2

Job

Job and His Family

There was once a man in the land of Uz whose name was Job. That man was blameless and upright, one who feared God and turned away from evil. There were born to him seven sons and three daughters. He had seven thousand sheep, three thousand camels, five hundred yoke of oxen, five hundred donkeys, and very many servants; so that this man was the greatest of all the people of the east. His sons used to go and hold feasts in one another's houses in turn; and they would send and invite their three sisters to eat and drink with them. And when the feast days had run their course, Job would send and sanctify them, and he would rise early in the morning and offer burnt-offerings according to the number of them all; for Job said, 'It may be that my children have sinned, and cursed God in their hearts.' This is what Job always did.

Attack on Job's Character

One day the heavenly beings came to present themselves before the Lord, and Satan also came among them. The Lord said to Satan, 'Where have you come from?' Satan* answered the Lord, 'From going to and fro on the earth, and from walking up and down on it.' The Lord said to Satan, 'Have you considered my servant Job? There is no one like him on the earth, a blameless and upright man who fears God and turns away from evil.' Then Satan answered the Lord, 'Does Job fear God for nothing? Have you not put a fence around him and his house and all that he has, on every side? You have blessed the work of his hands, and his possessions have increased in the land. But stretch out your hand now, and touch all that he has, and he will curse you to your face.' The Lord said to Satan,* 'Very well, all that he has is in your power; only do not stretch out your hand against him!' So Satan went out from the presence of the Lord.

Job Loses Property and Children

One day when his sons and daughters were eating and drinking wine in the eldest brother's house, a messenger came to Job and said, 'The oxen were ploughing and the donkeys were feeding beside them, and the Sabeans fell on them and carried them off, and killed the servants with the edge of the sword; I alone have escaped to tell you.' While he was still speaking, another came and said, 'The fire of God fell from heaven and burned up the sheep and the servants, and consumed them; I alone have escaped to tell you.' While he was still speaking, another came and said, 'The Chaldeans formed three columns, made a raid on the camels and carried them off, and killed the servants with the edge of the sword; I alone have escaped to tell you.' While he was still speaking, another came and said, 'Your sons and daughters were eating and drinking wine in their eldest brother's house, and suddenly a great wind came across the desert, struck the four corners of the house, and it fell on the young people, and they are dead; I alone have escaped to tell you.'

Then Job arose, tore his robe, shaved his head, and fell on the ground and worshipped. He said, 'Naked I came from my mother's womb, and naked shall I return there; the Lord gave, and the Lord has taken away; blessed be the name of the Lord.'

In all this Job did not sin or charge God with wrongdoing.

Attack on Job's Health

One day the heavenly beings came to present themselves before the Lord, and Satan also came among them to present himself before the Lord. The Lord said to Satan, 'Where have you come from?' Satan answered the Lord, 'From going to and fro on the earth, and from walking up and down on it.' The Lord said to Satan, 'Have you considered my servant Job? There is no one like him on the earth, a blameless and upright man who fears God and turns away from evil. He still persists in his integrity, although you incited me against him, to destroy him for no reason.' Then Satan answered the Lord, 'Skin for skin! All that people have they will give to save their lives. But stretch out your hand now and touch his bone and his flesh, and he will curse you to your face.' The Lord said to Satan,' 'Very well, he is in your power; only spare his life.'

So Satan went out from the presence of the Lord, and inflicted loathsome sores on Job from the sole of his foot to the crown of his head. Job took a potsherd with which to scrape himself, and sat among the ashes.

Then his wife said to him, 'Do you still persist in your integrity? Curse God, and die.' But he said to her, 'You speak as any foolish woman would speak. Shall we receive the good at the hand of God, and not receive the bad?' In all this Job did not sin with his lips.

Job's Three Friends

Now when Job's three friends heard of all these troubles that had come upon him, each of them set out from his home—Eliphaz the Temanite, Bildad the Shuhite, and Zophar the Naamathite. They met together to go and console and comfort him. When they saw him from a distance, they did not recognize him, and they raised their voices and wept aloud; they tore their robes and threw dust in the air upon their heads. They sat with him on the ground for seven days and seven nights, and no one spoke a word to him, for they saw that his suffering was very great.

The Parable of the Good Samaritan

Luke 10:25-37

Just then a lawyer stood up to test Jesus. 'Teacher,' he said, 'what must I do to inherit eternal life?' He said to him, 'What is written in the law? What do you read there?' He answered, 'You shall love the Lord your God with all your heart, and with all your soul, and with all your strength, and with all your mind; and your neighbour as yourself.' And he said to him, 'You have given the right answer; do this, and you will live.'

But wanting to justify himself, he asked Jesus, 'And who is my neighbour?' Jesus replied, 'A man was going down from Jerusalem to Jericho, and fell into the hands of robbers, who stripped him, beat him, and went away, leaving him half dead. Now by chance a priest was going down that road; and when he saw him, he passed by on the other side. So likewise a Levite, when he came to the place and saw him, passed by on the other side. But a Samaritan while travelling came near him; and when he saw him, he was moved with pity. He went to him and bandaged his wounds, having poured oil and wine on them. Then he put him on his own animal, brought him to an inn, and took care of him. The next day he took out two denarii, gave them to the innkeeper, and said, "Take care of him; and when I come back, I will repay you whatever more you spend." Which of these three, do you think, was a neighbour to the man who fell into the hands of the robbers?' He said, 'The one who showed him mercy.' Jesus said to him, 'Go and do likewise.'

The Chapter Of Women

The Quran *IV* (Medina)

In the name of the merciful and compassionate Allah.

O ye folk! fear your Lord, who created you from one soul, and created there from its mate, and diffused from them twain many men and women. And fear Allah, in whose name ye beg of one another, and the wombs; verily, Allah over you doth watch.'

And give unto the orphans their property, and give them not the vile in exchange for the good, and devour not their property to your own property; verily, that were a great sin. But if ye fear that ye cannot do justice between orphans, then marry what seems good to you of women, by twos, or threes, or fours; and if ye fear that ye cannot be equitable, then only one, or what your right hands possess. That keeps you nearer to not being partial.

And give women their dowries freely; and if they are good enough to remit any of it of themselves, then devour it with good digestion and appetite."

But do not give up to fools' their property which Allah has made you to stand by; but maintain them from it, and clothe them, and speak to them with a reasonable speech. [sJ Prove orphans until they reach a marriageable age, and if ye perceive in them right management, then hand over to them their property, and do not devour it extravagantly in anticipation of their growing up. And he who is rich, let him abstain; but he who is poor, let him devour in reason, and when ye hand over to them their property, then take witnesses against them; but Allah sufficeth for taking account.

Men should have a portion of what their parents and kindred leave, and women should have a portion of what their parents and kindred leave, whether it be little or much, a determined portion. And when the next of kin and the orphans and the poor are present at the division, then maintain them out of it, and speak to them a reasonable speech. [IO] And let these fear lest they leave behind them a weak seed, for whom they would be afraid; and let them fear Allah, and speak a straightforward speech. Verily, those who devour the property of orphans unjustly, only devour into their bellies fire, and they shall broil in flames.

Allah instructs you concerning your children; for a male the like of the portion of two females, and if there be women above two, then let them have two-thirds of what (the deceased) leaves; and if there be but one, then let her have a half; and as to the parents, to each of them a sixth of what he leaves, if he has a son; but if he have no son, and his parents inherit, then let his mother have a third, and if he have brethren, let his mother have a sixth after payment of the bequest he bequeaths and of his debt.

Your parents or your children, ye know not which of them is nearest to you in usefulness:-an ordinance this from Allah; verily, Allah is knowing and wise! And ye shall have half of what your wives leave, if they have no son; but if they have a son, then ye shall have a fourth of what they leave, after payment of the bequests they bequeath or of their debts. And they shall have a fourth of what ye leave, if ye have no son; but if ye have a son, then let them have an eighth of what ye leave, after payment of the bequest ye bequeath and of your debts.

[IsJ And if the man's or the woman's (property) be inherited by a kinsman who is neither parent nor child,' and he have a brother or sister, then let each of these two have a sixth; but if they are more than that, let them share in a third after payment of the bequest he bequeaths and of his debts, without prejudice. An ordinance this from Allah, and Allah is knowing and clement!

These be Allah's bounds, and whoso obeys Allah and the Apostle He will make him enter into gardens beneath which rivers flow, and they shall dwell therein for aye;—that is the mighty happiness.

But whoso rebels against Allah and His Apostle, and transgresses His bounds, He will make him enter into fire, and dwell therein for aye; and for him is shameful woe.

Against those of your women who commit adultery, call witnesses four in number from among yourselves; and if these bear witness, then keep the women in houses? until death release them, or Allah shall make for them a way.

[20] And if two of you commit then hurt them both! but if they turn again and amend, leave them alone, verily, Allah is easily turned, compassionate.

Allah is only bound to turn again towards those who do evil through ignorance and then turn again. Surely, these will Allah turn again to, for Allah is knowing, wise. His turning again is not for those who do evil, until, when death comes before one of them, he says, 'Now I turn again'; nor yet for those who die in misbelief. For such as these have we prepared a grievous woe.

O ye who believe! it is not lawful for you to inherit women's estates against their will; nor to hinder them? that ye may go off with part of what ye brought them, unless they commit fornication manifestly; but associate with them in reason, for if ye are averse from them, it may be that ye are averse from something wherein Allah has put much good for you.

But if ye wish to exchange one wife for another, and have given one of them a talent,[10] then take not from it anything. What! would you take it for a calumny and a manifest crime?"

[25] How can ye take it when one of you has gone in unto the other, and they have taken from you a rigid compact?

And do not marry women your fathers married,—except bygones,—for it is abominable and hateful, and an evil way; unlawful for you are your mothers, and your daughters, and your sisters, and your paternal aunts and maternal aunts, and your brother's daughters, and your sister's daughters, and your foster mothers, and your foster sisters, and your wives' mothers, and your step daughters who are your wards, born of your wives to whom ye have gone in; but if ye have not gone in unto them, then it is no crime in you; and the lawful spouses of your sons from your own loins, and that ye form a connexion between two sisters,—except bygones,—verily, Allah is forgiving, merciful; and married women, save such as your right hands possess,—Allah's Book against you!—but lawful for you is all besides this, for you to seek them with your wealth, marrying them and not fornicating; but such of them as ye have enjoyed, give them their hire as a lawful due; for there is no crime in you about what ye agree between you after such lawful due, verily, Allah is knowing and wise.

But whosoever of you cannot go the length of marrying marriageable women who believe, then take of what your right hands possess, of your maidens who believe;- though Allah knows best about your faith. Ye come one from the other; then marry them with the permission of their people, and give them their hire in reason, they being chaste and not fornicating, and not receivers of paramours.

[30] But when they are married, if they commit fornication, then inflict upon them half the penalty for married women; that is for whomsoever of you fears wrong; but that ye should have patience is better for you, and Allah is forgiving and merciful.

Allah wishes to explain to you and to guide you into the ordinances of those who were before you, and to turn towards you, for Allah is knowing, wise. Allah wishes to turn towards you, but those who follow their lusts wish that ye should swerve with a mighty swerving! Allah wishes to make it light for you, for man was created weak.

O ye who believe! devour not your property amongst yourselves vainly, unless it be a merchandise by mutual consent. And do not kill yourselves; verily, Allah is compassionate unto you.

But whoso does that maliciously and unjustly, we will broil him with fire; for that is easy with Allah.

[35] If ye avoid great sins from which ye are forbidden, we will cover your offences and make you enter with a noble entrance.

And do not covet that by which Allah has preferred one of you over another. The men shall have a portion of what they earn, and the women a portion of what they earn; ask Allah for His grace, verily, Allah knows all.

To everyone have we appointed kinsfolk as heirs of what parents and relatives and those with whom ye have joined right hands leave; so give them their portion, for, verily, Allah is over all a witness.

Men stand superior to women in that Allah hath preferred some of them over others, and in that they expend of their wealth: and the virtuous women, devoted, careful (in their husbands') absence, as Allah has cared for them. But those whose perverseness ye fear, admonish them and remove them into bedchambers and beat them; but if they submit to you, then do not seek a way against them; verily, Allah is high and great.

And if ye fear a breach between the two, then send a judge from his people and a judge from her people. If they wish for reconciliation, Allah will arrange between them; verily, Allah is knowing and aware.

[40] And serve Allah, and do not associate aught with Him; and to your parents show kindness, and to kindred, and orphans, and the poor, and the neighbour who is akin, and the neighbour who is a stranger, and the companion who is strange, and the son of the road, and what your right hands possess, i} verily, Allah loves not him who is proud and boastful; who are miserly and bid men be miserly too, and who hide what

Allah has given them of His grace;—but we have prepared for the misbelievers shameful woe.

And those who expend their wealth in alms for appearance sake before men, and who believe not in Allah nor in the last day;—but whosoever has Satan for his mate, an evil mate has he.

What harm would it do them if they believed in Allah and in the last day, and expended in alms of what Allah has provided them with? but Allah knows about them.

Verily, Allah would not wrong by the weight of an atom; and if it's' a good work, He will double it and bring from Himself a mighty hire.

[4s] How then when we bring from every nation a witness, and bring thee as a witness against these on the day when those who misbelieve and rebel against the Apostle would fain that the earth were levelled with them? But they cannot hide the news from Allah.

O ye who believe! approach not prayer while ye are drunk, until ye well know what ye say; nor yet while polluted,—unless ye be passing by the way,—until ye have washed yourselves. But if ye are sick, or on a journey, or one of you come from the privy, or if ye have touched a woman, and ye cannot find water, then use good surface sand and wipe your faces and your hands therewith; verily, Allah pardons and forgives.

Do ye not see those who have been given a portion of the Book? They buy error, and they wish that ye may err from the way! But Allah knows best who your enemies are, and Allah suffices as a patron, and sufficient is Allah as a help.

And those who are Jews, and those who pervert the words from their places, and say, 'We hear but we rebel, and do thou listen without hearing: and (who say) 'rd'hind', 's distorting it with their tongues and taunting about religion. But had they said, 'We hear and we obey, so listen and look upon us: it would have been better for them and more upright;—but may Allah curse

them in their misbelief, for they will not believe except a few.

[50] O ye who have been given the Book! believe in what we have revealed, confirming what ye had before; ere we deface your faces and turn them into hinder parts, or curse you as we cursed the fellows of the Sabbath." when Allah's command was done.

Verily, Allah pardons not associating aught with Him, but He pardons anything short of that to whomsoever He pleases; but he who associates aught with Allah, he hath devised a mighty sin.

Do ye not see those who purify themselves? Nay, Allah purifies whom He will, and they shall not be wronged a straw.

Behold, how they devise against Allah a lie, and that is manifest sin enough.

Do ye not see those to whom a portion of the Book has been given? They believe in Jibt and Taghut's and they say of those who misbelieve. 'These are better guided in the way than those who believe: [55] These are those whom Allah has cursed, and whom Allah has cursed no helper shall he find.

Shall they have a portion of the kingdom? Why even then they would not give to men a jot.'?

Do they envy man for what Allah has given of His grace? We have given to Abraham's people the Book and wisdom, and we have given them a mighty kingdom. And of them are some who believe therein, and of them are some who turn from it, but Hell is flaming enough for them.

Verily, those who disbelieve in our signs, we will broil them with fire; whenever their skins are well done, then we will change them for other skins, that they may taste the torment. Verily, Allah is glorious and wise.

[60] But those who believe and do aright, we will make them enter gardens beneath which rivers flow, and they shall dwell therein for ever and aye, for them therein are pure wives, and we will make them enter into a shady shade. Verily,

Allah bids you pay your trusts to their owners, and when ye judge between men to judge with justice. Verily, Allah, excellent is what He admonishes you with; verily, Allah both hears and sees.

O ye who believe! obey Allah, and obey the Apostle and those in authority amongst you; and if ye quarrel about anything, refer to Allah and the Apostle, if ye believe in Allah and the last day; that is better and fairer as a settlement.

Do ye not see those who pretend that they believe in what has been revealed to them, and what was revealed before thee; they wish to refer their judgement to Taghut, but they are bidden to disbelieve therein, and Satan wishes to them into a remote error. And when it is said to them, 'Come round to what Allah has sent down and unto the Apostle: thou seest the hypocrites turning from thee, turning away.

[65] How then when there befalls them a mischance through what their hands have sent on before? Then will they come to you, and swear by Allah, 'We meant naught but good and concord: These, Allah knows what is in their hearts. Turn thou away from them and admonish them, and speak to them into their souls with a searching word.

We have never sent an apostle save that he should be obeyed by the permission of Allah; and if they, when they have wronged themselves, come to thee and ask pardon of Allah, and the Apostle asks pardon for them, then they will find Allah easy to be turned, compassionate.

But no! by thy Lord! they will not believe, until they have made thee judge of what they differ on; then they will not find in themselves aught to hinder what thou hast decreed, and they will submit with submission. But had we prescribed for them, 'Kill yourselves, or go ye forth out of your houses: they would not have done it, save only a few of them; but had they done what they are admonished, then it would have been better for them, and a more firm assurance.

[70] And then we would surely have brought them from ourselves a mighty hire, and would have guided them into a right path.

Whoso obeys Allah and the Apostle, these are with those Allah has been pleased with, of prophets and confessors and martyrs and the righteous; —a fair company are they.

That is grace from Allah, and Allah knows well enough.

O ye who believe! take your precautions and sally in detachments or altogether. Verily, there is of you who tarries behind, and, if a mischance befalls you, says, has been gracious to me, since I am not with them a martyr:

[75] But if there befalls you grace from Allah, he would say-as though there were no friendship between you and him. 'O would that I had been with thee to attain this mighty happiness!' Let those then fight in Allah's way who sell this life of the world for the next; and whoso fights in Allah's way, then, be he killed or be he victorious, we will give him a mighty hire.

What ails you that ye do not fight in Allah's way, and for the weak men and women and children, who say, Lord, bring us out of this town" of oppressive folk, and make for us from Thee a patron, and make for us from Thee a help'?

Those who believe fight in the way of Allah; and those who disbelieve fight in the way of Taghut: fight ye then against the friends of Satan, verily, Satan's tricks are weak.

Do ye not see those to whom it is said, 'Restrain your hands, and be steadfast in prayer and give alms'; and when it is prescribed for them to fight then a band of them fear men, as though it were the fear of Allah or a still stronger fear, and they say, 'O our Lord! why hast thou prescribed for us to fight, couldst thou not let us abide till our near appointed time?' Say, 'The enjoyment of this world is but slight, and the next is better for him who fears'; but they shall not be wronged a straw.

[80] Wheresoever ye be death will overtake you, though ye were in lofty towers. And if a good thing befall them, they say, 'This is Allah: but if a bad thing, they say, This is from thee. Say, 'It is all from Allah: What ails these people? They can hardly understand a tale.

What befalls thee of good it is from Allah; and what befalls thee of bad it is from thyself. We have sent thee to mankind as an apostle, and Allah sufficeth for a witness.

Whoso obeys the prophet he has obeyed Allah; and he who turns back we have not sent thee to watch over them.

They say, 'Obedience!' but when they sally forth from you, a company of them brood by night over something else than that which thou hast said; but Allah writes down that over which they brood. Turn then from them and rely on Allah, for Allah sufficeth for a guardian. Do they not meditate on the Quran? if it were from other than Allah they would find in it many a discrepancy.

[85] And when there comes to them a matter of security or fear they publish it; but if they were to report it to the Apostle and to those in authority amongst them, then those of them who would elicit it from them would know it; but were it not for Allah's grace upon you and His mercy ye had followed Satan, save a few.

Fight, then, in the way of Allah; impose not aught on any but thyself. and urge on the believers; it may be that Allah will restrain the violence of those who misbelieve, for Allah is more violent and more severe to punish.

Whoso intercedes with a good intercession shall have a portion therefrom; but he who intercedes with a bad intercession shall have the like thereof, for Allah keeps watch over all things.

And when ye are saluted with a salutation, salute with a better than it, Or return it;—verily, Allah of all things takes account.

Allah, there is no Allah but He! He will surely assemble you on the resurrection day, there is no doubt therein; who is truer than Allah in his discourse?

[90] Why are ye two parties about the hypocrites, when Allah hath overturned them for what they earned? Do ye wish to guide those whom Allah hath led astray? Whoso Allah hath led astray ye shall not surely find for him a path. They would fain that ye misbelieve as they misbelieve, that ye might be alike; take ye not patrons from among them until they too flee in Allah's way; but if they turn their backs, then seize them and kill them wheresoever ye find them, and take from them neither patron nor help,—save those who reach a people betwixt whom and you is an alliance—or who come to you while their bosoms prevent them from fighting you or fighting their own people. But had Allah pleased He would have given you dominion over them, and they would surely have fought you. But if they retire from you and do not fight you, and offer you peace, then Allah hath given you no way against them.

Ye will find others who seek for quarter from you, and quarter from their own people; whenever they return to sedition they shall be overturned therein: but if they retire not from you, nor offer you peace, nor restrain their hands, then seize them and kill them wheresoever ye find them;—over these we have made for you manifest 'power.

It is not for a believer to kill a believer save by mistake; and whosoever kills a believer by mistake then let him free a believing neck;" and the blood money must be paid to his people save what they shall remit as alms. But if he be from a tribe hostile to you and yet a believer, then let him free a believing neck. And if it be a tribe betwixt whom and you there is an alliance, then let the blood money be paid to his friends, and let him free a believing neck; but he who cannot find the means, then let him fast for two consecutive months—a penance this from Allah, for Allah is knowing, wise.

[95] And whoso kills a believer purposely, his reward is Hell, to dwell therein for aye; and Allah will be wrath with him, and curse him, and prepare for him a mighty woe.

O ye who believe! when ye are knocking about in the way of Allah be discerning, and do not say to him who offers you a salutation, 'Thou art no believer: craving after the chances of this world's life.' for with Allah are many spoils! So were ye aforetime. but Allah was gracious to you, be ye then discerning; verily, Allah of what ye do is well aware.

Not alike are those of the believers who sit at home without harm, and those who are strenuous in Allah's way with their wealth and their persons. Allah hath preferred those who are strenuous with their wealth and their persons to those who sit still, by many degrees, and to each hath Allah promised good, but Allah hath preferred the strenuous for a mighty hire over those who sit still,- degrees from him, and pardon and mercy, for Allah is forgiving and merciful.

Verily, the angels when they took the souls of those who had wronged themselves said, 'What state were ye in?' they say, 'We were but weak in the earth'; they said, 'Was not Allah's earth wide enough for you to flee away therein?' These are those whose resort is Hell, and a bad journey shall it be!

[100] Save for the weak men, and women, and children, who could not compass any stratagem, and were not guided to a way; these it may be Allah will pardon, for Allah both pardons and forgives.

Whosoever flees in the way of Allah shall find in the earth many a spacious refuge; and he who goes forth from his house, fleeing unto Allah and His prophet, and then death catches him up, his hire devolves on Allah, and Allah is forgiving and merciful.

And when ye knock about in the earth, it is no crime to you that ye come short in prayer, if ye fear that those who disbelieve will set upon you; verily, the misbelievers are your obvious foes.

When thou art amongst them, and standest up to pray with them, then let a party of them stand up with thee, and let them take their arms; and when they adore, let them go behind you, and let another party who have not yet prayed come forward and pray with thee; and let them take their precautions and their arms.

Fain would those who misbelieve that ye were careless of your arms and your baggage, that they might turn upon you with a single turning. And it is no crime to you if ye be annoyed with rain or be sick, that ye lay down your arms; but take your precautions,—verily, Allah has prepared for those who misbelieve a shameful woe.

But when ye have fulfilled your prayer, remember Allah standing and sitting and lying on your sides; and when ye are in safety then be steadfast in prayer; verily, prayer is for the believers prescribed and timed!

[IOS] And do not give way in pursuit of the people; if ye suffer they shall surely suffer too, even as ye suffer; and ye hope from Allah, but they hope not! and Allah is knowing, wise.

Verily, we have revealed to thee the Book in truth that thou mayest judge between men of what Allah has shown thee; so be not with the treacherous a disputant; but ask Allah's pardon: verily, Allah is forgiving, merciful.

And wrangle not for those who defraud themselves; for Allah loves not him who is a fraudulent sinner. They hide themselves from men; but they cannot hide themselves from Allah, for He is with them while they brood at night over speeches that please Him not;-but Allah doth compass what they do!

Here are ye, wrangling for them about this world's life;-but who shall wrangle with Allah for them on the day of judgement, or who shall be a guardian over them?

[no] Yet whoso does evil and wrongs himself, and then asks pardon of Allah, shall find Allah

forgiving and merciful; and whoso commits a crime, he only commits it against himself, for Allah is knowing, wise.

And whoso commits a fault or a sin and throws it on the innocent, he hath to bear a calumny and a manifest sin.

Were it not for Allah's grace upon thee, and His mercy, a party of them would have tried to lead thee astray; but they only lead themselves astray; they shall not hurt you in aught: for Allah hath sent down upon thee the Book and the wisdom, and taught thee what thou didst not know, for Allah's grace was mighty on thee.

There is no good in most of what they talk in private; save in his who bids almsgiving, or kindness, or reconciliation between men; and whoso does this, craving the good pleasure of Allah, we will give to him a mighty hire.

But he who severs himself from the prophet after that we have made manifest to him the guidance, and follows other than the way of the believers, we will turn our backs on him as he hath turned his back; and we will make him reach Hell, and a bad journey shall it be.

Verily, Allah forgives not associating aught with Him, but He pardons anything short of that, to whomsoever he will; but whoso associates aught with Allah, he hath erred a wide error.

Verily, they call not beside Him on aught save females; and they do not call on aught save a rebellious devil.

Allah curse him! for he said, 'I will take from thy servants a portion due to me; and I will lead them astray; and I will stir up vain desires within them; and I will order them and they shall surely crop the ears of cattle; and I will order them and they shall surely after Allah's creation'; but he who takes the devil for his patron Instead of Allah, he loses with a manifest loss. He promises them, and stirs up vain desires within them, but the devil promises only to deceive.

[120] These, their resort is Hell; they shall not find an escape there from! But those who believe, and do what is right, we will make them enter into gardens beneath which rivers flow, to dwell therein for aye,-Allah's promise in truth; and who is truer than Allah in speech? Not for your vain desires, nor the vain desires of the people of the Book. He who doeth evil shall be recompensed therewith, and shall not find for him beside Allah a patron, or a help. But he who doeth good works,—be it male or female,—and believes, they shall enter into Paradise, and they shall not be wronged a jot.

Who has a better religion than he who resigns his face to Allah, and does good, and follows the faith of Abraham, as a hanfj?-for Allah took Abraham as a friend.

[51] And Allah's is what is in the heavens and in the earth, and Allah encompasses all things!

They will ask thee a decision about women; say, 'Allah decides for you about them, and that which is rehearsed' to you in the Book; about orphan women to whom ye do not give what is prescribed for them, and whom ye are averse from marrying; and about weak children; and that ye stand fairly by orphans; and what ye do of good, verily, that Allah knows.

And if a woman fears from her husband perverseness or aversion, it is no crime in them both that they should be reconciled to each other, for reconciliation is best. For souls are prone to avarice; but if ye act kindly and fear Allah, of what ye do He is aware.

Ye are not able, it may be, to act equitably to your wives, even though ye covet it; do not however be quite partial, and leave one as it were in suspense; but if ye be reconciled and fear, then Allah is forgiving and merciful; but if they separate, Allah can make both independent out of His abundance; for Allah is abundant, wise.

[130] Allah's is what is in the heavens and what is in the earth! We have ordained to those

who have been given the He hath revealed this to you in the Book.: "that when ye hear the signs of Allah disbelieved in and mocked then sit ye not down with them until they plunge into another discourse, for verily, then ye would be like them. Verily, Allah will gather the hypocrites and misbelievers into Hell together.

[140] Those who lie in wait for you, and if the victory be yours from Allah. say, 'Were we not with you?' and if the misbelievers have a chance, they say, 'Did we not get the mastery over you, and defend you from the believers?' But Allah shall judge between you on the resurrection day; for Allah will not give the misbelievers a way against believers.

Verily, the hypocrites seek to deceive Allah. but He deceives them; and when they rise up to pray, they rise up lazily to be seen of men, and do not remember Allah, except a few; wavering between the two, neither to these nor yet to those! but whomsoever Allah doth lead astray thou shall not find for him a way.

O ye who believe! take not misbelievers for patrons rather than believers; do ye wish to make for Allah a power against you?

Verily, the hypocrites are in the lowest depths of hell-fire, and thou shalt not find for them a help.

[145] Save those who turn again, and do right, and take tight hold on Allah, and are sincere in religion to Allah; these are with the believers, and Allah will give to the believers mighty hire.

Why should Allah punish you, if ye are grateful and i believe? for Allah is grateful and knowing.

Book before you, and to you too that ye fear Allah; but if ye misbelieve verily, Allah's is what is in the heavens and what is in the earth, and Allah is rich and to be praised!

Allah's is what is in the heavens and what is in the earth! and Allah sufficeth for a guardian!

If He will He can make ye pass away, O men! and can bring others;—Allah is able to do all that.

He who wishes for a reward in this world,-with Allah is the reward of this world and of the next, and Allah both hears and sees.

O ye who believe! be ye steadfast in justice, witnessing before Allah though it be against yourselves, or your parents, or your kindred, be it rich or poor, for Allah is nearer akin than either.

Follow not, then, lusts, so as to act partially; but if ye swerve or turn aside, Allah of what ye do is well aware.

[135] O ye who believe! believe in Allah and His apostles, and the Book which He hath revealed to His Apostle, and the Book which He sent down before; for whoso disbelieves in Allah, and His angels, and His Apostle, and the last day, has erred a wide error.

Verily, those who believe and then misbelieve, and then believe and then misbelieve, and then increase in misbelief, Allah will never pardon them, nor will He guide them in the path.

Give to the hypocrites the glad tidings that for them is grievous woe!

Those who take the misbelievers for their patrons rather than believers, do they crave honour from them? Verily, honour is altogether Allah's!

Allah loves not publicity of evil speech, unless one has been wronged; for Allah both hears and knows.

If ye display good or hide it, or pardon evil, verily, Allah is pardoning and powerful!

Verily, those who disbelieve in Allah and His apostles desire to make a distinction between Allah and His apostles, and say, 'We believe in part and disbelieve in part, and desire to take a midway course between the two': [ISO] these are the misbelievers, and we have prepared for misbelievers shameful woe! But those who believe in Allah and His apostles, and who do not make a distinction between anyone of them, to these we will give their hire, for Allah is forgiving and merciful!

The people of the Book will ask thee to bring down for them a book from heaven; but they asked Moses a greater thing than that, for they said, 'Show us Allah openly'; but the thunderbolt caught them in their injustice. Then they took the calf, after what had come to them of manifest signs; but we pardoned that, and gave Moses obvious authority. And we held over them the mountain at their compact, and said to them, 'Enter ye the door adoring'; and we said to them, 'Transgress not on the Sabbath day': and we took from them a rigid compact.

But for that they broke their compact, and for their misbelief in Allah's signs, and for their killing the prophets undeservedly, and for their saying, 'Our hearts are uncircumcised':-nay, Allah hath stamped on them their so that they cannot believe except a few,—[ISS] and for their misbelief, and for their saying about Mary a mighty calumny, and for their saying, 'Verily, we have killed the Messiah, Jesus the son of Mary, the apostle of Allah' ... but they did not kill him, and they did not crucify him, but a similitude was made for them. And verily, those who differ about him are in doubt concerning him; they have no knowledge concerning him, but only follow an opinion. They did not kill him, for sure! nay, Allah raised him up unto Himself; for Allah is mighty and wise!"

And there shall not be one of the people of the Book but shall believe in him before his death; and on the day of judgement he shall be a witness against them.

And for the injustice of those who are Jews have we forbidden them good things which we had made lawful for them, and for their obstructing so much the way of Allah, and for their taking usury when we had forbidden it, and for their devouring the wealth of people in vain,-but we have prepared for those of them who misbelieve a grievous woe.

[160] But those amongst them who are firm in knowledge, and the believers who believe in what is revealed to thee, let what is revealed before thee, and the steadfast in prayer, and the givers of alms, and the believers in Allah and the last day, unto these we will give a mighty hire.

Verily, we have inspired thee as we inspired Noah and the prophets after him, and as we inspired Abraham, and Jacob, and the tribes, and Jesus, and Job, and Jonas, and Aaron, and Solomon; and to David did we give Psalms.

Of apostles we have already told thee of some before; and of apostles some we have not told thee of; But Moses did Allah speak to, speaking; apostles giving glad tidings and warning, that men should have no argument against Allah, after the apostles, for Allah is mighty, wise!

But Allah bears witness to what He has revealed to thee: He revealed it in His knowledge, and the angels bear witness too; though Allah is witness enough.

[r651] Verily, those who misbelieve and obstruct the way of Allah, have erred a wide error.

Verily, those who misbelieve and are unjust, Allah will not pardon them, nor will He guide them on the road- save the road to Hell, to dwell therein for aye;-that is easy enough to Allah!

O ye folk! the Apostle has come to you with truth from your Lord: believe then, for it is better for you. But if ye misbelieve, then Allah's is what is in the heavens and the earth, and Allah is knowing, wise.

O ye people of the Book! do not exceed in your religion, nor say against Allah aught save the truth. The Messiah, Jesus the son of Mary, is but the apostle of Allah and His Word, which He cast into Mary and a spirit from Him; believe then in Allah and His apostles, and say not 'Three'. Have done! it were better for you. Allah is only one Allah, celebrated be His praise that He should beget a Son! His is what is in the heavens and what is in the earth; and Allah sufficeth for a guardian.

[170] The Messiah doth surely not disdain to be a servant of Allah, nor do the angels who are

nigh to Him; and whosoever disdains His service and is too proud, He will gather them altogether to Himself.

But as for those who believe and do what is right, He will pay their hire and will give increase to them of His grace. But as for those who disdain and are too proud, He will punish them with a grievous woe, and they shall not find for them other than Allah a patron or a help.

O ye folk! proof has come to you from your Lord, and we have sent down to you manifest light. As for those who believe in Allah, and take tight hold of Him, He will make them enter into mercy from Him and grace; and He will guide them to Himself by a right way.

They will ask thee for a decision; say, 'Allah will give you a decision concerning remote kinship?'

If a man perish and have no child, but have a sister, let her have half of what he leaves; and he shall be her heir, if she have no son. But if there be two sisters, let them both have two thirds of what he leaves; and if there be brethren, both men and women, let the male have like the portion of two females. Allah makes this manifest to you lest ye err; for Allah all things doth know.

Section 2

God and Humanity

God

Clive Marsh

Theology begins with god. There would be no justifiable God-talk were it not believed that it makes sense to use the term 'God' in human speech, and that there are traditions of God-talk to which one can relate, and within which one can live one's life. Most who refer to God believe that the word 'God' refers to a reality beyond the thought and experience of the speaker. 'God' names a reality within which one lives, moves and has one's being. Religious traditions are therefore seeking to present in speech a reality to which adherents relate in their daily lives.

God-talk can happen without there being a God (atheists believe this is what happens anyway). But most who use God-talk of any kind believe that human beings are trying to get to grips with a reality which, whilst 'wholly other', must nevertheless be grasped in linguistic form so that that reality may be talked about at all. God's 'wholly otherness' would be uncommunicable without being turned into images, verbal or otherwise. if people are to grasp hold of any sense of God, then there has to be some tradition about the reality of God upon which people can draw in order to come to an understanding of what is being talked about. Only on that basis do people have a chance to test out their experience of human life and work out whether or not they believe that living life 'in relation to God' is either possible or desirable.

The reality of God and concepts of God are not, of course, to be equated. All verbal or visual images of God are at one stage removed from God's reality. God is being 'pictured' in words or images. The reality being pictured remains mysterious, though is usually assumed to be good: the source of all goodness indeed, the goal of creation as well as its originator, supreme benevolence, the ultimate and most just judge of all. But such precision is what has yet to be disclosed, and differences exist across religious traditions. The mysterious reality—God—is not at the beck and call of religious efforts to describe God. But the gap between God as reality and God as described in human images is an important one to respect. The belief that God is, and that God wills what is good for the world, still leaves much open about how humans grasp God and what God wills for the world, and how they fashion the world accordingly. That is the task that theology plays within religious traditions, and within the wider societies of which religions are a part.

All seven chapters in this second part of the book are about grasping hold of a Christian doctrine of God. But there is still a specific task of identifying 'concepts of God' as they appear in society. For it is not immediately apparent to those outside of a religious tradition that, say, notions of human being, heaven, or redemption necessarily have anything to do with God. So we begin in this chapter with concepts of God as they appear in film. In the process of examining a small sample of Western filmic portrayals of God in critical comparison with Christian understandings of God it will be possible to identify some parameters within which all the discussion in this part of the book takes place.

God has been portrayed in a number of different ways in film. From the dramatic actions of God in *The Ten Commandments,* through the white-haired old man of *Oh, God,* to God as a woman in *Dogma,* the images have varied as have the genres of films in which God has 'appeared'. From revered off-screen character (silent or otherwise) to figure of fun (rarely irreverently presented), God has not surprisingly proved a difficult role to play, and still more difficult to cast. Of course, the Christian conviction that when people have to do with Jesus Christ they are dealing with God leads to the reminder that Jesus-films are portrayals of God too. Though true up to a point, even Christians know that the incarnation of God in the person of Jesus Christ does not mean that the whole of God is revealed. Despite Jesus-films, then, there is still an issue about how God is portrayed on screen. Mention of Jesus-films does, however, highlight the fact that for Christians the figure of Jesus Christ is central in theology and religious practice. Even if a Jesus-film is not a direct image of God, then

how God is being imaged is contained within a portrayal of Jesus.

In this opening chapter of Part II, I have opted to explore a recent humorous portrayal of God in film—Morgan Freeman's 'God' in *Bruce Almighty*—and a topical and controversial Jesus-film—Mel Gibson's *The Passion of the Christ.* Alongside these two portrayals I shall refer also to *The Truman Show* in which a God-like figure appears, the overall impact of whom within the film's narrative raises telling questions about what it means to live within a defined 'world' of thought or practice. In this way I am able to examine in general terms how images of God take shape at the cinema and also to begin addressing the question how concepts of God function in Christianity.

Films

Bruce Almighty (Tom Shadyac, *2003*)

Bruce Almighty is a comedy in which Bruce Nolan (Jim Carrey) is a TV reporter who is given the opportunity to play the role of God whilst still living within his normal, everyday world. In response to a rant against God for what he perceives to be an unfair world, after Nolan has had a particularly bad day, God (Morgan Freeman) hands Bruce divine powers. There are just two caveats to his exercise of divine powers: he cannot let people know whose powers he possesses, and he cannot bypass people's exercise of free will.

The result, however, is that Bruce has the chance to put obstacles in the way of his competitors for positions in the TV company for which he works. Bruce's discovery is that the possession of such powers presents him with a frightening, stifling level of responsibility, and that even so, because he cannot make anyone love him, possession of such powers has limited value. Sobered through his encounter with God, he returns to his life appreciative of what he has and of the love of those around him.

The Passion of the Christ (Mel Gibson, 2004)

Much has already been written about this rather unusual film. Hugely successful in terms of viewing figures, *The Passion of the Christ* is a biblical epic in Latin and Aramaic that presents a meditation on the last twelve hours of the life of Jesus of Nazareth, portraying the crucifixion of Jesus with graphic realism. The broader context of the circumstances surrounding Jesus' death is supplied through a series of twelve flashbacks which provide some clue about his earlier life. In the main, however, the focus is on the political intrigue between Jewish and Roman authorities which led to Jesus' conviction and execution and the horror of the acts of humiliation and crucifixion themselves. Notoriously, in the first box-office version of the film (2004) the flogging scene lasted twenty minutes.

The Truman Show (Peter Weir, 1998)

The Truman Show is a satire on the power of the media, and specifically on the genre 'reality TV'. Again starring Jim Carrey, the film portrays the life of Truman Burbank, a figure who lives his life unaware that he is himself the subject of a reality TV show. All other characters who are part of his life are actors, even including his wife (Laura Linney). Burbank's life is lived within a huge TV studio. His every move is monitored and his life orchestrated by Christof (Ed Harris), a TV producer. When blunders begin to occur in the staging of Truman's life he begins to become suspicious. His dramatic discovery of the fabricated nature of his existence occurs when he undertakes a sea journey, survives a staged storm, and makes

it to the edge of the TV studio to confront his 'creator'/producer.

Viewing experiences

These three recent films present explicit and implicit images of God in very different ways. Cognitively, the films present a playful, homely image of a God who supports people in their discovery of love (*Bruce Almighty*), a God entangled in some way in the violence of the world (*The Passion of the Christ*) and, implicitly, as a director-like figure who seeks to control people's every move (*The Truman Show*). Only in the case of the first film is the God-image fully explicit. And through portrayal of God by a black, male actor (Morgan Freeman), though a clear anthropomorphism, a basic stereotype of God-image (as an old, bearded white-man) is undermined. It is, however, not at all clear whether the viewer is intended to 'use' the image of God only as a means to focus on human love (for viewers 'know' that images of God are but stories). Alternatively, the playfulness exercised with the God image in the film can remind viewers that images of God are necessary in human life, though do undergo change. The film may receive either of these responses from viewers. *Bruce Almighty* thus opens up questions both about the function of images of God, and how they relate to any reality 'God'.

The Passion of the Christ offers an image of Christ within a portrayal of the story of Jesus. Without familiarity with the tradition, however, the viewer of this film can be at a great disadvantage. It could be argued that the image of God communicated by this film is that of a bloodthirsty God. Where reference to God and God's will is made explicit in the film, the focus is inevitably on God requiring this suffering from Jesus. The focus is, after all, upon the last hours of Jesus' life. Jesus wonders whether he can carry the weight of the sins of the world (and it is assumed that this is necessary, i.e. that God requires it). When carrying the cross, Jesus expresses his awareness that he is fulfilling the Father's will.

It is the stark presentation of the Passion Narrative (the final chapters in each of the four New Testament Gospels) in relative isolation from the rest of Jesus' life that creates this rather distorted image. In Christian terms, then, the image of God implied is incomplete. A Christian viewer inevitably receives a fuller view of God than a viewer dependent on the film itself (in which a truncated set of Christian convictions is displayed). Knowledge of more of the Christian Gospel narratives than just the endings—not to mention the content of the rest of the Christian Bible—is thus necessary to ensure that a Christian reading of the circumstances of Jesus' life, death and resurrection is grasped. As it stands, *The Passion of the Christ* purports to offer a Christian view of God, though conveys only a partial picture. It leaves a theologically interested viewer merely with a further question: why on earth would early Christians ever have thought that insight into a loving God could be gained through reflection on a crucifixion and its aftermath?

Christof, the director/producer of *The Truman Show*, need not, of course, be seen as a God-figure at all. For the film is clearly about the way in which the boundary between reality and fantasy can be smudged by the way that communication media affects people's perceptions of what is. If seen as a God-figure, then, Christof represents a sinister, lurking, controlling hand. The media have become like a God because of the extent of their influencing of people's experiences and reactions. But if God is like this, the film implies, then this is not a figure who is to be welcomed within human experience.

Affective responses to the three films take us further in our consideration of the God-images they present. Viewers are likely to feel warm towards the God of *Bruce Almighty*. The film's

humour makes us feel good. Morgan Freeman's God, as a supportive presence, helps both Bruce and viewers to develop as people. We are to learn the same lessons as Bruce. And yet we are given mixed messages. We are to leave the cinema also reminded that we are on our own. We may feel good, and feel supported in our endeavours (even by God) to 'be the miracle' (to be active in loving others, and not expect everything to be done for us). But God has disappeared back into the loft (back to heaven?) and has left the task of living to us. The pleasure of the humour viewers experience hides the symbolism of the isolation in which they are left.

In response to *The Passion of the Christ*, as many published reviews have indicated, disgust has mixed with moral outrage for many viewers. Whether Christian or not, viewers have reacted badly to the suggestion that any god would require the brutal execution of a human being in order for the divine will to be fulfilled. The film may be prefaced with words from the prophet Isaiah. It may well be presented as a theological meditation of the death of Jesus. But its affective impact upon many viewers is that grotesque brutality is somehow required by God. The numbing effect of the portrayal of the violence perpetrated against Jesus leads viewers who do not already inhabit a Christian theological thought-world to be immune to the potentially salvific message which such a death might eventually produce.

Christof need not be a God-figure. But the emotional impact of *The Truman Show* as a film can make him more of a God-figure than was intended by the makers of the film. Any form of viewer identification with Truman culminates in the possibility of Truman's liberation from his confinement in the constructed world of 'The Truman Show' as soon as he reaches the edge of the studio. Whether or not motifs such as control of the sea are explicitly acknowledged by viewers as features that link Christof with God the creator, the viewer is invited to share in an experience of breaking out from whatever confines or restricts. In the film, the creator cannot also be the liberator without also destroying the whole experiment. Allowing Truman his freedom from the reality TV show means the end of the show. Viewers of the show *within* the film are all rooting for Truman, urging him to break free (even though they know their voyeuristic fun will end too). Viewers of *the film* are encouraged to become anti-Christof. In so doing they are being invited to break out of whatever contains them, or shapes them against their will, or whatever makes them conform. The film thus promotes individual, existential liberation. It could also imply, for some viewers, that the only way that this is achievable is by opposition to all institutional contexts in which we live and move, or via the discovery that God and God-figures are ultimately not supportive of human freedom. Alternatively, it could mean that the media and institutional contexts within which we live must be exposed and critiqued. But at an affective level, despite its feelgood ending, the film can promote a constructive rage in the viewer: whatever constrains the viewer must be destroyed.

Connecting questions and issues

To enable the films' engagement with questions about God to be more fully explored, it is now necessary to distil from the above summaries of the film plots and themes and viewer responses to them a series of questions which will make theological discussion possible and fruitful.

- What more can be said about the images of God offered in and through the films?
- What is being done with these images?
- What 'reality value' are we expected, as viewers, to attach to the God portrayed in these images?

- What does it mean to 'have', to 'use', or to 'carry' an image of God?
- What do these films tell us, if anything, about a society's functioning and the transmission of images of God within it?
- What relationships and tensions are there between a culture's carrying of God-images and the religious traditions which claim primary responsibility for preserving and working with them?
- What is to be made of the distinction between the 'reality' and the 'image' of God in religions and societies? How do responses to these films help us, if at all, to address the question of realism and non-realism in discussing the meaning of the word 'God'?

The next section will work within a framework created by these questions.

Explorations: images and traditions; power and freedom

The fact that the subject of God is treated humorously in film is intriguing. It may suggest a lack of reverence. Or it may be a challenge to an inappropriate degree of reverence shown to the topic of God within cultures which have lost a sense of what it means to speak of God in a more matter-of-fact way, clearly related to everyday life. Whatever the intention behind *Bruce Almighty*, the film brings discussion of God into mainstream popular culture through the medium of comedy. Humour is, however, two-edged. Are God and religion being laughed at? Are they artistic devices to enable the film to handle the subject-matter of human love?

Bruce Almighty is a clever film in that by virtue of its having a clear 'moral' it proves accessible and enjoyable for those with little or no sympathy for the concept of God or religion. A key question of the film's reception and interpretation, however, is the extent to which its theological theme is essential to what viewers take from it. It is evidently essential to the plot. But does the film imply that for the miracle of human love to occur God is indispensable?

Certainly, in order to get the most from the film within its own terms, a viewer needs to bring a broad appreciation of theistic belief in order to grasp some of the jokes and allusions made. Some of these are common to most religious traditions. Others are specifically Jewish or Christian. The film assumes a basic appreciation of such motifs as God giving signs (via road-signs, billboards, TV adverts), God as light/source of light (God as an electrician fixing lights), God's being one ('I am the One') and God's hearing/answering prayers. More specifically, there is reference to the Exodus (Bruce 'parts the waves' in his soup bowl) and to walking on water (by both God and Bruce).

It is, however, unlikely that a viewer—if aware of such allusions—would take time or care to disentangle them all. A film like this works in a nonspecific way, making jokes about allusions to 'the divine' ('the Almighty', 'the guy upstairs') in a general manner. Such generality, however, creates problems if it is then assumed that a film like this can somehow contribute to a culture's carrying of an image of God. For it offers a number of mixed messages about who and what God is supposed to be, and be about. In addition to the allusions already cited, the view that 'everything happens for a reason' is expressed by Grace (Jennifer Aniston), as if God is responsible for all things that occur. The departure of God back into his loft suggests deism rather than theism: human beings are left to their own devices by a God who has set creation up, but then ceased to interact with it. Furthermore, the lingering presence of the divine in the human realm is even given a Gnostic twist ('you have the divine spark'), in a way which suggests God's presence as only spiritual, as opposed to spiritual *and* material in the world.

Two central questions therefore emerge from this film and its reception. What is the value of the imagery of God for the viewer beyond the film?

What is to be made of the absence of specificity of the image/s of God presented? I shall return to these in the 'Working conclusions' section in due course.

The Passion of the Christ offers a very different range of theological issues and questions to the viewer. Here, the image of God is highly specific. From humour and the generalized image of 'the divine' of *Bruce Almighty*, we have turned to a specific form of Christianity and a particular interpretation of the doctrine of the atonement. This is a film about Jesus. As such, in any culture where it is recognized that in Christian understanding God-talk is undertaken with respect to the person of Jesus Christ, then the film presents an image of God. In this sense, the film reflects Christianity's inevitable Christocentrism. The film will surely, in time, be grouped within the emerging canon of 'Jesus-films'. Despite this, the film implies that it is primarily, or only, in the death of Jesus that God is at work. By not doing very much to interpret the death of Jesus in the light of his life it presents a limited view of the Christian understanding of God.

Gibson's Jesus may thus seem utterly orthodox. I suggest, however, that the film and its reception highlight two issues about the relationship between religious communities and the wider culture of which they are a part, and thus about the way in which concepts of God are carried culturally. First, the film and its reception indicate the sheer difficulty of offering a concept of God outside of the context of a living religious community. Religious communities seek to 'live' their understandings of God. This means that images and concepts of God are complex symbols that are hard to communicate. The theological significance of the observation that The Passion of the Christ is only in a restricted sense a 'Jesus-film' (because it does not offer the viewer enough about the life of Jesus) may not be apparent to many viewers.

Second, the distinction between religious communities and wider society is crucial. It may be possible to talk of societies 'carrying' a number of images of God. But unlike religious communities, societies do not choose to 'carry' specific images of God. They incorporate the pluralism of images which religions carry with them, and societies' members—whether they consider themselves religious or not—adopt, reject or adapt images and concepts of God in a complex variety of ways. Any exploration of a concept of God therefore has to take account of whose concept of God it is. To note that all God-concepts are tradition-related and community-specific does not then make them the inventions or projections of those communities. The observation merely respects the life-involving character of God-concepts. No-one can say 'I believe in God' in any meaningful way without this also connecting with who they relate to, what they think about themselves and the world, and about how they choose to live their lives. The distinction between society (as a whole) and religious traditions (in particular) thus indicates that any interpreter of God-concepts needs to be clear about which particular traditions are 'carried' (and 'lived within') by which particular communities. Only on the basis of such detailed examination, I suggest, is *The Passion of the Christ* and its reception comprehensible.

The truncated nature of the image of God implied in *The Passion of the Christ*—its blood-thirsty God—does, however, find echoes in a very different form in *The Truman Show*. As already stated, Christof need not be seen directly as God-figure at all. He is God-like in so far as he runs the show (literally). But again, if the comparison with God is to be drawn then it is a limited comparison. It is God's omnipotence that is being either parodied or criticized. The importance of the way that *The Truman Show* works theologically as a film is, however, two-fold. First, its theological possibilities are implicit rather than explicit. The film therefore primarily does emotional work on viewers—enabling them to get inside Truman's story and the stories of the viewer of *The Truman Show within* the film. The possibility of a comparison between Christof and God can then be warmly received by a viewer who is anti-religion, or beyond it ('I am glad I do not live within such a world'). It can also be received appreciatively by a theist who does not believe in this dominant kind of God, a God who leaves little de facto freedom to God's creatures. It could, however, be a shock in its implications for a believer who draws the comparison and is then faced for the first time with the question of possible limits to God's omnipotence. Perhaps God cannot do everything (if creatures are in any sense 'free'). Furthermore, what are the implications for God's creatures if there is no escape from God?

With *The Truman Show* we have come full circle. We are back facing, in a significantly different way, some of the same basic issues about what it means to believe in God, and what God might be like, as were presented in *Bruce Almighty*. In the latter film, God is quite upfront in handing over his powers: Bruce could not tell people he was God and he could not undermine human freedom. (Problematically, of course, God and Bruce still seem able to 'do everything' when it comes to moving objects around, changing the weather and generally defying the laws of nature.) In *The Truman Show*, the expression of qualified omnipotence is more sinister. But the challenge for the viewer is more intense precisely because of the emotional commitment which the viewer is lured into making: it really does matter that God is not like Christof.

Working conclusions

This juxtaposition and brief discussion of three recent films demonstrate that the question of the nature of God is alive and well within popular Western culture. They do not pose in any direct way the question of God's existence, but they all accept that cultures contain within them images of God with which its people interact. Only one—*The Passion of the Christ*—makes explicit a direct link with a specific religious tradition, and I have suggested that the link it makes with Christianity is inadequate.

Nevertheless the films and their reception suggest that exploration of images of God remains culturally and existentially necessary. Examination of issues of omnipotence, dominance, freedom and the possibility of love and concern for others, what it is that human beings may need releasing from, and whether God requires suffering (e.g. that of Jesus) for such release to occur will be necessary within such theological exploration. The examination of such topics is not, however, ultimately possible in any generalized way. Concepts of God are tradition-specific and community- related. There can be comparative theological studies across religion. Philosophers may also continue to speak of a 'concept of God' in a generalized sense. But religious belief deals with God in more specific ways because of the ritual practices of which it is comprised and the ethical conduct that flows from them. Images of God can, in Western culture, be explored through many different religious channels, for all major religious traditions are part of Western culture. From here on I shall be examining in more detail a Christian view of God, through the component parts of a Christian systematic theology. This is partly because there is much residual Christian thought lurking throughout popular culture (and you have to have some hooks to link onto—theological exploration never occurs in a vacuum). But it is also because a choice has to made about a tradition on which to major, and within which to work.

It will take six further chapters for this book even to begin to address some of the specifically Christian forms of questions about God. By beginning to address such questions 'through film', the film-watcher/reader will, however, already be developing a 'whole person approach' to the task of theology (relating to body, mind and spirit). The enjoyment and challenge of watching/experiencing and responding to film becomes theological exploration in which emotions and aesthetic responses play a crucial part alongside thinking. From here on, the book invites the film-watching student of theology constantly to ask: and has Christian theology insights to offer the process of my response to and reception of this film?

And likewise: does this film, and my response to and reception of it draw out anything specific from, or question or sharpen any aspect of, Christian tradition?

For further study

Before more films are watched and discussed, however, it is vital that the history of Christian theology be allowed its say. The following texts would be useful in introducing readers to some of the major treatments in Christian history of the basic questions about who and what 'God' is. From the Bible, the following are worth exploring:

Genesis 1.1-2.3 One of the accounts of God with which the Bible opens. Exodus 3 The account of God's appearance to Moses, where the divine name 'I am who I am' is revealed to Moses.

Exodus 19-20 The account of the giving of the Ten Commandments on Mount Sinai. Psalm 33 A psalm which gives expression to the way in which God is held to watch over the earth.

Jonah This short book from the Hebrew Bible/Old Testament is intriguing because of the way it shows God having a change of mind (to Jonah's annoyance) in order to be merciful.

Colossians 1.15-20 Often thought to have been an early Christian hymn (then included within this letter to the church in Colossae), this passage speaks about Christ but indicates how Christians have always done their God-talk by speaking about Christ.

I John 4.7-21 One of the clearest passages in the New Testament about God's nature as love.

The following texts from later Christian history will help readers think further how human beings speak of God, about aspects of God's relation to the world, and some of the different ways of understanding the death of Christ which have been offered in Christian history.

Anselm and Abelard (late eleventh century) offer two views on the death of Christ (in McGrath, pp. 340-3). Anselm offers a 'satisfaction' theory of atonement, according to which the death of Christ pays the necessary price for human sin. Abelard sees that Christ has died 'for us', but wants to put greater stress upon the way in which God, in Christ, invites people to loving action in response to Christ's death.

Calvin, 'God's Providence Governs All' in Hodgson and King, pp. 123-8. This is a classic sixteenth-century statement on the sovereignty of God, and expresses the view that lies behind Grace's statement in *Bruce Almighty* ('everything happens for a reason'). God is here portrayed not simply as having created the world, but as continuing to direct its course in some detail.

Hegel, 'Without the World God is not God' (in Hodgson and King, pp. 132-6). This text from a famous nineteenth-century philosopher-theologian opens up the thorny question of whether, having created the world, God is in some sense dependent on it.

'Karl Barth on Revelation as God's Self-Disclosure' (= *Church Dogmatics* 1/1 [1932, E.T. 1976]), pp. 191, 193-94; in McGrath, pp. 138-40; longer extract in Hodgson and King, pp. 97-101). This extract from a seminal work by one of the most influential of twentieth-century theologians argues for the priority of God's self-revelation in all thinking about God.

Moltmann, 'On the Suffering of God' (in McGrath, pp. 117-20). This highly influential twentieth-century text probes the question of what was happening to God at the point of Jesus' crucifixion. It therefore focuses on many of the issues left unclear or unresolved by *The Passion of the Christ*.

James Cone, 'God is Black' (in Thistlethwaite and Engel, pp. 101-14). These reflections by a leading black theologian offer a critique of much theological thinking in showing how images of God and human experience interrelate.

Human Being

Clive Marsh

From discussion of who and what God is and how God relates to the world, we turn to the created order itself. Who and what are human beings and what is their place within the created order as a whole? Why call the world we know 'the created order' at all? In this chapter I juxtapose four very different films in order to enable the reader to examine the doctrines of creation and human being.

Films

Koyaanisqatsi (Godfrey Reggio, 1983)

Koyaanisqatsi has been variously described as 'a rather pointless, very beautiful, and finally rather boring experience' and 'perhaps the most powerful film about nature ever'. It is an evocative, dialogue-less, film which juxtaposes striking visual images of nature, space and human beauty with the sometimes ugly aspects of human habitation: smoky cities, heavy industry and car-filled freeways. 'Koyaanisqatsi' means 'a state of life that calls for another way of living' or 'life out of balance' in Hopi, a Native American language. The film's purpose is thus to reflect back to the viewer what is happening to the world, and what role human beings are playing in damaging it. Despite its visual and aural beauty as a film (Philip Glass's music enhances the viewing experience), its message appears bleak. But the contrast between its apparent narrative purpose (the world was beautiful but human beings are destroying it) and the experience of viewing will be worth examining further in due course.

Eternal Sunshine of the Spotless Mind (Michel Gondry, 2004)

The second film to be looked at focuses on human beings. It is a love story and a humorous but by no means formulaic romantic comedy. Joel (Jim Carrey) and Clementine (Kate Winslet) have been in a relationship before. When they meet at the start of the film, however, neither we nor they know this. We discover that they have had their memories of each other erased. The film tracks the ups and downs of the relationships between two quite different people: shy and withdrawn Joel, and lively, demanding Clementine. Using clever dialogue, trickery with time, and striking camerawork, Gondry and scriptwriter Charlie Kaufman take the viewer through their meetings, their fallings out, their parting, their memory-erasure (complete with Joel's regrets and struggles to prevent it happening) before leaving us and them back where they started: meeting again on Valentine's Day.

Do the Right Thing (Spike Lee, 1989)

This influential and challenging film by Spike Lee tackles race relations head-on. Using a (hot) day in the life of a Brooklyn street, and focusing on the owners and customers of a pizzeria ('Sal's Famous'), Lee—who wrote, directed and acted in the film—draws out the complexity of urban race relations in a powerful way. Lee plays Mookie, a pizza delivery man whose links with all the main characters through his work form a focal point of the plot. Sal's pizzeria is run by an Italian immigrant and his two sons, is frequented by many people from the predominantly black neighbourhood and is located opposite a grocery store run by a Korean couple. The pizzeria is thus a concrete site of the encounter of ethnicities and cultures. The plot revolves around the tensions between the various groups, and the diverse ideological outlooks of different individuals and groups. A particular emphasis in the film is the tension within the black community between the different ways of Martin Luther King and Malcom X with respect to whether or not violence should ever be contemplated when one encounters injustice. However, the film skillfully presents many aspects of the way that ethnic difference both creates a rich cultural mix, and also produces a social context in which great demands are placed on the human capacity to handle such difference.

Though fully representative of a black perspective, Lee has successfully made a film which makes it clear that all the characters are ambiguous (none wholly good, none wholly bad) and that no single ethnic group deserves special favour.

Notting Hill (Roger Michell, 1999)

In stark contrast to *Do the Right Thing* the films of Richard Curtis present a very different view of urban life. They deal mostly with the lives of white, affluent English city dwellers (all three considered here are London-based). They all deal with the making and breaking of relationships and risk presenting near caricatures in the stereotypical characters used. They trade off some stock British/American contrasts. They are for the most part fantasies, comedies with clever plots and some nice twists. I want to read *Notting Hill* in the context of the three main films in which Richard Curtis has thus far been involved (i.e. alongside *Four Weddings and a Funeral* and *Love Actually*). I suggest that *Notting Hill* can be read in the light of what *Love Actually* is getting at, and in the light of the motif of the demands and depths of love which, despite all their apparent superficiality, each of these three films in practice presents.

'Seems to me that love is everywhere. Often it's not particularly dignified, or newsworthy—but it's always there—fathers and sons, mothers and daughters, husbands and wives, boyfriends, girl-friends, old friends.' These words are part of the opening voiceover by the Prime Minister (Hugh Grant) at the start of *Love Actually*. The speech signals what is going to be celebrated in the film. Despite the location of his films within the genre of comedy or romantic comedy, however, the celebrations of love offered go beyond the formulaic requirements of such films. The love celebrated, as Grant's speech indicates, is not only romantic or sexual love. It is the love found in families and in friendships. And where love is sexual it is not only heterosexual. Nor is the love 'easy' despite many fantasy and 'happy ending' elements across the films. *In Four Weddings and a Funeral*, the funeral is of Gareth (Simon Callow), a gay man, whose homosexuality had been hidden even from his closest friends. There is thus the pain of the death for his partner, Matthew (John Hannah), and his family and friends, but also of the knowledge that the couple had felt the need to hide their sexuality.

In *Notting Hill*, a marriage is celebrated: not the impending one of the two main characters William (Hugh Grant) and Anna (Julia Roberts), but that between Bella (Gina McKee) and Max (Tim McInnerny). They are clearly well off—both are lawyers—and their practical struggle is only alluded to, through Max's carrying Bella upstairs. But the fact of Bella's physical incapacity and her newly discovered childlessness are contained within their loving relationship, and borne by it. In *Love Actually*, the pain present in two of the ten relationships stands out: that caused for Karen (Emma Thompson) by Harry's (Alan Rickman) infidelity, and that borne within Sarah's (Laura Linney) relationship to her mentally ill brother Michael (Michael Fitzgerald).

Beyond the fantasy elements in each of these films (financial worries are not prominent in the films, film-stars don't usually walk into small bookshops, travel abroad doesn't automatically lead to a range of satisfying trouble-free sexual relationships with beautiful people), there is a conservatism of both form and content. However, whether the conservatism of content (e.g. marriage is still worth striving for, real happiness is heterosexual) is ultimately determinative of their impact and value as films depends on their reception. For alongside the fantastic and the simple the plot and character elements just mentioned point to a level of satisfying complexity in the films. The films are to be enjoyed and make us feel good. But they also leave the viewer, as we shall see below, with more than the feelgood factor.

Viewing experiences

These films offer four distinctly different types of viewing experience. *Koyaanisqatsi* depends for its effect upon colour, striking imagery, the interplay of mostly non-verbal sound (especially music) and image, and the willingness of the viewer to participate in the task of interpreting images and their juxtaposition. Whether viewers are inspired or bored will depend on whether they are willing to stay with the film and work at the task of interpretation. Consideration of this film marks the first point in this study where one of the differences between a 'popular' and an 'art' film becomes evident. For the viewer who stays with it, the challenge of locating oneself as a responsible human being within the world is both ethical and emotional. Viewers *feel* their co-responsibility within the world for resisting any human tendency towards neglect or destruction. The aesthetic experience of viewing thus opens up a cognitive challenge to think of the 'world' in terms of 'creation', that is as a gift.

Unlike *Koyaanisqatsi*, *Eternal Sunshine of the Spotless Mind* is more widely known through its release in multiplexes. It is, however, in its own way a demanding film. It is not an easy film to follow. The viewer has to move behind what is portrayed in screen time to be able to unravel what is mixed up in the times of both plot and story. For a viewer disinclined or unable to do this, the film will simply end up confusing and confused. Whether the film then functions as an enjoyable and challenging stimulus to reflect upon 'the centrality of memory in defining one's personality' (McCarthy) will depend upon how much the viewer has been prepared for the film, that is, made ready to handle the film's reversing of the story, or is prepared to reflect on it afterwards.[2]

The experience of viewing *Eternal Sunshine of the Spotless Mind* can, however, prove disturbing as well as disorientating. Whatever is to be made of Joel's regression scene (described by McCarthy as 'downright odd'), the clever range of camera and sound techniques—especially the blurring and slurring as memories are being erased—seek to accentuate the level of damage to one's self-awareness which memory loss would cause. Viewers are thus exposed through such technical skill to more than a mere cognitive reflection on the question 'what would it mean to lose my memory?'

Do the Right Thing is demanding in a different way again from *Koyaanisqatsi* and *Eternal Sunshine of the Spotless Mind*. Unlike the former but like the latter, the focus is again upon the inter-human. The film deals less with the intra-human, however, than on the ethnic and cultural groups into which people are born, find their identity and out of which they experience the world and encounter the 'other'. It leaves no viewer emotionally unaffected. *Eternal Sunshine of the Spotless Mind* had not ignored the importance of memory for linking people together. Memory is seen to be always in part memory of having been related to others, and thus one's identity in part depends on the memory of others as well as oneself. But the film largely focused on individuals. *Do the Right Thing* presents plausible, interesting, ambiguous individual characters but it is keenly interested too in the groups and traditions within which each is located and in and through which they discover and shape their identities.

The power of the experience of watching *Do the Right Thing* depends on the nature and degree of identification on the viewer's part. Many middle-class white viewers might conclude that they cannot 'get into' the film much, except through the character of Clifton (John Savage), the well-meaning new local resident who, in response to the query why he lives in a black neighbourhood, indicates he is 'under the assumption that this is a free country and one can live where he pleases'. Wealthy white liberal cinema-goers may indeed find this as an emotional point of access to the film. Yet they may overlook, on grounds of class and on the level of (lack of) immersion in urban culture, potential identification with Sal and his sons, and with the police who patrol the area and are then involved in the killing which sparks off the riot which brings the film to its climax. Diverse groups within the black community—based on age, gender, and ideological outlook—are opened up by Lee. They offer a range of opportunities for black viewers to locate themselves specifically within the film's plot and action. In a way which viewers of other ethnic backgrounds might not be able fully to appreciate, Lee invites black viewers to explore their backgrounds, identities, commitments and prejudices in the context of exploration of the intensity of experience presented in the film, and the reality of tensions between groups, between black and black, black and white, black and Asian. No potential tension is left unexplored, and thus there is no emotional hiding place for any viewer prepared to open up to the impact of their own ethnicity, gender, class and age upon their identity. Film critic Roger Ebert declared: 'I have only been given a few filmgoing experiences in my life to equal the first time I saw *Do the Right Thing*. Most movies remain up there on the screen. Only a few penetrate your soul.' Ebert is surely not alone in feeling the deep emotional impact of the film. And as with any great film, its work is only fully done when people respond and work with their reactions to it, so that the viewing experience does not remain only an evening's entertainment.

The Curtis films take us in a different direction again. They may seem light and superficial compared to the other films considered so far. They are slick packages designed for a good night out and the cultivation of a warm glow for the twenty- and thirty-something cinema-going public for whom they are clearly intended. My use of them here derives largely from evidence adduced from teaching experience. What 'lingers in the mind' of many viewers, beyond the feelgood factor, is an element in their respective plots of the disruption of the romance and the comedy of each. Hence, the funeral in *Four Weddings and a Funeral* stands out, and collections of poems by W H. Auden sold millions of copies as a result of his 'Stop the Clocks' being used in that scene. In *Notting Hill*, the quality of relationship between Max and Bella overshadows the fantasy romance of Anna and William, because enough is glimpsed (and felt) by the viewer of what they have to struggle with together within their relationship, despite their material wealth. In *Love Actually*, the two plots with loose ends, already referred to above, are the ones that are remembered, not the ones that are tied up neatly or seem far from real life.

In other words, across all three films there is a motif of stark real life, always containing an element of sadness, yet not always consumed by negativity, which disrupts the genre in and through which the films are packaged and marketed. These disruptions become important in the films' reception as they are what viewers commonly remember and therefore 'work with' beyond first or ensuing viewings ('O, I feel so sorry for the Emma Thompson character').

Connecting questions and issues

A wide range of questions arises from these films about what it means to be a human being. These include:

- What is the place of humanity within the whole of the created order? Are humans somehow special?
- What does it mean to speak of 'the created order' as opposed to 'the world' or 'the universe'? (For does not talk of 'created order' already imply a purpose, thoughtfulness or design which may not actually be there?)

- How does human identity emerge? Is it 'discovered' or 'constructed'?
- What place do life-experience and memory play in the discovery or construction of human identity? Is memory solely individual? If it is both individual and communal, then how is memory 'carried'?
- What part is played in the formation of identity by the different groups to which we belong and the diverse commitments that we have? How do we deal with the fact that some of these may be chosen (e.g. ethical, political, religious) and others not (age, gender, ethnicity)?
- What does 'love' mean? What types of love might there be, given that there is something of love which seems identifiably the same across human cultures, and yet even within single cultures there are different expressions of love (e.g. within families, in friendships, in sexual relationships)?
- How are the frailties and limitations of human experience (including illness, accidents, evil, death) to be handled?

These form the framework within which the explorations will be conducted.

Explorations: gift and gratitude; individual and social sin; memory and identity; love and Trinity

Human beings do not come out very well in *Koyaanisqatsi*. It looks as though we are being identified by its director as the villain of the piece. Creation, it seems, would be fine if we had not messed it up. The viewing experience means that reception of the film is, however, more complex than this. The film is beautifully photographed, and the music is haunting. Whether or not we feel good at the end, or have 'got' the message that Reggio seems to want us to hear, if we have stayed with the film we have enjoyed a rich aesthetic experience. The experience of watching, then, itself encapsulates the ambiguity of humanity's place within the world/creation. We are puny when compared to nature's awesome power, but that only puts us appropriately in our limited place within the universe. We (humanity) are part of the problem, and yet have the capacity to resist at least some of our tendencies to damage our environment. Human creativity and technological know-how could be put to better use. And the film itself, in presenting itself to us, is evidence of that. It confronts us, by beautiful means, with the world's beauty.

In Christian theology, accounts of the limited but important place of humanity within the created order, and of the ambiguity of human experience are ready to hand (Genesis 1—4, Psalm 8, Romans 7). In its focus on salvation Christianity has, however, sometimes not been good at attending to the salvation of the earth as a whole, or on being positive about human capacity to contribute to God's continued saving of creation. This film both presents the ambiguity and embodies evidence of how the ambiguity can be, if not overcome, then at least lived with. The creative skills of human beings are to be turned towards respect for the earth; human communities are to be mended so that people do not need to be isolated.

The film is not, of course, overtly theist. The conclusions drawn by a humanist might be identical to those just summarized. The difference in reception lies in the way in which the world and human beings are understood in the light of the 'givenness' of creation and human nature. Whatever and whoever God is understood to be, the existential conviction that God creates means that human life and its environment are received as gifts. These gifts are received in sometimes complex and fraught circumstances. The freedom of a created order that includes earthquakes and volcanic eruptions, droughts and floods, and produces human bodies that are all imperfect in some way, leaves many questions to be asked of God. But Christian theology suggests a disposition of gratitude as a starting point for the acceptance of who one is and what the world is like. On that basis it becomes possible to assess and develop what one is capable of. It is on the same basis that one's environment may be regarded not in a hostile manner. The surroundings are not to be subdued but treasured and cared for. To treasure and care for who one is and the surroundings within which one lives would, in Christian understanding, be undertaken with a deep sense of the ambiguity to which *Koyaanisqatsi* refers.

Without the final sentence of the previous paragraph, it could be argued that a Christian approach to human living was all too comfortable: written out of comfort for a world in which few problems are identified. Notions of 'gift' and 'gratitude' may be all very well for those who find immediate cause to be thankful (for material wealth, good health, safe surroundings, no environmental threats, political stability). The intensity of human experience portrayed in *Do the Right Thing* stands in sharp contrast to such ease and comfort.

There is gracefulness, tenderness, care and concern between people, and love and respect within and across generations in *Do The Right Thing*. But above all, alongside such positive aspects of human relations, there is profound ambiguity (people can be all those positive things and something more negative besides). And beneath all, because of such persistent, present negativity, a simmering rage lurks within many human interactions. It is this simmering rage, related to complex ethnic and ideological loyalties, which explodes violently at the end of the film and which stuns, and lingers with, the viewer. But it stuns and lingers in part because the viewer has been drawn into the emotional, social and political complexity of human living which Lee examines in this film. What theological explorations does a viewer's response evoke?

First, the essential ambiguity of a human being evident from the film invites being put alongside Christian exposition of human beings as always sinful, even whilst still being identifiably made in God's image. In Christian understanding, every human being possesses a tendency to turn damagingly inwards, away from others, away from God, and yet by virtue of being human continues to bear the hallmarks of being created by God. Being 'created' means not being in full control of one's origins or destiny. There are constraints on one's personality and identity (of time, place, gender and ethnicity). But being created in love *by God* means being created by One who desires freedom for those who populate the created world. Human beings are specific; 'humanity' does not exist in the abstract, only in particular forms, as real people, in a particular time and place, and with all the limitations of contingency which go with that specificity. But the degree of freedom which human beings possess, within the constraints of particularity, seems inevitably to carry with it dire consequences. Human exercise of freedom reveals the ever-present tendency to 'sin' (i.e. to neglect God).[4]

Lee's exposition of human relations in *Do The Right Thing* accentuates particularity to the full. The ambiguity and complexity of all the leading characters is real. People are only people in the context of particular locations (here, literally, in the context of one block within a New York neighbourhood). This block does not stand for 'humanity in general', however. The film shows that humanity is only human because it is particular. There is no 'humanity in the abstract'. Christian reflection on humanity is thus challenged both by the starkness of Lee's attention to particularity, and by the reminder that despite the clear presence of lurking rage (evil beneath the surface, evidence of 'original sin', even) goodness can still emerge in human interactions. And yet Christian theology also knows, despite what it has often implied throughout its history, that there is no 'humanity in the abstract'. The doctrine of incarnation (God enfleshed, supremely in the person of Jesus Christ) commits Christianity to close attention to concreteness and particularity. Because of this, Christian theology can work with such cultural-artistic expositions of human experience as *Do The Right Thing* to explore what it means in real situations to be both made in God's image *and* sinful (at one and the same time). 'Image of God' and 'sin' can too easily become abstract terms when not explored through the particularity of human experience within which they take form.

What has Christian theology made of 'sin'? Typically, sin has been understood as self-interest or pride. Human beings turn themselves into gods by worshipping their own selves. This expresses itself in many forms of self-interested behaviour such as the acquisition of wealth and the pursuit of pleasure for its own sake. Common to all such activities is the lack of thought for consequences on others. So-called 'sins' are, however, to be understood as the symptom of the sin of self-interest and neglect of God. This very typical view of sin has been rightly challenged, especially by women theologians, who have pointed out that it assumes a way of operating as a human being in which one has the *choice* to behave in this way. The experience of many women, past and present, across the world has been a *lack* of choice. Sin may thus be better defined as a lack of appropriate self-assertion. On this understanding, neglect of God takes the form of disregard for the God-given goodness of the human self. If human beings are made in God's image, the presence of that image in the human person is to be celebrated by acknowledgement of the human potential for creativity, for relationship, for goodness, for care of others and the earth's resources.

Both of these understandings of sin—as pride/exaggerated self-interest or lack of appropriate self-assertion—are, however, individualistic. They focus upon human sin as an individual disposition. *Do The Right Thing* presses viewers to think about corporate aspects of human identity and self-discovery, and thus of the way that the negative aspects of ambiguous humanity are inextricably woven within social forms of human life. The individual aspect of sin need not be overlooked here. Human beings continue, as individuals, to participate in structures of wickedness. But Lee's film, without letting the protagonists off the hook, shows how complex race, class and gender—and their interweaving—actually are. Furthermore, viewers, like the lead characters, are brought into the complexity. We are left confronting our own ambiguity as we think about the personal, social background which has made us, and makes us, who we are.

The film therefore offers a challenge to Christian thought not only to keep particularity rather than abstractness at the forefront of its exploration of human being. It also reminds theology to address the *social* complexity of human formation. As we shall see in Chapter 9 in due course, Christian theology has a social sense of what it means to be human at its heart. But Christianity sometimes moves too quickly towards a notion of 'church' as a form of human community which seeks to anticipate 'the Kingdom of God' (a kind of ultimate vision of what is possible for human beings to become). In its undue haste, Christianity is prone to overlook the 'kingdoms of sin' within which all human beings live. In other words, notions of 'original sin' have often been too individualistically conceived. The inevitability of human wickedness has thus not been adequately explored in Christian thought in relation to the social and political complexity of human life. *Do The Right Thing* is therefore theologically provocative because it relates the inevitability of human ambiguity to unavoidable social aspects of what it means to be human (ethnicity, above all). In so doing it poses a question about how creative, positive human potential (celebration of God's image) and human wickedness (as the expression of the universality of sin) are to be both understood, and the former encouraged, the latter resisted, given the scale and intensity of social pressures.

There is hope and humour in *Do The Right Thing*. Characters are immersed in the particularity of their neighbourhood. But some also step back from it at times. Mister Senor Love Daddy (Samuel Jackson) offers a commentary—a sort of soundtrack—on all that goes on. Black debates with black as to what kind of black-consciousness and action is appropriate. And, strikingly, at a point when it looks as though the Korean shop-owners may have their store wrecked, they are protected by black residents who can identify with them because of their own past experience. The role of black memory is thus important in the film not only for black people themselves but also as a way of enabling group-interest (in this case ethnicity) to be transcended. Whether as viewers we can 'survive our inevitable multiculturalism' is Lee's challenge. It is also a challenge to Christian theology, which must likewise work with and through the powerful loyalties engendered by group experience, and resist overlooking their force through too lazy and hasty an appeal to transcendence. As we shall see further in Chapter 9 below, 'church' as a concept invites people to find a new loyalty, and to participate in a different corporate memory than that delivered to people solely by the circumstances of their birth and ethnic background. But without attending to the significance and complexity of what our origins and ethnicities entail, perhaps no fully theological understanding of human being or church will be possible.

Eternal Sunshine of the Spotless Mind is also concerned with memory. Here we switch back to considering individual human beings. But because this film focuses upon the importance of memory for how human beings relate to each other, the emotions experienced by, and the questions posed for, viewers are instructive for exploration of the social formation of the human self. The potential disorientation experienced by the viewer of this film accentuates memory's importance for understanding who one is (What have I done? Who are my friends? What beliefs have I been living by?). A basic question left after the viewing experience (What would it mean for me to lose my memory?) is, however, supplemented by many others. How dependent am I on others for remembering who I am? (For others carry their memory of me on which I can depend when I continue my relationship with them.) Who are the most significant memory-carriers for me? What am I to do with the fact that some groups I am part of I did not choose (family, neighbourhood in early life), whilst others I did choose (neighbourhood in later life—though not neighbours; type of work—though not necessarily colleagues; religious community—possibly)? I am thus dependent on the collective memories of all of these groups in which I participate for part of my identity. I only exist as an interdependent person.

There is surprisingly little direct reflection on memory and the human self in the history of Christian thought. A well-known passage from the early church theologian St Augustine (345—430 CE) uses memory within a triad of memory, understanding and will as an analogy of the doctrine of the Trinity. Interestingly, as this is one of Augustine's psychological analogies, the memory and God are both being considered together within reflection on God being like a human

individual. There are then two further major areas in Christian theology where remembering and forgetting has proved vital: confession, and Holy Communion. In any act of penitence—the asking for God's forgiveness—religious believers are asking God to remove from them the consequences of actions which they believe or know to have been wrong. The recollection of them (not the forgetting) is important. It is, then, God who does the forgetting, in the sense that God releases the person confessing from any lingering guilt for past actions, from any burden of memory, and from any sense that God will punish a person for their deeds. Healing thus comes in the context of making public one's repentance of recalled evil actions. In the resolve to live a renewed life, the memory is not then a burden and need not be repressed. Within a life lived in relation to God, then, an individual's good and bad memories can be borne because an individual's own story (identity) rests within a larger story: that of the life of God.

The second main area of Christian life and thought within which memory has always played a crucial part is in the celebration of Mass/Eucharist/Holy Communion/Lord's Supper/Breaking of Bread. A full exploration of what Christians have deemed to occur (to the bread and wine, and to the participants) in the context of a service of Holy Communion cannot be entered into here. In all versions of the celebration of Communion, however, recollection is crucial. The Last Supper that Jesus shared with his immediate disciples is recalled, and words deemed to have been used by Jesus at that event are used again. Two aspects about this eucharistic recollection should be noted. First, the recollection is celebrated not simply as a past event, but as one which stimulates belief, thought and action in the present. Second, the act of recollection is not dependent on the individual memories of those participating. How could it be, of course, for none of us was there! The point is that the memory is contained within the words (of the liturgy or the free prayer used to recall the Last Supper) which the community of Christians who meet carry with them.

Beyond these three uses of memory in Christian tradition, as a subject of enquiry in its own right, 'memory' is otherwise a relatively modern subject for theological and philosophical reflection, receiving particular attention since the rise of interest in consciousness. *Eternal Sunshine of the Spotless Mind* reflects this modern post-Freud concern. Conscious and unconscious memories are recognized as crucial for the understanding and shaping of human identity. There has also been a huge interest in recent years in the healing of memories, individual and corporate. Indeed, it looks in many ways in the West as though the therapeutic role played in the past by religion (especially Christianity) is now being played throughout society by counsellors and therapists. So what is to be made of these parallel declarations of interest in the role of memory for the human being?

Eternal Sunshine of the Spotless Mind taps into a widespread current concern about the relationship between memory and identity. The film confronts the horrific prospect of memory loss in an imaginative way. It demonstrates that to be human means to live with a combination of good and bad memories about oneself and others. It suggests the sub-humanity of wanting to be rid of bad memories. It provokes the viewer to think about the interdependence of a person with others for how memories are carried, whilst leaving unresolved the question of how one actually lives with bad memories.

The weight of Christian thought, ironically, is concerned less with what a human being remembers than with what God will 'forget'. This is the overarching framework within which Christianity places the acts of remembering and forgetting. The

individual has long been known to struggle with bad memories. But because Christianity's concern is fundamentally with the salvation of the human person, it is the release from the impact of bad memories and the desire to enable people to live more constructively and purposefully within the story of God that are paramount. This has proved therapeutic for individuals throughout Christian history. Ultimately, however, Christianity is less concerned with the individual, than with the individual within the scope of the fate of the whole of humankind within the created order. It is for this reason that Christianity, building on a Jewish preoccupation with a collective memory, a story of a people (the people of the Exodus), is more concerned with the corporate memory of the church, as a form of the people of God. Unlike the collective memories within which people live in *Do The Right Thing*, the church's corporate memory is not based on ethnicity but on a memory, held corporately, about who God is. The response for a Christian to the question 'who are you?' could thus rightly be: 'I am one of God's people.' It is the participation in the people of God (via church) which gives a Christian person an identity. All other aspects of what it means to be human which pertain to memory—recollections of one's participation within an ethnic group, a social class, a family, or memories of aspects of one's individual life-story—are to be understood within this framework.

In this way, when a person 'loses one's memory' one is also then 'held', as if within the memory of God's own self, by the church which carries a collective memory of the story of God.

The interplay between *Do The Right Thing*, *Eternal Sunshine of the Spotless Mind* and Christian reflection on the human person thus proves provocative on a number of fronts. Central to the exploration have been the role of memory, the many ways in and through which one discovers, explores and/or constructs a human identity, and the relationship and tension between the individual and the group. But even if human beings find or construct an identity for themselves, and work out a place for themselves within the created order in which the image of God within them may be respected, what is it all for? What are human beings to do?

One of the most famous Christian statements about what human beings are for occurs in the seventeenth-century Westminster Shorter Catechism in response to the question 'what is the chief end of human beings?' Human beings, the Catechism states, are to glorify God and to enjoy God forever. 'Enjoyment' is sometimes not associated with Christianity, so this should be noted! But what does it mean to 'glorify' and 'enjoy' God? A simple answer can be given: human beings are to love. In loving, they are glorifying and enjoying. In Christian understanding, they will be able to do this all the more when loving as a human practice is understood as a reflection of who God is. All Christian theology can thus be understood as an attempt to grasp what it means to worship a God of love.

Christology and soteriology—the exploration of the person and work of Jesus Christ—are to be seen as ways of understanding what kind of god God is, for 'in Christ' God has made Godself known. The doctrine of the Trinity is an attempt to tease out what God must be like, given that God has made Godself known in Christ: God *is* love, *is* loving relationship in God's own self. The doctrine of the Holy Spirit is the main way in which Christian theology wrestles with the generous, overflowing in the whole of creation of the free creativity of God. God's love for creation is not confined to a past moment in time (incarnation in Jesus), or even to where we may say that Jesus Christ continues to be present today (as 'Church' or in the form of manifestations of God's Kingdom in the world). God's presence in the world will always, for Christians, be identifiably Christ-like,

but attention to the Holy Spirit enables Christians to see the love of God for creation present in many forms. When human beings attempt, then, to explore what love is, they are, in Christian understanding, inevitably working in theological territory. When love songs are sung, love poems are written and films about love are made, then the love of God, as reflected in and through human love, is being celebrated and explored. It is on this basis that the three films of Richard Curtis being examined in this chapter become resource material for theology.

One of the drawbacks when talking about 'love songs', 'love poems' or 'films about love', of course, is that it is often assumed that romantic, heterosexual love is what is being talked about. This is indeed often the case. In the case of the Curtis films, however, as I have already shown, more is being explored. Yes, the customary features of romantic comedy remain present (man/boy meets woman/girl, there's a rocky relationship, but they get together in the end). But as indicated earlier, other features are mixed in. These allow real life to intrude into the fantasy and give the viewer more to 'work with'.

The features of the three Curtis films which viewer-response highlights, and which are especially interesting for Christian theology, are these. First, love is not always romantic. *Love Actually* includes within its narratives the love between brother and sister, and between parents and children. It can admittedly be argued that the Curtis films do trade off an interest in erotic forms of love, and in so doing also feed a contemporary Western cultural tendency to idolize sexual love. But the presence and exploration of other relationships within the films qualifies the way in which sexual love is presented as a norm. Love understood as loving relationship is present in the films. This is also a central concern for Christian theology.

Second, love includes suffering. Sarah's love for her brother Michael entails suffering for both.

Harry's infidelity makes Karen suffer. It does not remove her love. Matthew suffers when his relationship with Gareth is broken by Gareth's death. In one sense these are merely real-life examples of what anyone who loves knows. No relationship of any depth which lasts over time will be devoid of such suffering. Such a profoundly human experience is, in Christian understanding, not merely illuminated when parallels are drawn between contemporary human experience and the story of Jesus. By the Jesus story being understood as a crucial part of 'the story of God' and of God's relating to the world, then such forms of human suffering are seen to be forms of human participation in the divine life. This matches the way in which God has chosen to participate in creation, risking 'in Christ' all that costly loving entails.

Third, love bears all things. Suffering is not to be idolized. It is never 'acceptable' in the sense of being sought and welcomed. But it happens, and sometimes has to be borne, not being able to be eradicated. This aspect of love becomes clear in Max and Bella's relationship in *Notting Hill*. The reason that their relationship, and not that of William and Anna, is a good model for people to copy is not simply that they are married. Theirs is a lasting, loving pain-bearing relationship because they have had to face suffering, and yet still they love. As viewers we have confidence that they will bear together, in love, whatever life will present to them.

Where can true love be found?: in God. For film-viewers not already predisposed to offer this answer, however, the meaning of such a response has to be grasped via a circuitous route. In response to all the films looked at in this chapter we see that the meaning of human beings' 'glorifying God and enjoying God forever' takes shape in the context of human loving. Human love, of creation and of one human being for another, is participation in the love of God for the created order. This can only be celebrated in concrete form, however much it may be reflected upon in the abstract.

Working conclusions

A number of important theological themes have emerged from engagement with the six films looked at in this chapter. Many of these themes overlap directly with the subject-matter of other chapters. Here I simply highlight the themes that have emerged and the way in which this chapter's treatment of them links to other material in the book.

First, we have been reminded that human beings are made in God's image. This means being created for relationship—between human beings and between human beings and creation as a whole. Discovery of what it means to be in relationship both occurs within given patterns of human relationship—families, ethnic groups—and within those relationships that we choose to live within—friendships of all kinds. These relationships reflect who God is in so far as Christian theology makes the claim, via its doctrine of the Trinity, that God is relational in God's own self.

Second, who we are as loving beings is not only discovered, but also constructed. The formation of our identity as persons occurs in relation both to the groups we are given to belong to, and those we choose. These groups carry a memory for us, a tradition of believing and behaving which shape the meanings we adopt, sometimes by clear choice, sometimes without knowing. The fashioning of personal identity is thus always an individual and a social exercise. Christian theology recognizes this, and also the many different communal forms (families, friendships, ethnic groups) through which memory is carried and the self is shaped. 'Church' enters into this mix as a challenge to the social forms in and through which what it means to be made in God's image (to relate, to love, to be a steward of God's earth) is discovered and explored. More will be said on this in Chapter 9 below.

Third, obstructions to what makes it possible for human being to celebrate the divine image in their self-understanding and living also have to be addressed. Whatever mars the recognition and enjoyment of God's presence in the world (sin), whether that takes individual or social form, has to be opposed. This links with many of the chapters below. Chapter 7 explores redemption: how human beings are enabled by God to be human in the face of internal and external factors which prevent loving relationship. Chapter 8 explores key ritual practices (sacraments) through which Christianity enables people to recognize their God-givenness, and the way that God goes on loving and shape them in their everyday living. The sacraments, like the church itself, embody in concrete form the tradition and the memory by which people are carried through life. Keeping a focus on what it means to be made in God's image and resisting all that blocks recognition of that image therefore entails being appropriately dependent on others. It is not an individual's task to maintain the image: human beings are made in God's image. They need support of many kinds to respect what having such a gift means in practice.

For further study

Biblical passages worth exploring include:

Genesis 1-3 The opening chapters of both the Hebrew and Christian Bibles, in which there are two accounts of creation (1.1—2.4a and 2.4b—25) and an account of 'the Fall', i.e. a story which seeks to characterize human disobedience, and distance from God.

Psalm 8 A statement about the dignity of human beings before God.

Proverbs 8.22-31 A poetic passage praising Wisdom, and Wisdom's fundamental role in creation.

John 1.1-5 One of the most famous passages in the New Testament, linking Jesus Christ with God the Creator via attention to 'the Word'.

Romans 7.7-25 A passage which finds the Apostle Paul vexed by his experience of being unable to do what, in his mind, he knows he wants to do. It is a classic expression of existential struggle.

Texts from the history of Christian thought worth exploring include:

'Augustine on the Trinity' (= extracts from *De Trinitate* IX.i.1-v.8; in McGrath, pp. 187-90). This famous passage finds Augustine exploring the doctrine of the Trinity using lots of different imagery drawn from human psychology.

John Calvin on knowledge of God and knowledge of the self (= *Institutes of the Christian Religion* [1559] 1.1.1 and 1.2.1; in Madges, pp. 103-5). Here, Calvin notes the close relationship between knowing ourselves and knowing God. At the same time, Calvin observed that there is a stark distinction between who God is and who we are.

John Calvin on human awareness of divinity (= *Institutes of the Christian Religion* III.1, 3 [1559]; in Ahlgren, pp. 40-1). These extracts find Calvin expressing the way in which people maintain an awareness of God no matter how far from God they may seem to be.

Sarah M. Grimké on the image of God (= *Letters on the Equality of the Sexes and the Condition of Woman* [1838], pp. 3-5 and 8-10; in Placher,Vol. 2, pp. 119-20).Written in the context of the fight for the abolition of slavery in the USA, this powerful text interprets 'the image of God' in relation to equality between the sexes.

Reinhold Niebuhr on human nature (= *The Nature and Destiny of Man, vol. l; Human Nature* [1964], pp. 150, 161, 163-4, 178-9, 270-2; in Ahlgren, pp. 54-7). These extracts from an influential set of 1939 lectures contain Niebuhr's understanding of sin as pride.

Emil Brunner on 'the Image of God' (= *The Christian Doctrine of Creation and Redemption; Dogmatics Vol. 2* [1952], pp. 55-8; in McGrath, pp. 442-5). This passage offers a fine exposition of a relational understanding of the term 'image of God'.

'Richard Swinburne on the Concept of Creation' (= *The Coherence of Theism* [1977], pp. 12631; in McGrath, pp. 222-5). This text sets out with philosophical clarity what it means to speak of 'creation' within a theistic world-view.

John Mbiti on the cultural influences upon understandings of creation (= 'The Encounter of Christian Faith and African Religion', *The Christian Century* [27.8-3.9. 1980]; in Placher, vol. 2, pp. 197-8). In this extract from a journal article, Kenyan theologian John Mbiti points out how the universality of the claim for God as creator influences the way in which local histories are understood.

Sara Maitland on 'Ways of Relating' (in Loades, pp. 148-57). Novelist Sara Maitland reflects on how what it means to 'relate' connects with fundamental questions about how people talk of God.

Vitor Westhelle on a view of creation from Latin America (in Thistlethwaite and Engel, pp. 146-58). This challenging text brings to the topic of creation the insights of theology done in relation to displaced peoples. The concept of 'image of God' is interpreted relationally against this background.

Images of God

Ray Billington

If God made us in his own image, we have certainly returned the compliment.
(Voltaire)

The aim of this book is to show that, while religion is fundamental to the human condition, God is not. Religion is natural, God is artificial; religion is unavoidable, God is redundant. Why it remains the case that people still turn to God in their millions will be the subject of the next chapter. At this stage I wish to examine what it is that people have in mind when they reflect on the idea of God, or gods. It would clearly be impossible to describe every nuance of belief without making a whole book of a single chapter, but I shall attempt to outline those concepts which are most broadly expressed. In a situation where people can speak freely of 'God as we understand him'—to quote a fixed phrase of one self-help organisation—it should not surprise anyone that even a broad canvas yields a plethora of images to compare and contrast.

Deism

While there are several forms of deism, its general use stems from the seventeenth century, the Age of Enlightenment, when science had begun to provide the authority for people to cope with the complexities of the universe without falling back on the concept of God. God was viewed by deists as one who, having created the universe (in whatever time it took: the debate on that issue was just beginning to warm up) then retired for a well-earned rest, lasting for the remainder of eternity.

There is, in fact, a certain logic in this belief. Granted that since he was perfect, he could hardly create something imperfect (unless he was being deliberately devious, like the manufacturers of obsolescent light-bulbs); it follows that the world, being a perfect product of a perfect being (how else do we know of his perfection except through the evidence of his works?), no longer requires his assistance. Deism is the product of a broad human need, which we shall examine in the next chapter, to see a purpose in and a cause of everything. With time being viewed as lineal, God is used as a shorthand term to explain what otherwise seems inexplicable. Apart from its use of God as a *deus ex machina,* deism generally avoids the concept that there is any form of direct communication between God and his creatures. He has left them to work out their own salvation, with the result that, so far as they are concerned, their experience of him is not dissimilar to that of agnostics if not atheists.

Pantheism

The etymology of this word (as with most of the others to be examined) lies in the Greek language. 'Pan' means 'all' and 'theos' means 'God'. So the core of this theory is that God is all and all is God; in fact, it would not be inapposite to transliterate pantheism as 'all-God-ism'. Many pantheists define 'all' in terms of 'all that lives'—from *Homo sapiens* to the amoeba, from the mustard seed to the oak tree. But since nothing that has being in this world can exist independently of the surroundings in which the process of being is set, some 'hard' pantheists include inanimate objects along with sentient beings, stones, rivers and mountains alongside grass, insects, birds, fish and mammals, as manifestations of God.

Among modern philosophers, nobody expressed pantheism more directly than Spinoza. In his *Ethics* (1: 18) he wrote:

> All things that are, are in God, and must be conceived through God, and therefore God is the cause of things which are in Himself. This is the first point. Further, no substance can be granted outside God, that is, nothing which is outside God exists in itself; which was the second point. Therefore God is the immanent, but not transcendent, cause of all things.

The words 'immanent' and 'transcendent' are descriptive of, on the one hand, the divine presence within us (and, for pantheists, within all other beings) and, on the other, the divine manifested through the universe 'out there'. As we saw, deists refer (and occasionally defer) to this distant God: pantheists, on the contrary, rejoice in one who is manifested in our midst, within human beings and all other creatures. Even this statement is not entirely accurate, however, since it still retains a dualistic notion (*God* in *me, I* in *God)* which is alien to the deepest pantheistic ideas. God **is** me, and I *am* God would be a more accurate statement, though, as we shall see, statements of that kind should be used with the utmost caution if their meaning is not to be distorted.

What worries many about pantheism is its lack of belief in a God with moral qualities. Its viewpoint is, in fact, a logical inference from its basic image of God. If it is the case that the divine is expressed in every living being, then, at least so far as the human examples are concerned, no moral judgment can be made on behaviour, whether it be the kind of which we usually express approval, such as goodwill, tolerance, fair play and so on, or that which usually receives condemnation such as malice, greed and destructiveness. If everything we do and feel is an expression of God, all moral distinctions are irrelevant. This may seem like a *reductio ad absurdem* of the case, and perhaps it is not so heinous a situation as Westerners, raised on an either-or, good-bad mentality on ethical matters, are apt to judge it; but it remains a stumbling-block for many people. To state that we recognise God throughout the whole of his creation may seem acceptable, even desirable, to those who can sincerely sing of 'all things bright and beautiful', but how heartily can one sing this in the light of 'nature red in tooth and claw', where the stoat kills the rabbit and the ivy stifles the tree? Shelley could write in 'Adonais' of his friend Keats, recently dead:

He is made one with Nature: there is heard
His voice in all her music, from the moan
Of thunder, to the song of night's sweet bird.

And, presumably, in the hiss of the pit viper and the howl of the jackal. Maybe that comment betrays an anthropocentrism which is inappropriate, even impertinent, in pantheistic thought; but what can be said unequivocally is that nature is amoral, so that, inasmuch as it is viewed as a reflection of God's nature, he, too, is amoral. From the pantheist perspective, therefore, all the moral castigations over the ages, made by preachers in God's name, have been a total waste of breath. We shall see the soundness of this outlook as we proceed, specifically in Chapter 10.

One other criticism of pantheism relates to our human sense of initiative and freedom. If all is God, it is asked, what place is there for those qualities which seem (to the enquirer at any rate) integral to her sense of individuality, self-consciousness and autonomy? The resolution of this dilemma (if there is one) must remain until we discuss the mystical experience in Chapter 5.

Animism

Strictly, animism does not belong to any account of differing philosophies of God, but its affinity with some aspects of pantheism justifies a mention here. It derives from the Latin anima, meaning 'soul' (the same root as for the word 'animal', which is ironic in view of the fact that the official view of Christianity—to name but one world religion—is that they do not have souls). The primitive view expresses two beliefs. First, all human beings possess, or, perhaps more accurately, are possessed by, souls. These can exist both within and, more significantly, independently of the body. In dreams a person sees the souls of others besides himself appearing as phantoms or eidola —images of their physical appearances. It is also believed that these phantoms have been seen in visions or hallucinations, including phantoms of the dead. It is the absence of the soul which makes all the difference between a corpse and a living being.

By extension, it is believed, at least by some animists, that features of nature also have an anima. A particular rock, or tree, or stream will instil in the onlooker an aura, which he may interpret in terms of the supernatural or holy. Animistic thought is reflected in the Old Testament: in Genesis 28: 22, Jacob dedicates to God the stone on which he has laid his head to sleep with the words, 'This stone which I have set up as a sacred pillar shall be a house of God'. The rock which Moses struck in the wilderness, from which water flowed (Numbers 20: 7-11) may reflect similar thinking. The Christian doctrine of transubstantiation, with its view that the bread and wine become the actual body and blood of Christ, has been described as animistic in its conception, in the sense that physical objects assume a supernatural quality or essence.

Animism was seen by John Le Patourel (from *Chambers Encyclopedia*) as:

> not itself a religion, but a sort of primitive philosophy which controls not only religion but the whole life of the natural man. It represents a stage in the religious evolution which is still represented by the so-called nature-religions, or rather by the poly-daemonistic tribal religions.

Associated with animism is the term *mana*, referring, like animism, to an occult supernatural power which attaches itself to certain sacred objects. Distinctive to the idea of mana is the belief that, being sacred, these objects are therefore *tabu*, which literally means 'not to be lightly approached'. In Melanesia, mana is always connected with some individual who directs it, often wearing on his person a relic of a successful warrior, which gives him the aura he seeks. In other parts of the world the sacred object is described as a fetish. Common to all expressions of animism is the belief in a mystic, quasi-impersonal force which draws from observers a sense of awe and of the supernatural. In the religion of ancient Rome this was described as *numen* and Rudolph Otto, in his *The Idea of the Holy* (*Das Heilige*), has developed from this his concept of the numinous, referring to holiness as a state of mind which is brought about by a reaction to the mysterious, the abnormal and the uncanny. His view of religion, which we shall return to in Chapter 5, is a form of religious dread which he describes as *mysterium tremendum*—a mystery giving rise to both fascination and self-abasement. Otto stands in a tradition which is a far cry from that of animism, but I shall be suggesting that his philosophy represents a step, inspired by primitive concepts, towards the acceptance of religion without God. Animism and its cognates may be out of range of what I shall be proposing, but it is not out of bounds.

Theism

Theism expresses the image of God which is the most widely held in the world today, since it is the view taught in the three interconnected world religions which found their earliest expressions in the Middle East: Judaism, Christianity and Islam. The Greek word *theos*, like the Latin *deus*, means God, and the use of two different linguistic sources makes for clarity in designating the differing views. Effectively, theism combines both deism and pantheism, though with its own distinctive gloss. It accepts the transcendental God of the former, but adds the immanent God (gods) of the latter, and the combination gives its believers an image of a God who is both all-powerful and all-loving, terrible in his judgment on the wicked, merciful towards those who truly repent of their sins. The God of theism is thus an intervening God, not the absentee God of deism. It presents the view that, whatever his original intention for the world which he has created, his creatures, consequent to the freedom of choice which he has granted them, have gone astray and so constantly need his counsel and comfort if they are not to be overcome by folly (sin) and despair.

Although today almost all followers of the three religions just mentioned are unlikely to find this a problem, it should be added that, strictly speaking (that is, to be etymologically and, to a lesser extent, historically accurate), the correct word in this context is *monotheism*, where belief in only *one* God is made explicit. So long as we retain the concept of theism as, so far as Judaism, Christianity and Islam are concerned, belief in a supreme being, we are not likely to be confused on this matter.

Two supplementary concepts should be mentioned here. The first is *henotheism*, which reflects a stage between polytheism and monotheism. It acknowledges belief in a supreme being, but one who coexists with other, lesser, divine beings or gods. It is expressed, interestingly enough, in the first of the Ten Commandments: 'You shall have no other gods before me' (Exodus 20: 3). There *are* other gods, but compared with Jehovah they are impotent and worthless. A second view which similarly exemplifies a halfway-house between polytheism and monotheism is *monolatry*, literally only one to worship (Greek *latreia* means worship): again, the existence of other gods is not denied, but, it is affirmed by monolatrists, only their God is *worth* worshipping or, to avoid tautology (since the etymology of both words is the same—worship = 'worthship', or 'weorthscipe' in Old English), is *to be* worshipped. Again this is reflected in the Ten Commandments (the second): 'you shall not bow down to them or serve them; for I the Lord your God am a jealous God'.

Dualism (Ditheism)

As the name suggests, this school of thought affirms a belief in two gods, one of whom is normally 'good', the other 'evil', and sees both the history of the world and the battle that occurs within people's souls as arenas for the (inevitable) conflict between the two. It is an attempt to make sense of a world, allegedly created and ruled by a benevolent God, in which evil is continually encountered, whether in human behaviour, or, on a wider canvas, in the 'four horsemen' of the Apocalypse: death, famine, pestilence and war.

The most overtly dualistic of the world's religions is Zoroastrianism, the religion of the followers of the Iranian prophet, Zoroaster (or Zarathustra as it is transliterated from Persian). It is still adhered to by the Guebres of Iran (where they suffer persecution for their beliefs) and the Parsees of India. It expounds the view that the world is governed by a wholly good God, Ahuro Mazda, who is opposed by the evil Angra Mainyu. The Zoroastrian *Gathas* declares:

> Now at the beginning the twin spirits have declared their nature, the better and the evil, in thought and word and deed . . . And when these two spirits came together, in the beginning they established life and non-life.
>
> (Yasna, 30)

Although the ultimate defeat of evil is assured (which is why some Zoroastrian scholars deny that this system of belief is ditheistic), the battle between the two is still proceeding, and followers of this religion are there- fore called to commit themselves totally to goodness. It was because of this emphasis on morality that Nietzsche chose the founder of this religion as a focal point of his ground-breaking work *Thus Spake Zarathustra*: he was, Nietzsche believed, the most moral of all the world's religious leaders.

In its attempt to come to terms with the problem of evil in a world allegedly ruled by a benevolent God, theism has not shied away from this expression of dualism. Christianity, for example, has resorted to a personification of evil in the form of Satan, whose power, it teaches, has been dealt a mortal blow through the sacrifice of Jesus the Christ. C. G. Jung (1959) contends that the implication of this belief is that Christianity is ditheistic, since, even if Satan is damned, 'he is *eternal* in his state of damnation'. He adds: 'If Christianity claims to be a monotheism, it becomes unavoidable to assume the opposites as being contained in God.' (The fact is, as has been clear since Hume's famous analysis *Enquiry Concerning the Principles of Morals*, that belief in one supreme God who is both omnipotent and at the same time benevolent founders on the problem of evil. As Hume stated, either God can destroy evil but will not, in which case he is malevolent; or he wants to change things but cannot, in which case he is impotent. Evil is thought of as a 'problem' only because we feel that the situation ought to be otherwise: but that is to anticipate later discussion, especially in Chapter 10.)

The Hindu scripture the *Bhagavad-gita* (the key section of the massive *Mahabharata*) illustrates the symbolic nature of dualism. The *Mahabharata* is an account of the battle for the kingdom of Bharata waged between two families, the evil Kauravas and the virtuous Pandavas. Book 6, the *Bhagavad-gita*, contains the instructions before the battle given by the God Krishna to Arjuna, one of the five Pandava brothers. The battle is, in fact, symbolic of the eternal conflict in every individual between the ego and 'higher nature'—or, quite simply, between the good and the bad in everyone. The yin-yang philosophy of China expresses dualism is a different way, suggesting that 'good' and 'bad' cannot exist independently of each other: that we, in fact, can understand the one only in contrast with the other. Consequently, it is false to depict the two as rival forces and, even more harmful, unrealistic to symbolise or personify them as two eternally coexisting rival Gods. Both 'good' and 'evil', as I shall further indicate in Chapter 10, depend on each other to have any meaning at all.

Polytheism

Literally 'many gods', this form of belief has been expressed in numerous societies, both primitive and advanced. The classical world of both the Greeks and the Romans had its pantheons, that is, many gods, each with his or her area of responsibility. Many other civilisations had a similarly wide range of gods and goddesses, for example in Egypt, Mexico, and among the Celts and the Norse. While there is generally a hierarchy among their gods and goddesses, where the highest achieve that status because of the importance of their responsibilities (gods of war are more important than household gods, for instance—perhaps reflecting the male dominance in constructing these pantheons), there is generally no one God who is viewed as being in overall charge.

This is an aspect of polytheism which varies between cultures, however. The Hindus, for example, express belief in many gods, such as Rama, Vishnu, Shiva and his consort Kali, but Brahman is held to be the ultimate source of all that exists. In some communities the idea is held that while there is one supreme God who retains ultimate responsibility for the world and its happenings, he has delegated his authority to divine functionaries who work as directed by, and are responsible to, him. Maybe, as Geoffrey Parrinder suggests (*Religion in an African City*), we need 'to devise a term which would denote religions that have a supreme God and also worship other gods'. Many expressions of polytheism fall into this category since, as William James suggests (1960,

p. 141), it has 'shown itself well satisfied with a universe composed of many original principles, provided we be allowed to believe that the divine principle remains supreme, and that others are subordinate'.

Panentheism

This is the doctrine that, while God is manifested in all living creatures, as pantheists believe, that is not the whole story: if it were, it would imply that God exists only so long as Nature exists; so when, as is inevitable eventually, the world comes to an end, he will die with it. The word means 'all-in-God' and was rescued from obscurity by John Robinson in his sequel to *Honest to God, Explorations into God*. He argued that the panentheistic view, in a way not always found in theism, made explicit apropos of God that he was both immanent and transcendent, present in all living things but not dependent on their existence for his own: he is omnipresent and eternal throughout the universe and, if need be, beyond. Add to this the interventionist theology of theism, and, Robinson suggested, we have the most philosophically satisfying view of God's being, and of his relationship both with the universe in general and all forms of life, human or otherwise, in particular.

These, then, are some of the major delineations of God, or gods, which have found acceptance among human beings since the earliest historical times. The list is not totally comprehensive, but I hope that enough categories have been included to embrace the ideas of most people who affirm a belief in the deity. Two issues remain to be reflected upon before turning to the question of *why* people have come to any of these beliefs.

A classification of types

From the amalgam just presented, I think it is possible to classify the various expressions of belief under three main headings. The first, and most primitive, is the polytheistic and animistic set of beliefs. While sometimes expressing the idea of one supreme being who delegates some of his powers to subordinates, the more general picture is of a large number of deities, each with a particular area of responsibility. Some areas are more extensive, and the gods responsible for them consequently more 'important', than others, but the general scene is one of a cabinet (with perhaps a *primus inter pares*), and not a dictatorship.

The second category is monotheism. Where this is the belief, it is held that there is one God only who has revealed his power through the original creation of the universe and apart from in classical deism, continues to reveal himself throughout the world in his role as guide and guardian of the people whom he has created. It is to him that they are continuously, and will be ultimately, answerable.

The third type is more difficult to name, since it contains facets of most of the categories mentioned earlier. It includes elements of pantheism, especially in its emphasis on the harmony of an individual with the natural world, the unavoidable context of his living, and on the sense of the divine which runs through him. Otto's conception of the numinous is close to what I am implying. Perhaps the most convenient word is mysticism, and we shall remain with that for the present, recognising, as will be outlined later, that we need to give it a connotation and context which broadens it out from its traditional usage.

Most of the world's religions have elements of all three types in their belief systems, though normally one is dominant. The religion which affirms all three without making a value judgment about their respective merits is Hinduism. This religion will be discussed in some detail in Chapter 6, but it is worth noting here that the Hindu scriptures—the Vedas, with the Upanishads, the *Mahabharata*, with the *Bhagavad-gita*, the *Ramayana* and so on—include all three types. Sometimes they express a belief in many gods—Brahman, Vishnu, Krishna, Shiva and numerous others; at other times a belief in one absolute God, Brahman; and elsewhere a belief in the mystical experience as the ultimate reality, the discovery of the oneness of the individual Atman with the Brahman, the ground of being—a discovery which means entry into the state of moksha, enlightenment, where one can say with total certainty, 'tat tvam asi': thou art (or I am) that.

I shall be arguing that it is along this path that we need to tread if we are to experience religion which is unencumbered either by ancient mythology or modern pseudo-psychology; here faith is replaced with experience and knowledge. But the path is wider than that to which even Hinduism, the most religious of the world's religions, bears witness.

Attributes of God

Monotheists declare that God is perfect, and this concept is the basis, as we shall see, of the ontological argument for his existence. 'Perfect' sounds a straightforward-enough term, but what it means exactly becomes more difficult to determine the more closely it is examined. It can be used casually, of course, as when we describe someone as a perfect fool, or as looking like a perfect angel, but in this usage the epithet adds little to the name; we may have a perfect copy of a document, in the sense that it is an exact replica of the original, but would we be justified in describing a copy of a famous painting as 'a perfect forgery'? Generally, we use the term to mean 'that which cannot be improved on' which, so far as human beings and their inventions and creations are concerned, is impossible. There is, for instance, no such thing as a perfectly tuned motor engine: with more sophisticated equipment we should be able to increase, however infinitesimally, its accuracy; similarly, there is no such person as a perfect lady or gentleman, no perfect body or perfect mind. Similarly, there is nobody who is morally perfect. Even assuming that we could reach a consensus about what the word 'good' means in reference to a human character, which is expecting the impossible since we are dealing with an evaluative term about whose meaning there will always be wide-ranging disagreement (as will be further discussed in Chapter 10), it is inconceivable that everyone everywhere would agree that any particular person had attained such a standard of goodness that he or she could not be better. Yet the New Testament calls for this quality: 'You must be perfect, as your heavenly father is perfect' (Matt 5: 48).

The attributes of God which theologians and philosophers of religion (who do not always belong to the same stable, of course) have extrapolated over the centuries to categorise his perfection will be readily agreed on. God is:

- almighty (omnipotent in the latinised version of the word): he *can do anything*;
- all-knowing (omniscient): he *knows everything*;
- all-present (omnipresent): he *is everywhere*;
- everlasting (eternal): he *is without beginning or end*;

(these last two characteristics are contained in the word universal, often ascribed to God)

- unchangeable (immutable): he *is forever the same*;
- limitless (infinite): a word which embraces several of the foregoing designations, meaning that he is *inexhaustible*, and illustrated in the hymn 'O God thou bottomless abyss'.

The trouble with this list is that though the qualities referred to spring readily to people's lips when talking of God's perfection, it is beyond the mind of man to picture what any of them means in actuality. If, for instance, God is almighty, does that mean he can do anything he decides to do, even act against logic by arranging that every other day a triangle can have four sides, or that on the Sabbath an object can both exist and not exist at the same time, breaking the Law of Contradiction? If he cannot achieve these, does that mean that his almightiness is bound by the rules of logic? A monotheist may well argue that, since God created the rules, and since he is unchangeable, he is simply abiding by what he himself established. But if that is the case, does it not suggest that his immutability is inconsistent with his omnipotence? The monotheist might reply that what is not broken doesn't need mending—and that the laws of logic fit into this category. (The scriptural fundamentalist has, of course, no problem with logic: he can, for instance, cheerfully accept the two contradictory accounts of the creation contained in Genesis 1 and 2, with the defence that these differences simply illustrate St Paul's affirmation that 'the foolishness of God is wiser than men'. Thus do some people break the first commandment, which includes loving God with all the mind.)

Karen Armstrong (op. cit.) has shown in her comprehensive survey that, whether or not God is himself immutable, his image over the centuries and in different cultures has certainly changed. The monotheist may defend his position by affirming that, while human understanding of him may have changed, he has been always the same—waiting, it may be presumed, to be fully discovered and understood. If this is the case, it follows that any statements about God, like those made about the physical world (as Popper has indicated) can be seen as no more than provisional, however certain they may seem from our current perspective.

Perhaps the monotheist will eventually be able to resolve the dilemma created by another of God's attributes—his omniscience. If God knows everything, this knowledge must be of the future as well as the past (and the present, if there is such a thing: time, after all, is the continuous process of the 'not yet' moving inexorably into the 'no longer'). If he knows only what has happened up to now (which, as I write, is already in the past), then he knows no more than what can be known by a *very* knowledgeable scholar—or, at any rate, a group of scholars—who, or most of whom, would hardly wish to claim to be gods. Yet if God knows the future, this implies that he knows all that is to become of us. What price, then, freewill, autonomy and personal initiative?

The situation here is bristling with problems, which are hardly eased by the attribution of human qualities to the infinite being: a process of *anthropomorphism*, meaning 'in the form of man'. These qualities describe God in terms which are more readily accessible to mortal beings because we encounter them among our fellows on a daily basis. Thus God is proclaimed as one who loves his creatures, cares for them, guides them when they are perplexed, comforts them in times of sorrow, strengthens them in times of trial, forgives them their sins and, if all goes well, finally rewards them with an eternal place in his presence. There is also another side to his nature, equally expressive of human qualities. He can be jealous, wrathful, destructive, vengeful and, ultimately, condemnatory as he sits in judgment on his creatures. Armstrong illustrates from theistic sources how the latter qualities were gradually replaced by the former in the minds of the authors of those scriptures; but the anthropomorphism remains: God possesses human qualities to the highest conceivable extent, all, in short, perfectly expressed. He is the ideal father, the most considerate lover, the wisest advocate and the most unbiased judge.

The problem with these anthropomorphic characterisations, as opposed to the more philosophical terms used earlier, is that they have the effect of bringing God down to human level, and depend for their effectiveness on what, for human beings, always requires physical organisms. Thus God is (almost) always male; he is the father of his people, the bridegroom to his faithful worshippers. It may be argued that if we called God 'she' we would have the same anthropomorphic problem, which is intensified if we call him 'it'. (To affirm that we need a new pronoun which means 'he and/or she and/or it' simply begs the question raised in this book: why speak of God at all?—but we will hold that topic over until Chapter 5.) At this stage of the enquiry, it is enough to be aware that any kind of talk about God, who is perfect, is bound to be expressed inadequately, and that what words we use are the best we can manage after many generations of reflection on the matter. To realise that all God-talk is inadequate is to recognise a situation very little different from that of a musician attempting to characterise the inspiration behind his compositions, or a poet describing his muse.

The philosopher Ludwig Feuerbach (1804-72) argued that God, as an image held in people's minds, was nothing more than a product of anthropomorphism. In his most famous book *Das Wesen des Christentums*, translated by George Eliot as *The Essence of Christianity*, he described religion as 'the dream of the human mind', arguing that human beings project their own ideals and natures on to an illusory God. God was thus the personification of the best thinking of which the human mind was capable, with a character which epitomised the best behaviour which they could engage in and the noblest principles which they could follow. For Feuerbach, theology was concerned with the nature of man rather than God: man was, he argued, the only true *ens realissimum*, or most real being ('ens' is the present participle of the Latin 'esse', to be, and 'realissi-mum' the superlative of the adjective 'reale', which is self-explicatory).

Process theology

A view on the nature of God which was first expounded a century ago, but has yet to be accommodated into theistic teaching, is process theology. It was first openly discussed by the philosopher A. N. Whitehead (1861-1947), but was given a wider public through the writings of Pierre Teilhard De Chardin (1881-1955), especially in his book *The Phenomenon of Man*, which, initially refused an imprimatur by the Roman Catholic Church, was eventually published in 1959 after his death, publication having been refused despite the fact that he was a Jesuit priest, but perhaps because he was also a palaeontologist. It is significant that the introduction to this book was written by the humanist, Julian Huxley.

Process theology teaches that God cannot be understood in the theistic tradition alone, but only if to this tradition are added the main developments in science, especially the science of evolution. God's way of working in the world is a slow process, so that we are given a picture of him working to overcome the evil that is present in the universe, together with the element of chance, or accident, which it contains.

God is thus viewed as one who is not so much self-sufficient as involved in the long, patience-demanding process of bringing about what Teilhard termed the *noosphere*, a state beyond the biosphere, where the mind is the supremely active agent of events. This idiosyncratic representation of God's immanence almost reaches the point of declaring that he is not omnipotent, because he cannot do what he wants where and when he wants, but must work alongside his creation to bring about the new higher state: a process which seems to imply that God is also not unchangeable, as earlier described. This theology has appealed to numerous modern theologians and philosophers of religion; but it, like earlier views, still remains fixed on the view of God's necessity, which is precisely the issue under discussion. It is time to turn our attention to the question of why this point of view has such a hold on *Homo sapiens*.

Section 3

Religion and Nationhood

Interpretation of Politics and Religion

Laura Olson

I spent years in looking for men wise enough to solve the problems that puzzled me, not in religion or politics so much as along the wavy line between the two.

—Lord John Acton

During the mid-nineteenth century, Herman Melville portrayed the ties that linked political and religious values. For him, many Americans infused the nation with spiritual values. As he commented in *White-Jacket or The World in a Man-of-War*: "We Americans are the peculiar, chosen people—the Israel of our time. … The political Messiah … has come in us, if we would but give utterance to his promptings. … To be efficacious, Virtue must come down from aloft, even as our blessed Redeemer came down to redeem our whole man-of-war world; to that end, mixing with its sailors and sinners as equals" (Melville 2002:151, 229). In his later novel, *Moby Dick*, Melville held that the individual owed a higher loyalty than to the national ship of state engaged in warfare, injustice, and oppression.

Preaching to congregants in the New Bedford, Massachusetts chapel, Father Mapple concluded his sermon about the sailor Jonah with this hosanna: "Delight,—top gallant delight is to him who acknowledges no law or lord but the Lord his God, and is only a patriot to heaven" (Melville 1961:64). Horrified by the injustices reflected in the "bloody massacres" and national wars, Melville recognized the gap between the "wisdom of heaven" taught by Jesus and the "practical wisdom of earth" implemented by government officials (Melville 2002:324). Echoing Jesus' teachings, he asserted that citizens' identity rested mainly on ultimate spiritual values that assumed a universal perspective, not loyalty to the nation-state.

Political Attitudes and Religious Values

Just as during the nineteenth century, so today the impact of religious values has attracted extensive attention in the United States. Issues of justice linked to war, nationalism, and legal rights stimulate divergent interpretations. Disputes arise about the meaning of procedural and distributive justice. Threats to national security jeopardize support for civil liberties. Legalization of rights to abortion and homosexual relationships provoke controversies among churches and political parties. Procedures for expanding gender equality arouse disagreements about women's rights. On matters of distributive justice, ideological differences split those who favor government policies for greater income equality from groups that prefer more promarket programs.

This essay explores the diverse ways that religious values influence political attitudes toward procedural and distributive justice. Whereas procedural justice emphasizes the means to achieve goals, distributive justice pays greater attention to the results, especially to the actual allocation of income and wealth. Both religion and politics place high importance on the laws, rules, and norms that regulate human interactions. Distributive justice involves the link between individual interests and the common good. Equitable treatment of the poor, marginals, and outcasts forms a major issue considered by religious and political texts.

Three related questions become crucial to the analysis of justice. First, why do individuals and groups hold distinctive theological views about spiritual justice, and why do these beliefs change?

Second, in what ways do theological interpretations influence concepts of political justice? Third, how and why do these perceptions of justice shape political preferences held by religious liberals and conservatives, both among the elite as well as the mass public? Despite a few differences, the Social Gospel and New Thought best represent liberal positions toward politics and theology. Table 1.1 illustrates the crucial variables explaining political attitudes. These explanations include the historical context, theological assumptions about spiritual justice, and orientations toward political justice.

How do theological interpretations of God, the individual, and society shape beliefs about spiritual justice? Hierarchy, individualism, egalitarianism, and fatalism represent four types of justice. To what degree do persons stress deference to authority versus opposition to hierarchy? Do they give priority to individual autonomy or to personal interdependence with the community? When interacting with others, some people prefer inclusive, egalitarian relationships, whereas others lean toward more elitist, exclusive connections. How fatalistic or efficacious do individuals feel about changing the status quo? If efficacious feelings dominate, faith, righteous beliefs, good works, obedience to law, prayer, and education comprise possible ways to achieve personal

Table 1. Explanations for Political Attitudes

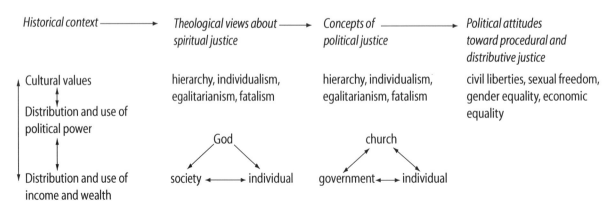

salvation and societal redemption (see Andrain and Smith 2006:94–103; Douglas and Ney 1998:96–185; Lockart 2003; Thompson, Verweij, and Ellis 2006; Wildavsky 1998).

What explanations lie behind the links between theological interpretations and concepts of political justice? A functional theory of attitudes at the micro (individual) level, a meso approach to church organizations and their ties to political parties, and a macro concern for the historical context—cultural values, political and economic structures—provide some tentative explanations. Interacting with the structural situation, religious beliefs can fulfill several needs: the search for meaning, the establishment of community solidarity, and defense against threats (Smith, Bruner, and White 1956). These beliefs then influence interpretations of political justice about the interactions among the church, government, and individual.

How do interpretations of political justice influence specific attitudes toward procedural and distributive justice, particularly preferences for civil liberties, legal abortion, gender equality, and economic equality? Particularly when religious values become closely aligned with ideological identifications, prospects rise for the political importance of religious issues. Liberals and conservatives articulate different concepts of justice. Conservatives who affirm hierarchy, individual freedom for property-owners, unequal economic outcomes, and resignation to established traditions will probably give lower support to civil liberties, sexual choice, gender equality, and activist government programs intended to promote greater income equality. By contrast, most liberals express opposite beliefs about justice. They reject hierarchical authority, prefer more equal distribution of resources, feel high personal efficacy, and uphold individual liberty from domination by government, corporate, and ecclesiastical bureaucracies. According to liberals, public policy

officials should support civil liberties, legal abortion, gender equality, and egalitarian government programs that provide comprehensive, generous social services. Under these polarizing ideological conditions, liberal and conservative activists in churches, business firms, unions, political parties, and social movements link their theological beliefs to public attitudes. Activists who can mobilize the most cohesive networks and form alliances with powerful government officials attain the greatest influence over the public policy agenda.

These questions about religious values and political justice pose important issues that pertain to everyone's life. Despite the "wavy line" separating religious values from political ideologies, both discourses highlight similar issues, feature a similar structure of thought, and fulfill the same functions. Even if specific interpretations differ, major topics of communication revolve around justice, equality, liberty, civic virtue, the public good, and ethical behavior. However divergent their orientations, theologians and political leaders stress hierarchy, individualism, egalitarianism, and fatalism as key perspectives toward justice. Politics and religion also focus on power. Whereas government officials accumulate and use power to make public decisions, many New Thought adherents view God as Omnipotence, infinite power, and creative, ultimate energy (Cady 1995:29–31).

The thoughts elaborated by political and religious adherents show similar structural dimensions: coherence, consistency, and interdependence of ideas. These vary according to the degree of an individual's active involvement. Political leaders and activists express a greater coherence than do more passive party supporters and voters among the general public. Similarly, whereas theologians and ministers often articulate coherent beliefs, the laity, especially inactive members who rarely attend religious services, hold more fragmented, *ad hoc*, inconsistent interpretations (see Bennett 2006; Converse 1964, 2006; Friedman 2006).

Interpretations of religious and political communications fulfill similar functions. They provide meaning, social solidarity, and defense against threats (Jervis 2006). In the political arena, ideologies specify one's place in the political system, the meaning of citizenship, and the degree of activism. Theologies concentrate on the search for meaning through issues of faith that involve the individual's relation to God, the nature of reality, the role of spiritual values in human affairs, and ethical behavior toward others.

Faced with a complex situation filled with contradictions, puzzling dilemmas, injustice, and uncertainty, religious values may offer meaning. Especially to those suffering injustice, evil, misfortune, and hopelessness, belief in transcendental, ultimate values can give a plausible interpretation of events, reasons for living, hope for eventual justice, and the causes of suffering. The Hebrews perceived liberation from Egyptian oppression by the Pharaoh and conquest of the "promised land" as hope of victory over initial tragedy. Early Christians viewed the Roman crucifixion of Jesus and his resurrection as divine signs of their triumph over political oppression, economic exploitation by the wealthy elites, and cultural humiliation. For both Jews and Christians, justice brought not only redemption to the individual but also to the whole society. Nineteenth-century Christians in the United States struggled for temperance, women's suffrage, and the abolition of slavery. During the twentieth century African Americans, liberal white Christians, and Jews campaigned for an integrated society that expanded voting rights, civil liberties, economic equality, educational opportunities, and access to public accommodations. Supporting world peace, liberal Christian churches and Jews protested against the wars in Vietnam and Iraq. They also led movements to secure public policies

that would reduce poverty, enhance immigrants' rights, protect sexual choice, and secure a healthy environment. For them, a clear separation of state from church control would enable the individuals to realize their full potentialities through reason, education, and an enlightened conscience.

Cultural interpretations scarcely remain constant or uniform. They change over time and space. Their meaning depends on the historical context that shapes both the communicator and the audience. Hence, analysts cannot uncover a single, original meaning to a specific scriptural passage or ideological phrase. Because meanings represent transactions among individuals—the formulator of a text and the user of that text—they become pluralist and complex, not unified or simple. Depending on the historical context and the specific audience, the same religious or political text will attribute divergent meanings to the same symbolic "truths" about justice, salvation, virtue, liberation, and equality (Berryman 2005; Meeks 2005).

Since meanings largely depend on social interactions, the degree of solidarity provided by theological or political beliefs functions as a key benefit to individuals. Local political networks—clubs, political parties, interest groups, popular movements—as well as more inclusive ties to the national community represent contemporary forms of social cohesion. Similarly, in the religious sphere solidarity may emerge from local religious networks (churches, temples, synagogues, mosques) and from more universal ties to a denomination and an ideal spiritual community, whether Christian, Jewish, Islamic, or Buddhist. For many persons, the benefits of belonging to a local religious community that provides fellowship and social services outweigh the costs of participation, such as contributing finances, attending services, meeting in Bible circles, and serving as church officers. Sharing the dominant beliefs of the congregation merges one's personal identity with the collective identity. Particularly when a religious association supplies not only meaningful values but also tangible social services, solidarity increases. Since the mid-nineteenth century, U.S. Catholic charities have provided social benefits such as job interviews, housing, health care, education, child care, and neighborhood assistance to immigrants from Ireland, Italy, Spain, Poland, and Latin America. Prayers, rituals, and other ceremonies strengthen this solidarity.

Interpersonal ties can stem from cooperative or adversarial interactions with other groups. If individuals belong to a heterogeneous religious or political association with members of diverse social backgrounds, they develop an inclusive stance that reflects a commitment to civil values: tolerance, mutual respect, compromise, and dialogue with others who hold divergent interests. Interaction with other groups embodies the same accommodating spirit that brings solidarity within each separate group. Reconciliation strengthens transactions with diverse groups. Minimal hostility emerges between "pure" ingroups and "decadent" outgroups. Civic solidarity promotes support for democratic principles. Yet often religious solidarity rests on adversarial relations with different groups. Dominant loyalty attaches to a monolithic, homogeneous religious institution. Instead of building bridges, the religious group remains a separate island with hostile attitudes toward other groups that fail to support their dominant beliefs. Even if conflict with outgroups intensifies intragroup solidarity, it lessens enthusiasm for such notions of procedural justice linked to civil liberties, individual rights for all citizens, and political equality (Andrain and Smith 2006:76–84).

Particularly when conflictual interactions strengthen solidarity, defense against threats becomes a crucial function of both political and religious beliefs. All over the world, individuals face many threats to their security. Some arise from their own fear of death or the actual deaths of loved ones. Threats from marginal groups—homosexuals, AIDS victims, drug addicts, people of a minority ethnic or religious association—often pose dangers to those feeling insecure. National unemployment, declining wages, growing poverty, and high inflation cause widespread worries about economic well-being. The dysfunctional aspects of modernization and globalization—rising joblessness, increased poverty, heightened income inequality, rapid changes in economic growth—often produce the threats that lead to membership in a religious community promising reassurance against all these perceived dangers. When domestic violence, wars, famines, hurricanes, and earthquakes strike a nation, the defensive urge rises. If defense against threats becomes a dominant motive, religious polarization may combine with political polarization to exacerbate conflict (Cesari 2005; Leustean 2005; Yamane 2007).

However important the resemblances between political and religious beliefs, they reveal crucial differences. A key dissimilarity stems from political leaders' greater concern for mundane, incremental, pragmatic issues that yield to compromise and accommodation. By contrast, religion stresses more transcendental, ultimate ends that provide meaning to human experiences, strengthen solidarity, and offer reassurance against threats. Particularly if these transcendental standards apply to all aspects of life, "true believers" cannot easily make compromises for fear of contaminating the purity of their spiritual interpretations. Regardless of these differences, the major focus of this book highlights the interaction—the reciprocal influence—that politics exerts on religion. How do religious values shape concepts of political justice? In what ways do political developments affect general interpretations of justice and their links to specific policy preferences?

Political and Spiritual Justice

Interpretations of religious and political justice focus on three dimensions: the content (meaning) of justice and its application to specific attitudes, such as civil liberties, gender equality, sexual freedom, and economic equality. For each dimensions, we can distinguish divergent liberal and conservative views most often assumed by well-educated activists, academicians, and theologians.

Meaning of Justice

Mary Douglas and Aaron Wildavsky formulated four types of justice that shape theological perspectives and political outlooks. They include hierarchy, individualism, egalitarianism, and fatalism (Douglas and Ney 1998:96–153; Wildavsky 1998). These four worldviews depend on the strength of group ties over the individual as well as the acceptance of role differentiation and externally-imposed rules. Hierarchy gives precedence to strong group ties, deference to rules imposed by elites, and norms that accord high-status persons the greatest privileges. Individualism ranks lower on group cohesion and rules imposed by external authorities. Rather than deferring to hierarchs' interpretation of rules, individualists in small groups negotiate the specific implications of general rules, so that they adjust to changing, ad hoc conditions. Competition becomes important as a way to motivate incentives for productive achievement and to allocate unequal rewards based on the degree of performance. Unlike individualists, egalitarians affirm the need for more equal rights to participation and resources. They want individuals to participate in communal networks where widespread, inclusive participation prevails among people who conduct discourse about rules for reconciling conflicts. Fatalism takes an atomized outlook on the world. Cynicism, social distrust, and alienation toward others deter individuals from group cooperation. Perceiving change as futile, fatalists resign themselves to accepting rules imposed by hierarchical institutions. Apathy and minimal participation in either a political or religious association result. In general, whereas liberals place priority on egalitarian, individualist concepts of justice, conservatives give greater emphasis to hierarchy and the need to obey the dictates of the collective *ethos* upheld by family and church heads.

Examining the main goals of justice, the sources of injustice, and ways for attaining greater justice, we can better comprehend the meaning of these four worldviews. The conservative hierarchs uphold order, loyalty, and harmony as primary goals. Injustice derives from deviations from the rules imposed by established institutions. Disobedience toward traditional ethical standards produces decadence, disorder, impurity, and moral anarchy. To strengthen justice, society must strengthen the traditional established institutions: the church, family, military, police, and courts. Besides educating the masses in ethical, spiritual standards, these institutions impose sanctions on individuals who deviate from customary rules. Society operates as an organic community based on loyalty to the established traditional order. Government assistance to church and patriarchal families strengthens social harmony.

Unlike hierarchs, who value order, libertarian individualists equate justice with the innovative freedom to compete and achieve success. For them, the main goals focus on performance, efficiency, and productivity: entrepreneurial values. This utilitarian view assumes that a just society grants higher rewards—income, promotion, status—to individuals who have made the greatest contribution to beneficial outcomes. The causes of injustice stem from both structural inequities and personal failings. An oppressive bureaucratic government may wield extensive control over business enterprises, so that individuals retain few choices. Social groups can discriminate against persons with high talents, abilities, and skills. Laziness, drug addiction, alcoholism, and irresponsibility may deter individuals from taking advantage of existing opportunities or creating new opportunities for achievement. Rather than egalitarian public policies administered by a bureaucratic government, voluntary associations and personal effort become the major strategies for attaining a more just society where benefits depend on individual contributions. Stable contracts, secure property rights, privatization, deregulation, flexible wages, and education in productive skills and attitudes that promote personal responsibility become crucial programs for securing procedural fairness. Under these policies, equal opportunities, however extensive, usually lead to unequal economic rewards.

By contrast, leftist egalitarians seek to enhance all dimensions of equality: cultural, economic, and political. Cultural equality focuses on treating all persons, whatever their social status, with respect and dignity. Economic equality connotes not only enhanced opportunities for everyone but a narrower gap separating rich from poor. Political equality encompasses equal treatment before the law, access to the government decision process, and equal influence over the policy agenda. Injustice emerges from structural domination: political repression, economic exploitation, and cultural humiliation by authoritarian churches, oppressive governments, and gigantic corporations. For egalitarians, the most effective strategies for obtaining justice involve more inclusive popular participation in decentralized governments, small-scale councils, consumer groups, nonbureaucratic unions, mass political parties, populist movements, and religious associations

such as *comunidades eclesiales de base* (Christian local communities teaching liberation theology). Upholding the need for equality between men and women, young and old, rich and poor, saints and sinners, these populist organizations campaign for universalist, inclusive public policies that grant social services to all persons, regardless of income, social status, political power, ethnicity, or religion. By implementing policies in a fair, nonarbitrary, nondiscretionary way, government administrators secure procedural justice. Distributive justice thrives when policies produce egalitarian consequences in a caring, sharing society.

Unlike the egalitarians, fatalists place little faith in ever securing either procedural or distributive justice. For them, justice seems futile, however desirable. Survival becomes a major goal. Injustice arises from conditions beyond one's personal control—luck, chance, accidents, karma, maybe even God or Satan. Life appears unfair, random, unpredictable, uncontrollable, and chaotic. Perceiving life as a lottery, fatalists have low personal and political efficacy. They rely on cleverness and manipulation, key strategies for survival. Although their sense of political impotence discourages active public participation, fatalists may support powerful patrons and charismatic leaders who promise immediate but dictatorial solutions to their personal frustrations about perceived injustice. Playing the public lottery often gives marginals the rare if random chance to win a fortune and alleviate deprivations stemming from unjust conditions.

Neither one individual nor the same society consistently upholds only a single worldview; divergent values compete for dominance and often combine to influence theological and political orientations. For example, corporate elites often synthesize individualism with hierarchy to justify their class rule. When the Swedish Social Democrats initially gained power, they blended organizational hierarchy with egalitarian social service benefits. Whereas the Social Gospel prophet Walter Rauschenbusch linked economic equality to collectivism, New Thought students in Unity and Religious Science harmonize cultural equality with individualism. If fatalism combines with equality, high alienation emerges against the elitist establishment; yet the radical dissidents lack the efficacy to engage in collective political action. The merger of hierarchy with fatalism reflects marginalization by rightwingers who see themselves victimized by leftist oppression but feel powerless to organize for sociopolitical change (Grendstad 2003).

Application of Spiritual Principles to Public Policies

Influenced by the four worldviews of justice, liberals and conservatives apply general principles to specific public attitudes toward procedural and distributive justice. These policy issues include civil liberties, sexual freedom, gender equality, prison reform, ecology, world peace, and income distribution. On all these issues, liberals rather than conservatives adopt a more optimistic, individualistic, and egalitarian perspective but show lower deference to established authority. As a result, they give greater support to civil liberties, gender equality, sexual choice, economic equality, and policies for expanding the scope of government authority to provide social service benefits for health care, urban assistance, and poverty reduction. By contrast, conservatives take a more pessimistic, hierarchical, elitist, communal outlook on these public issues. Social institutions, especially the church and family, wield communal control over individual will. Opposed to disorder, chaos, and anarchy, they show greater faith in hierarchical elites: men, elders, clergy, and the wealthy. However great the ideological consistency affirmed by conservative activists, class differences often split the conservative movement. Whereas wealthier members oppose government attempts to increase income equality, poorer conservatives show stronger support (Collins 1993; Grafton and Permaloff 2005; Greeley and Hout 2006:84–90, 121–27).

Given the diversity of meanings attached to religious concepts, notions of spiritual reality do not always congrue with interpretations of just policies. The most consistent stands occur among those who share a similar outlook toward spiritual and political justice. For example, William Sloane Coffin, John Shelby Spong, and Rabbi Michael Lerner all favor civil liberties, procedural democracy, gender equality, and more equal economic outcomes. Perceiving God as loving, nurturant Spirit, they view biblical truths in a symbolic, metaphorical, pluralist way. By contrast, Protestant fundamentalists like Pat Robertson, James Dobson, Tim LaHaye, and dominant Southern Baptist ministers take a self-styled "conservative" perspective on politics and religion. Compared with liberal clergy, they give less support to legalized abortion, homosexual rights, women's equality with men in church or government, and government programs to secure greater economic equality. Interpretations of truth rest on a monistic, literal reading of the Bible, regarded as an inerrant, infallible foundation of personal behavior, legal decrees, and even conclusions about evolution. For them, God plays a punitive role, judging sinners and punishing the wicked. Reflecting a polarized view, these fundamentalist leaders believe divine nurturance extends only to "born-again" Christians who have accepted Jesus Christ as their personal Savior.

Other religious leaders adopt less consistent perspectives toward politics and spiritual values. The founder of Sojourners, a national network that works for world peace, poverty reduction, and social justice, Protestant evangelical Jim Wallis holds "orthodox" theological doctrines derived from the Apostles' Creed. Although he displays limited enthusiasm for abortion and homosexual rights, he strongly backs public policies to secure expanded civil liberties, gender equality, and especially economic equality. Dorothy Day, the cofounder of the Catholic Worker movement, affirmed the theological concepts in the Apostles' Creed, the Nicene Creed, the seven sacraments of the Church, and the proclamations of the Vatican II Council. She remained actively committed to economic equality, women's rights, political dissent, and world peace yet took a skeptical stand toward sexual permissiveness, abortion, and homosexual behavior. Although Unity and Religious Science adherents affirm homosexual rights, they hold more conservative positions toward economic policies that uphold individual initiative, not government laws, as the better way to overcome poverty. Yet New Thought shares a liberal outlook on the spiritual interpretations of God, the individual, and society. Perceiving God as the spiritual Principle of life, light, and love, it places a high value on individual education, prayer, and meditation as effective ways to raise people's consciousness and thereby revitalize social conditions. Discourse becomes a crucial method for educating the public.

Religious Discourse and Political Change

Discourse analysis helps clarify the complex impact of beliefs about justice on public attitudes toward justice. Several related questions deserve attention. Why do individuals, both citizens and leaders, find meaning in discourse? Why does the content of discourse change? Under what conditions can a religious group secure greater influence over the policy process and thereby produce change in society?

The meanings attributed to discourse revolve around the three "i"s: ideas, institutions, individuals (Palier and Surel 2005). If religious values prove salient to individuals—offer clarity, coherence, and plausibility—they will adopt them. This acceptance particularly occurs when these ideas portray a vision of justice, virtue, hope, and redemption that gives meaning, cements social solidarity, and provides reassurance against threats to the self, group, and society. Effective discourse facilitates this importance, which most often prevails when powerful, cohesive institutions propagate the teachings. Governments, political parties, churches, popular social movements, and especially the mass media play a crucial role. With sufficient resources, networks, and cohesion, they can use both oral and written texts to mobilize supporters, demobilize opponents, and gain defections from rivals. Priests, ministers, pastors, rabbis, and imams function as key religious figures framing spiritual values. Political party leaders and government officials articulate their visions of the public interest. Entrepreneurs use economic resources to spread the message. Mass media personnel who communicate through radio, television, newspapers, magazines, and the Internet may reach a broad audience in modern societies. If audience members form a discourse community with relatives, friends, neighbors, and workmates, then the prospects rise for accepting the dominant interpretations of religious values as well as their application to specific policy issues (Besecke 2005).

Conflict stimulates changing interpretations. Inversionary discourse challenges the hegemonic, dominant concepts of authority with oppositional interpretations. Powerful sociopolitical networks communicate beliefs about justice that draw sharp contrasts between present empirical conditions and transformative ideals, such as equality, respect for marginals, and service to others. Inversionary discourse advocates profound role reversals. The last become first. Outsiders come inside. Marginals join the inner circle. Sinners gain redemption. Justice, righteousness, hope, efficacy, and life replace injustice, corruption, despair, fatalism, and decay. Conflicts between opposing ideas, competitive institutions, and different individuals facilitate the acceptance of inversionary discourse. Conflicting standards of justice produce changed meanings. When hierarchical, elitist, fatalistic views yield to greater stress on opposition to hierarchy, egalitarian interactions among all people, and personal efficacy, individuals will more likely adopt a liberal inversionary discourse. Particularly when structural conflicts wrack the society, opposing standards of justice intensify. Wars, depressions, floods, hurricanes, and earthquakes cause conflicts. Rapid modernization often produces dysfunctional consequences—rising poverty, higher unemployment, greater income inequality, more interpersonal violence, and cultural humiliation of outcast groups. Under these structural conditions, high risks result. A perceived loss in political power, wealth, and status often leads deprived individuals to reject the interpretations upheld by the establishment. Angered by injustice, they may turn to a religious or political group that promises hope for a better future. Personal leaders mobilize support behind the inversionary discourse. Charismatic heroes, populists, and radical prophets communicate messages that deconstruct old meanings, construct new orientations, and reinterpret formerly-dominant values. Only when leaders develop a powerful organization, gain widespread support, and weaken the sanctions imposed by the dominant establishment do the changed meanings actually produce egalitarian social change (Apter 2005, 2006a; Apter and Saich 1994; Mansbridge 2005; Wald, Silverman, and Friday 2005).

If religious or political activists aim to enact policies for social change, they need an innovative vision, a powerful organization, and the public support that comes from effective mobilization. The idealistic vision arouses interest and highlights the importance of specific policy issues that focus on current problems. Material interests congrue with moral-spiritual values that bring benefits to the self, group, and nation. Mass media transmit a shared language about the policy relevance of such issues as reproductive choice, gender equality, civil liberties, and economic redistribution. If electoral campaigns stress these issues and provoke conflict between competing political parties, public attentiveness grows. Churches, unions, and parties can mobilize higher participation among concerned citizens. Particularly when individuals perceive the discourse as cognitively believable, emotionally appealing, and relevant to their need for meaning, social solidarity, and reassurance against perceived threats, these persons will support the policy message for social change (Hutchings 2003; Mühlhäusler and Peace 2006).

Beginning with the Protestant reformations in the sixteenth century and extending to the present time, societies have become more modernized, differentiated, and open to conflicts that generate a changed discourse. Mobilizers pursuing an egalitarian, efficacious, individualist form of justice forge several struggles: economic conflicts, cultural struggles over legitimacy, and political competition to shape public policy performance. By forming unions, consumer associations, and other populist movements, formerly-excluded classes claim that the dominant classes pursue injustice, corruption, and private interests. In the religious sphere, conflicting symbols delegitimize the ecclesiastical authorities. Prophets who promise innovation struggle against religious officials who seek continuity with tradition. These prophets articulate a new discourse that deconstructs established hierarchical authority. Through dialogues with the public, the unjust absurdities of political life become unmasked. Particularly during crisis times when disasters, war, and economic stagnation threaten the society, prophetic heroes articulate new messages that promise the hope of change. Resignation yields to efficacy. The possible becomes probable. Improvement of worldly conditions appears feasible now, not in some future heaven. Structural crises bring the decay in traditions that used to legitimize the sociopolitical hierarchy. As the class and religious conflicts mount, change appears in the political sphere. Religious heresy leads to political dissent. Rhetorical appeals rally activists around a campaign for social justice, liberation, and equality. Combined with inclusive political organizations, the innovative discourse mobilizes liberal supporters (Bourdieu 1998a, 1998b; Engler 2003; Verter 2003).

Given the present conditions in the United States, the prospect for liberal churches securing fundamental transformations appears limited. Although several religious leaders articulate an innovative vision, they lack a national centralized organization to realize that vision. Since the 1968 assassination of the Reverend Martin Luther King, Jr., no charismatic prophet has arisen to mobilize a mass membership behind a spiritual campaign for social change. Most liberal church members, whether Unitarian, Congregational, or New Thought, come from high-status backgrounds with advanced formal education. Despite the calls for greater inclusiveness, few poor people belong to these churches. These denominations give lower priority to economic equality than to cultural freedom for women, homosexuals, abortion-seekers, and political dissidents. Their rational approach to the Bible downplays emotional commitment to a spiritual faith. Compared with orthodox Roman Catholics and especially fundamentalist-evangelical Protestants, liberal Christians and Jews display a weaker commitment to their religious values. For New Thought adherents, individual activities like prayer, meditation, and education take precedence over collective political mobilization. Like most other Americans, they perceive no feasible alternative

to the current economic or political system. Preferring incremental change, individuals who share a Social Gospel-New Thought ethos believe that an alliance with liberal Democrats will most effectively achieve civil liberties, gender equality, reproductive choice, reduced poverty, and a peaceful world (Taussig 2006).

Discussion Questions

1. What different views do religious liberals and conservatives take toward the relative importance of hierarchical and individualist values?
2. How do theological interpretations of justice influence political attitudes toward civil liberties, gender equality, legal abortion, and income distribution?
3. How and why does discourse in the mass media affect the decisions of religious persons to participate in political life? In what ways does religious discourse motivate social movements for political change?
4. In the United States why did liberal religious groups achieve greater policy successes during the 1960s than from 1980 to 2004?
5. How and why do the search for meaning, the commitment to social solidarity, and the defense against perceived threats explain attitudes toward civil liberties and income equality?

References

Andrain, Charles F., and James T. Smith. 2006. *Political Democracy, Trust, and Social Justice: A Comparative Overview.* Hanover, NH: University Press of New England.

Apter, David E. 2005. "Comparative Sociology: Some Paradigms and their Moments." In *Sage Handbook of Sociology,* ed. Craig Calhoun, Chris Rojek, and Bryan Turner. Thousand Oaks, CA: Sage Publications, pp. 103–26.

———. 2006a. "Duchamp's Urinal: Who Says What's Rational when Things Get Tough?" In *The Oxford Handbook of Contextual Political Analysis*, ed. Robert E. Goodin and Charles Tilly. New York: Oxford University Press, pp. 797–96.

Apter, David E., and Tony Saich. 1994. *Revolutionary Discourse in Mao's Republic*. Cambridge, MA: Harvard University Press.

Bennett, Stephen Earl. 2006. "Democratic Competence, Before Converse and After." *Critical Review* 18(1-3): pp. 105–41.

Berryman, Edward. 2005. "Beliefs, Apparitions, and Rationality: The Social Scientific Study of Religion after Wittgenstein." *Human Studies* 28(1): pp. 15–39.

Besecke, Kelly. 2005. "Seeing Invisible Religion: Religion as a Societal Conversation about Transcendent Meaning." *Sociological Theory* 23 (June): pp. 179–96.

Bourdieu, Pierre. 1998a. *Acts of Resistance: Against the Tyranny of the Market*. Trans. Richard Nice. New York: New Press.

———. 1998b. *Practical Reason: On the Theory of Action*. Stanford, CA: Stanford University Press.

Cady, H. Emilie. 1995. *Complete Works of H. Emilie Cady: Lessons in Truth, How I Used Truth, God a Present Help*. Unity Village, MO: Unity Books.

Cesari, Jocelyne. 2005. "Religion and Politics: Interaction, Confrontation and Tensions." *History and Anthropology* 16 (March): pp. 855–95.

Collings, Randall. 1993. "Liberals and Conservatives, Religious and Political: A Conjuncture of Modern History." *Sociology of Religion* 54 (fall): pp. 127–46.

Converse, Philip E. 1964. "The Nature of Belief Systems in Mass Publics." In *Ideology and Discontent*, ed. David E. Apter. New York: The Free Press of Glencoe, pp. 206–61.

———. 2006. "Democratic Theory and Electoral Reality." *Critical Review* 18(1–3): pp. 297–329.

Douglas, Mary, and Steven Ney. 1998. *Missing Persons: A Critique of Personhood in the Social Sciences*. Berkeley: University of California Press.

Engler, Steven. 2003. "Modern Times: Religion, Consecration and the State in Bourdieu." *Cultural Studies* 17 (May-July): pp. 445–67.

Friedman, Jeffrey. 2006. "Democratic Competence in Normative and Positive Theory: Neglected Implications of 'The Nature of Belief Systems in Mass Publics'" *Critical Review* 18(1-3): pp. i–xliii.

Grafton, Carl, and Anne Permaloff. 2005. "Liberal and Conservative Dissensus in Areas Of Domestic Public Policy Other than Business and Economics." *Policy Sciences* 38 (March): pp. 45–67.

Greeley, Andrew, and Michael Hout. 2006. *The Truth about Conservative Christians: What They Think and What They Believe*. Chicago: University of Chicago Press.

Grendstad, Gunnar. 2003. "Comparing Political Orientations: Grid-Group Theory versus the Left-Right Dimensions in the Five Nordic Countries." *European Journal of Political Research* 42 (January): pp. 1–21.

Hutchings, Vincent L. 2003. *Public Opinion and Democratic Accountability: How Citizens Learn about Politics*. Princeton, NJ: Princeton University Press.

Jervis, Robert. 2006. "Understanding Beliefs." *Politcal Psychology* 27 (October): pp. 641–43.

Leustean, Lucian N. 2005. "Towards an Integrated Theory of Religion and Politics." *Method and Theory in the Study of Relgion* 17(4): pp. 364–81.

Lockhart, Charles. 2003. *The Roots of American Exceptionalism: History, Institutions and Culture*. New York: Palgrave Macmillan.

Mansbridge, Jane. 2005. "Cracking through Hegemonic Ideology: The Logic of Formal Justice." *Social Justice Research* 18 (September): pp. 335–47.

Meeks, Wayne A. 2005. "Why Study the New Testament?" *New Testament Studies* 51 (April): pp.155-70.

Melville, Herman. 1961. *Moby Dick or The White Whale*. New York: New American Library.

———. 2002. *White-Jacket or The World in a Man-of-War*. New York: The Modern Library.

Mühlhäusler, Peter, and Adrian Peace. 2006. "Environmental Discourses." In *Annual Review of Anthropology,* vol. 35, ed. William H. Durham and Jane Hill. Palo Alto, CA: Annual Reviews, pp. 457–79.

Palier, Bruno, and Yves Surel. 2005. "Les 'Trois I' et 'Analyse de l'État en Action." *Revue Francaise de Science Politique* 55 (February): pp.7–32.

Smith, M. Brewster, Jerome S. Bruner, and Robert W. White. 1956. *Opinions and Personality*. New York: John Wiley.

Taussig, Hal. 2006. *A New Spiritual Home: Progressive Christianity at the Grass Roots*. Santa Rosa, CA: Polebridge Press.

Thompson, Michael, Marco Verweij, and Richard J. Elli. 2006. "Why and How Culture Matters." In *The Oxford Handbook of Contextual Political Analysis,* ed. Robert E.Goodin and Charles Tilly. New York: Oxford University Press, pp.319–40.

Verter, Bradford. 2003. "Spiritual Capital: Theorizing Religion with Bourdieu against Bourdieu." *Sociological Theory* 21 (June): pp.150–74.

Wald, Kenneth D., Adam L. Silverman, and Kevin S. Fridy. 2005. "Making Sense of Religion in Political Life." In *Annual Review of Politcal Science,* vol. 8, ed. Nelson W. Polsby. Palo Alto, CA: Annual Reviews, pp. 121–43.

Wildavsky, Aaron. 1998. *Culture and Social Theory*. Ed. Sun-Ki-Chai and Brendon Swedlow. New Brunswick, NJ: Transaction Publishers.

Yamane, David. 2007. "Beyond Beliefs: Religion and the Sociology of Religion in America." *Social Compass* 54 (March): pp. 33–48.

Religion and Politics: U.S.A.

Lisa Sowle Cahill

The 2008 election season was tumultuous, divisive, exhilarating, and historically unique. It yielded the first black president, Democratic candidate Barack Hussein Obama,[1] with the first

LISA SOWLE CAHILL, awarded her Ph.D. by the University of Chicago Divinity School, is now J. Donald Monan, S.J., Professor of Theology at Boston College where she specializes in theological ethics. Her recent publications include *Theological Bioethics: Participation, Justice, and Change* (2005); and *Genetics, Theology, and Ethics: An Interdisciplinary Conversation* (2005) which she edited. In progress is a book manuscript on the Bible, systematic theology, and social ethics.

[1] Although Obama is frequently characterized as African-American, that term is typically reserved for descendents of slaves, not recent immigrants or their children. Obama's father was Kenyan, his mother white. He was raised by his mother and grandparents after his parents divorced. No perspective is context-free; I served on the Catholic Advisory Committee of Barack Obama. Thanks to Thomas J. Reese, S.J., for many constructive suggestions on this essay. All Web sites referred to in this Note were accessed November 23, 2008.

Catholic vice president, Joseph Biden. Republican counterparts were John McCain, a decorated war hero; and Sarah Palin, governor of Alaska, potentially the first woman vice president.

Obama's campaign to empower his message at the "grassroots" was massively effective. It registered new African-American, Hispanic, and young voters, all of whom strongly favored Obama. Using frequent email appeals, Obama raised over $600 million from over three million donors—a virtual plebiscite on his popularity. Obama won 53% of the vote, compared to McCain's 46%. Catholics favored him 54% to 45%. Yet (non-Hispanic) whites overall favored McCain 55% to 43%, with a narrower gap among white Catholics—52% to 47%. This means that Latinos—66% pro-Obama—gained him the Catholic vote. Still, Obama did better with white Catholics than the two previous Democrats (Gore 2000, Kerry 2004).[2]

[2] See the Pew Forum survey, "How the Faithful Voted," http://pewforum.org/docs/?DocID=367. See also Mark Silk and Andrew Walsh, "A Past without a Future? Parsing

Though U.S. political and legal traditions separate church and state (government cannot establish a religion, nor directly fund religious activities), America is a religious country. Only 6.3% of Americans self-identify as "secular" and "unaffiliated" with any religion.[3] Religious leaders and groups are politically active and influential. The religious beliefs of candidates (all Protestant except Biden) were scrutinized. Catholics, a quarter of the electorate, were courted by both parties. Catholics are integrated into the American mainstream, yet Catholic identity is still stamped by 19th- and early 20th-century immigrant experiences.[4] Some recall or imagine a "vibrant culture of the Catholic ghetto" existing pre-Vatican II.[5] They resent lingering anti-Catholic sentiment that immigrant forebears evoked. Yet Catholic ethnic enclaves could be tainted by defensiveness and racism. Catholic calls for justice were not always inclusive.[6] Prioritizing issues like economic

equity, education, employment, and health care, Obama summoned all to the common good. McCain promised to win the war and identified himself as "pro-life" (yet supports embryonic stem cell research). Defense of life is central to Catholic moral tradition; it especially appeals to Catholics for whom "pro-life" serves as an identity marker amid cultural pluralism.[7]

Since 1975, the U.S. Conference of Catholic Bishops (USCCB) has issued political advisories. In November 2007, it overwhelmingly approved Forming Consciences for Faithful Citizenship to guide but not to "tell Catholics for whom or against whom to vote" (nos. 7, 58). Taking innocent life is not "just one issue among many" (no. 28), yet "other serious threats" including racism, the death penalty, unjust war, hunger, health care, and immigration "are not optional concerns" (no. 29). Abortion is an "intrinsic evil," but "racism" falls in the same category (no. 34), along with genocide, torture, and targeting noncombatants (no. 23). Faithful Citizenship calls for prudential discernment and "'the art of the possible'" (John Paul II, *Evangelium vitae* no. 73). Catholics must neither advocate intrinsic evil, nor be single-issue voters (no. 34). As the election neared, some bishops reclaimed abortion to define Catholic politics, equated opposition to abortion with commitment to make it illegal, and excluded the possibility of Catholics supporting Obama.[8] But judging the morality of abortion is logically and ethically dis-

the U.S. Catholic Vote," *America* 199.14 (November 3, 2008), http://www.americamagazine.org/content/article.cfm?article_id=11181; and Peter Steinfels, "Catholics and Choice (In the Voting Booth)," *New York Times* (November 8, 2008), http://www.nytimes.com/2008/ll/08/us/politics/08beliefs.html7_r=3&oref=slogin&pagewanted=print&oref=slogin.

[3]Pew Forum, "U.S. Religious Landscape Survey," http://religions.pewforum.org/.

[4]See James M. O'Toole, *The Faithful: A History of Catholics in America* (Cambridge, Mass.: Harvard University, 2008).

[5]Michael Sean Winters, *Left at the Altar: How the Democrats Lost the Catholics and How the Catholics Can Save the Democrats* (New York: Basic, 2008) 70. Winters rails against John F. Kennedy's relegation of religion to the private sphere, and finds hope in the influx of Latino Catholics.

[6]E. J. Dionne Jr., "There Is No Catholic Vote—And It's Important," in *American Catholics and Civic Engagement: A Distinctive Voice,* ed. Margaret O'Brien Steinfels (Lanham, Md.: Rowman & Littlefield, 2004) 258-59.

[7]On countercultural pro-life commitment see Jennifer Fulweiler, "A Sexual Revolution," *America* 199.1 (July 7, 2008) 11-13, http://www.americamagazine.org/content/article.cfm?article_id=10904.

[8]For example, Cardinal Justin Rigali and Bishop William Murphy, "Joint Statement," October 21, 2008, http://www.usccb.org/prolife/Rigali-Murphy-Joint-Statement.pdf; Michael Sean Winters, "Why They Didn't Listen," Tablet (15 November 2008), http://www.thetablet.co.uk/article/1227.

tinct from choosing political strategies to combat it; and distinct from judging morally or religiously those who choose differently.

A novel U.S. development is a bipartisan and ecumenical "progressive" coalition combining social justice and ecology with traditional "pro-life" causes. This movement connects through internet media, public events, and religious activism.[9] A surge of Catholic publications and organizations advances a similar "common good" agenda. Leading activists encouraged voters, "There has scarcely been a better opportunity for members of our church who are passionate about the common good to embrace their identity as Catholic Americans, and to help bring the light of our faith's message of justice and dignity to the farthest reaches of our nation and our world."[10]

Though most Americans and a majority of Catholics support legal abortion,[11] most (81%) want abortion reduction.[12] Prudence and realism question single-minded determination to reverse the 1973 Supreme Court decision *Roe v. Wade*, making abortion legal. Even with pro-life appointments by a Republican president, the court would maintain its bias toward established law (*stare decisis*). Overturning *Roe v. Wade* would return the matter to the states, and most would allow abortion. Furthermore, data shows that abortion rates decline as social programs rise. Latin American countries banning abortion still have high rates due to poverty and women's low status. Northern European countries with permissive abortion law and expansive programs of health care and family support have much lower rates than the U.S.[13] A bipartisan effort in Congress, The Pregnant Woman Support Act (H.R. 3192 and S. 2407), proposes to reduce abortions by promoting pregnancy assistance, adoption, and education and support for new mothers. The 2008 Democratic Party platform on abortion was expanded for the first time to include similar benefits.

Catholics prioritizing poverty, war, health care, immigration, or the environment; or limiting their abortion advocacy to socioeconomic measures, met swift and firm repudiation from

---

[9]See Jim Wallis, *God's Politics: Why the Right Gets It Wrong and the Left Doesn't Get It* (New York: HarperCollins, 2005); E. J. Dionne Jr., *Souled Out: Reclaiming Faith and Politics after the Religious Right* (Princeton, N.J.: Princeton University, 2008); Amy Sullivan, *The Party Faithful: How and Why the Democrats Are Closing the God Gap* (New York: Scribner, 2008); Sojourners Christians for Peace and Justice Web site (http://www.sojo.net/); Matthew 25 Network Web site (http://www.matthew25.org/); and evangelical pastor Rick Warren's Web site (http://www.rickwarren.com/).

[10]Chris Korzen and Alexia Kelley, *A Nation for All: How the Catholic Vision of the Common Good Can Save America from the Politics of Division* (San Francisco: Jossey-Bass, 2008) 123. Korzen and Kelley founded Catholics in Alliance for the Common Good (http://www.catholicsinalliance.org/) and Catholics United (http://www.catholics-united.org/), respectively. Another Web-based organization is Catholic Democrats (http://www.catholicdemocrats.org/). See also Clarke E. Cochran and David Carroll Cochran, *The Catholic Vote: A Guide for the Perplexed* (Maryknoll, N.Y.: Orbis, 2008); and Gerald J. Beyer, "Yes You Can: Why Catholics Don't Have to Vote Republican," Commonweal 135.12 (June 20, 2008) 15-18.

[11]See *The Faith and American Politics Survey: The Young and the Faithful*, at Faith in Public Life Web site, http://www.faithinpubliclife.org/content/faps.

[12]See "Religion in the 2008 Election: Post-Election Survey," by Catholics in Alliance, Faith in Public Life, and Sojourners, http://www.faithinpubliclife.org/content/post-electionpoll/.

[13]See Joseph Wright and Michael Bailey, *Reducing Abortion in America: The Effect of Social and Economic Supports*, sponsored by Catholics in Alliance for the Common Good, 2008, http://www.catholicsinalliance.org/files/CACG_Final.pdf.

some bishops who branded Obama unacceptable.[14] Douglas Kmiec, a Catholic Republican law professor, declared support for Obama,[15] was denied communion, then was denounced by Archbishop Charles J. Chaput of Denver. Chaput insists faith is relevant to politics, attacks anti-Catholicism, and warns against diluting Catholic identity.[16] Garnering less media attention were bishops insisting on symmetry of issues or stressing "intrinsic evils" like racism.[17]

In his U.S. visit, Pope Benedict XVI called for action on war, poverty, and the environment. Days before the election, Archbishop Celestino Migliore, papal nuncio to the UN, called for protection of the global climate, food security, human rights, a moratorium on the death penalty, basic health care, education, economic development, and all other "necessary efforts ... to create a society in which life is respected at all stages of development."[18] Yet Americans subordinated global concerns to domestic ones, especially the economy, the war in Iraq, universal health care, and energy policy.[19]

What are ramifications for Catholic ethics? First, *social ethics*. Does the election of Obama signal a new politics of social justice? Catholics by 71% support policies that "protect the interests of all and promote the common good," compared to 13% who focus on abortion and same-sex marriage.[20] Yet Catholic voters did not obviously favor "solidarity" and the preferential option for the poor over their families' welfare, especially economic security and health care. Political participation is crucial to healthy democracy and justice; the election enfranchised oppressed and disillusioned populations. Yet the gospel mandate to love one's neighbor as oneself remains a challenge in view of competition for economic resources, overt racism, negative stereotyping of Muslims, and constricted interest in foreign policy obligations.

Second, *moral theology's tools and methods*. Moral theology cannot set high stakes on individual decisions alone. The relation between acts and contexts has been a vexed topic since the proportionalist debates of the 1970s and 1980s. Faithful Citizenship's paired condemnations of abortion and social sins remind us that all agency is socially embedded, that individuals are responsible for social evil, and that acts are not more "directly" or "intrinsically" evil than practices and institutions. Cathleen Kaveny shows that "intrinsic evils" are not all equally grave.[21] Amelia Uelmen shows why

---

[14]See Steinfels, "Catholics and Choice"; and Winters, "Why They Didn't Listen."

[15]Douglas W. Kmiec, *Can a Catholic Support Him? Asking the Big Question about Barack Obama* (Woodstock, N.Y.: Overlook, 2008).

[16]Charles J. Chaput, *Render unto Caesar: Serving the Nation by Living Our Catholic Beliefs in Political Life* (New York: Doubleday, 2008).

[17]See Archbishop John C. Favalora (Miami), "Why We Don't Take Sides on Candidates," pastoral letter of September 12, 2008, http://www.miamiarchdiocese.org/Statement.asp?op=Column080912&lg=E; and Bishop Blase Cupich (Rapid City, S.D.), "Racism and the Election," America 119.13 (October 27, 2008) 5, http://www.americamagazine.org/content/article.cfm?article_id=11161.

[18]Catholic News Service, "Nuncio Talks to UN on Global Climate, Human Rights," October 29, 2008, http://www.uscatholic.org/news/2008/10/nuncios-talks-un-global-climate-human-rights.

[19]Jackie Calmes and Megan Thee, "Voter Polls Show Obama Built a Broad Coalition," *New York Times*, November 5, 2008. On Catholics, see Patricia Zapor, "Catholic voters mirror general electorate in support for Obama," Catholic News Service, http://www.catholic-news.com/data/stories/cns/0805649.htm.

[20]"Religion in the 2008 Election."

[21]M. Cathleen Kaveny, "Political Responsibility: Is the Concept of Intrinsic Evil Helpful to the Catholic Voter?" *America* 119.13 (October 27, 2008) 15-19.

they require prudential political analysis. She sees "intrinsic evil" as a "guardrail"; one could infer that "intrinsic evil" now functions more as a "prophetic" than a "casuistic" category,[22] especially as redeployed against social practices.

Third, *ecclesiology, ethics, and politics*. In the run-up to the election, some bishops disparaged Democrats, warned Catholics away from Obama, and advised dissenters to refrain from communion. A few demurred, and many were silent. But bishops were not the sole shapers of Catholic politics. Catholics of every stripe were remarkably active, going beyond academic publications, mainstream media, and Catholic magazines, to produce parish and campus panels, local action committees, and Web sites and blogs reaching a huge new audience. This too is a healthy development, despite frequently divisive rhetoric.

Benedict XVI sent Obama a congratulatory message, identifying "peace, solidarity and justice" as the "special issues" on which his administration should make progress.[23] The laity has shown that it is ready and able to join political discourse and action on "Catholic" terms. Targets include health care, economic recovery, poverty, energy, trade policy, immigration, Iraq and Afghanistan, nuclear reduction, and abortion reduction via programs that empower women and support families. Much can be accomplished through synergy among lay spokespersons and agencies, Catholics in public office, offices of the USCCB, local dioceses and parishes, Catholic-sponsored education, Catholic political groups, and fellow citizens of every tradition and faith.

Obama promises a bipartisan administration. U.S. Catholics deserve a bipartisan Church—for Democrats and Republicans, traditionalists and progressives, and older and younger Catholics uninterested in reliving or reinventing the liberal-conservative hostilities of an earlier era. Obama's campaign speech on race was hailed for its honesty, its empathy with fears and grievances of blacks and whites, and its call for forgiveness.[24] Catholic ethics and politics too should resist the "culture wars," forging a dynamic vision from constructive debate, respectful criticism, practical commitment, and a hermeneutic of generosity toward others' value priorities.

---

[22]Amelia J. Uelmen, "'It's Hard Work': Reflections on Conscience and Citizenship in the Catholic Tradition," *Journal of Catholic Legal Studies* 47 (2008) 338-39.

[23]Cindy Wooden, "Pope Sends Congratulatory Message to Obama," Catholic News Service, http://www.catholic-news.com/data/stories/cns/0805616.htm.

[24]Barack Obama, "A More Perfect Union," Philadelphia, March 18, 2008, http://www.npr.org/templates/story/story.php?storyId=88478467.

Introduction: What We Can Learn From Reinhold Niebuhr

By John Patrick Diggins

In 1939 Reinhold Niebuhr was selected to deliver the renowned Gifford Lectures at the University of Edinburgh. The annual series aims to promote the study of natural theology, the knowledge of God, and if the theme is meant to be profound, the setting that year was ominous. In October many of those listening to Niebuhr's second set of lectures in the university's Rainy Hall shuddered in dread. Not only was his theme, "The Nature and Destiny of Man," darkly foreboding, but during one lecture the roar of antiaircraft guns could be heard responding to a Luftwaffe attack on British ships docked in a nearby harbor.

During the next two years Great Britain would stand almost alone against Nazi Germany while an isolationist America watched nervously from distant shores. Western Europe capitulated to Nazi forces, and Hitler rained bombs on London, aiming to defeat Great Britain before abrogating his nonaggression pact with Joseph Stalin and turning east to conquer the Soviet Union. Niebuhr believed the West was intellectually as well as militarily unprepared to confront the menace of fascism, and he was deeply troubled as he surveyed the resources available to stand against Nazi Germany.

In many respects it seemed that the institutions of organized religion were as reluctant as Europe's democratic governments to firmly oppose tyranny. The Roman Catholic Church had adopted a strategy of accommodation. Relieved that the Black Shirts had saved Italy from communism, the Vatican negotiated the Lateran treaties with Benito Mussolini in 1929, securing its sovereignty and the church's status as Italy's state religion. In Germany the church protected itself with a *Reichskonkordat* worked out with Hitler's regime in 1933, and in Spain it sided with the Falangist movement and General Francisco Franco during the 1936 to 1939 civil war. "There is a peculiar pathos in the present anti-Communist campaign," wrote Niebuhr in 1939, "with its admission that the Church does not like Fascism but prefers it to Communism because Communism tries to destroy it while Fascism merely embarrasses it."

The Protestant churches in America and Europe were mostly antifascist and anticommunist and committed to liberal democracy. But many were also antiwar, steeped in doctrines of nonviolence and injunctions to love your enemy and turn the other cheek. Niebuhr felt his challenge here was to affirm the Christian conscience while demonstrating that pacifism was dubious for religion and dangerous in politics. With Hitler on the march, he insisted that Protestants recall the "sinfulness of human nature" that obstructs the ethic of pure love. Humanity's goodness is an illusion that could not stop Nazi tyranny. The theologian even drew upon pagan sources to drive home his point: Sin is as inevitable in Christianity as tragedy is in Greek drama, and there is no escape when the human condition is oppressed by fate rather than liberated by freedom. "The history of our era seems to move in tragic circles strangely analogous to those presented symbolically in Greek tragedy," he wrote in 1938. "The democratic nations of the world are involving themselves more inexorably in world catastrophe by their very efforts to avert and avoid it…Why are democratic nations so tragically committed to this dance of death?"

As for Judaism, it was the most tragic of faiths, imperiled by the hopefulness of its theology. As a prophetic religion that envisions God as present in history, Judaism is self-affirming and life- enhancing and, indeed, the instrument of the world's redemption.

In Judaism there is no Fall of Man. Humankind may be alienated from Yahweh and liable to punishment, but the soul is not stained by original sin and the eternal damnation that requires a divine savior. Judaism is not ironic but messianic; a living God acts in history to help his people overcome adversity and find fulfillment in "the world to come," the Kingdom of God.

All the more reason why Niebuhr grew alarmed about what was in store for the Jewish people at the time of the Anschluss, Germany's annexation of Austria in 1938:

With the entrance of the Nazis into Vienna their anti-Semitic fury has reached new proportions. Here was a city in which Jewish intelligence played a significant role in the cultural achievements of the nation, particularly in medicine and music. The Nazis swooped down upon the city and wreaked indescribable terror. The Jews have been spared no indignity…The tragic events since the taking of Austria allow us to see the racial fanaticism inherent in the Nazi creed in boldest outline. This is really the final destruction of every concept of universal values upon which Western civilization has been built.

If traditional religion hesitated before the evil of fascism, modern thought appeared unable to recognize it. Disavowing the spiritual and the supernatural, intellectuals in the 1930s looked to science for a naturalistic explanation of events. But though theorists might explain war as an aggressive biological urge or identify fascism as advancing the interest of a social class, they were unprepared for the events of 1939.

The decade's touchstones of naturalism—the ideas of Marx, Freud, and Darwin—were of little use. Marxists who had joined the Communist Party were shameless in defending Moscow's nonaggression pact with Hitler and opposed America's entry into the war. Sigmund Freud's death that year meant there would be no guidance from the father of psychoanalysis, who had once claimed humanity carried a "death instinct." And America's leading Darwinian, the philosopher John Dewey, who championed scientific inquiry as an instrument of social reform, surveyed the outbreak of war in Europe and gave his country six words of advice: "No matter what happens, stay out!" Even many of those adamantly opposed to fascism and revolted by the barbaric attacks on the Jews recoiled at the thought of going to war. Clearly modern thought needed a new voice.

When Reinhold Niebuhr came to prominence in the 1930s and 1940s, he warned that Christians would be tempted to invoke Jesus's Sermon on the Mount to justify refusing to take up arms against evil. In the face of the totalitarian threat, a religious aversion to violence seemed to him a delusionary conceit, the bad faith of a conscience trying selfishly to retain its innocence in an amoral and power-driven world.

Today the situation is different. At a Republican primary debate during the 2000 presidential election, Texas governor George W. Bush was asked to name the "philosopher" who most influenced his life. Bush replied, "Christ, because he changed my heart." The man who as president took America to war in Iraq thought Jesus was at his side. President Bush told reporter Bob Woodward that he sought counsel from "a higher father" on whether to go to war, and he delighted in saying with a cocky smile, "Bring 'em on." In our time the problem of religion is not its debilitating pacifism but its overbearing militarism. When "Mission Accomplished" adorned the tower of a US aircraft carrier in May 2003, genuine Christian humility was sacrificed on a banner of political vanity.

Niebuhr would dismiss the office-seeker who presumes to testify to God's will. While he thought it essential that religion play a vital role in public life, he believed its purpose was profoundly cautionary: religion could show Americans how to guard against the temptation to parade their righteousness. "Can the Church give a 'moral lead?'" he asked in 1959. He answered by suggesting how easily the church can misconceive its mission:

> If we seek to justify Christianity because it preserves democracy, or inspires a hatred for dictatorship, or makes a "free enterprise system" possible, or helps us to change our system into something better, or creates a "third force"—our utilitarian attitude debases the Christian faith to the status of a mere instrument of the warring creeds from which the world suffers.

In seeking to sensitize the American mind to the reality of sin in the world, Niebuhr was fond of William James's warning that "the trail of the human serpent is over everything." He believed the rhetoric of religious condemnation was nothing less than the sin of pride. "Let us judge not that we be not judged," admonished Lincoln in his second inaugural address, an admonition Niebuhr frequently recalled. Today, alas, piety serves power; our leaders go to war convinced they are right with God.

Niebuhr's voice guided America through World War II and the Cold War, but after the Vietnam War liberals ignored him, mistakenly equating his ideas with a reflexive anticommunism, while conservatives touted their own anticommunist credentials as badges of moral clarity, successfully tarring liberals as the proponents of a weak foreign policy born of moral relativism.

Today, in America's war on terror, Niebuhr's legacy is again invoked, but it continues to be misconstrued in the service of flawed political ends. Some contemporary liberals look to Niebuhr for counsel on ways to reclaim their lost reputation for muscular leadership in foreign policy. In 2006 the *New York Times Sunday Magazine* published "The Rehabilitation of the Cold War Liberal" by Peter Beinart, a former editor at the *New Republic,* accompanied by a full-page photo of Niebuhr. Beinart argued that after 9/11 America needed Niebuhr's wisdom because his example could show liberals how to assert American power, battle evil to win the war on terror, and recapture the glory days of liberalism.

One wonders why our neo-Niebuhrians think Niebuhr would have supported the invasion of Iraq, a preemptive war carried out unilaterally and for reasons that require continual revision. "We are not a sanctified nation," the theologian wrote in 1959:

> and we must not assume that all our actions are dictated by considerations of disinterested justice. If we fall into this error the natural resentments against our power on the part of the weaker nations will be compounded with resentments against our pretensions to virtue. These resentments are indeed a part of the animus of anti-Americanism throughout the world.

Niebuhr opposed the moral terms by which the Cold War came to be defined, and if he drew upon religion for political purposes, it was to foster skepticism and self-scrutiny, not to encourage arrogant self-assertion and rituals of righteousness.

Beinart claimed early Cold War liberals had demonstrated that capitalism could be coupled to domestic policy reform and international economic cooperation. But a market economy always lives uneasily with Christianity, and more recent attempts by neoconservatives to ground capitalism in Christian morality ignore Niebuhr's warnings against "our pretension to virtue." In *Wealth and Poverty* (1981), published at the start of the Reagan presidency, the writer George Gilder claimed that the public benefits of a commercial market are not the reward of avarice and self-interest but display the altruism of enterprise. Successful entrepreneurs work and invest to serve the needs of others. Similarly, the Catholic thinker Michael Novak was bold enough to deny the persuasive force of Max Weber's *The Protestant Ethic and the Spirit of Capitalism* by claiming that it was Catholicism that historically emphasized the creativity of entrepreneurship in service to God.

Niebuhr, who died in 1971, would hardly be surprised to see how profits are equated with piety and religion is used to rationalize material acquisitiveness. He agreed with Nietzsche's view that "altruistic actions are only a species of egoistic actions" and that in self-justification individuals deny the motives for their own behavior. With Augustine, Niebuhr understood that God implanted desire in human nature so that we never get as much as we want. Those who extol capitalism are romantics who exalt the self and its desires. But the Christian ideal of love, Niebuhr maintained, is heedless of the self and its craving for possession. Neoconservatives bear comparison to alchemists who conjure the identity of contraries, allowing humankind to indulge the pleasures of greed in the spirit of God—a transubstantiation Pascal called "treason." Americans may as well drive their SUVs through the eye of a needle.

If liberals have wanted Niebuhr to buttress their foreign policy credentials and neoconservatives need religion to support the market, radicals would just as soon forget religion and return to reason to attain the promise of freedom. Christopher Hitchens, once a Trotskyist and an ardent follower of Tom Paine, recently stated his position in the provocative and thoughtful *God Is Not Great*:

> Religion has run out of justifications. Thanks to the telescope and the microscope, it no longer offers an explanation of anything important. Where once it used to be able, by its total command of a world-view, to prevent the emergence of rivals, it can now only impede and retard—or try to turn back—the measurable advances that we have made. Sometimes, true, it will artfully concede

them. But this is to offer itself the choice between irrelevance and obstruction, impotence or outright reaction, and, given this choice, it is programmed to select the worse of the two. Meanwhile, confronted with the undreamed-of vistas inside our own cortex, in the farthest reaches of the known universe, and in the proteins and acids which constitute our nature, religion offers annihilation in the name of god, or else the false promise that if we take a knife to our foreskin, or pray in the right direction, or ingest a piece of wafer, we shall be "saved." It is as if someone, offered a delicious and fragrant out-of-season fruit, matured in a painstakingly and lovingly designed hothouse, should throw away the flesh and the pulp and gnaw moodily on the pit.

Hitchens has an answer to religion: "Above all, we are in need of a renewed Enlightenment." With the method of rational analysis bequeathed to us by the Enlightenment, we can study "literature and poetry" the way scientists approach "proteins and acids," and the "eternal ethical questions" dealt with in the humanities "can now easily depose the scrutiny of sacred texts that have been found to be corrupt and confected."

How easily? "Don't come to me with science," countered Nietzsche, for "it never creates values." Hitchens can praise what the telescope discovers, but, Nietzsche observed, "Since Copernicus man seems to have got himself on an inclined plane—now he is slipping faster and faster away from the centre into—what? into nothingness?" Humankind sees itself belittled, reduced to "nothing but a piece of bizarre conceit." Let us not delude ourselves, Nietzsche warned, by thinking that the philosophers of the Enlightenment were "emancipated from the theologians." Modern man thinks he attains knowledge, but everything he knows "does not merely fail to satisfy his desires but rather contradicts them and produces a sense of horror." Religion may have "run out of justifications," but the Enlightenment cannot justify itself.

Hitchens's insistence that we are "in need of a renewed Enlightenment" perpetuates the notion that the eighteenth-century philosophes broke free of Christianity. For the philosophe, evil is simple ignorance, a deficiency, not a depravity. Enlightenment thinkers assumed as axiomatic humankind's continuity with nature. For Niebuhr this was no less an illusion than assuming the continuity of man with God. Niebuhr liked to cite Carl Becker's intellectual history of the mind of the Enlightenment, *The Heavenly City of the Eighteenth-Century Philosophers* (1932), to show that Enlightenment thinkers took assumptions that sustained religion and carried them over into science: reason would replace faith and nature God, but what remained was the claim to omniscience, a conviction that one could comprehend a revealed body of knowledge.

The religious mind may "gnaw moodily on the pit" of theology and metaphysical curiosity, as Hitchens asserts. But is that not because the Enlightenment has proved impotent to answer the deepest questions of the human condition? Where in the "cortex" can we find answers to the mystery of love, the sweetness and sorrows of memory, the burden of conscience, guilt, and moral judgment, the riddle of the self, the opaqueness of knowledge, the elusiveness of truth, the meaninglessness of suffering, the purpose of life, and, the final insult, its cessation in death? "Here today, gone tomorrow" is both an empirical statement and a glib maxim that invites our casual indifference. The Enlightenment increased humanity's power over nature but failed to provide an answer to Tolstoy's two questions: Why was I born? and For what should I live? Nor could it answer Niebuhr's overriding question: How is it that "an evil which does not exist in nature could have arisen in human history?"

***

During the height of the Cold War, the eminent neoconservative intellectual Jeane Kirkpatrick, whom President Ronald Reagan appointed as US ambassador to the United Nations, grew understandably angry at the radical Left for its unrelenting criticisms of American foreign and domestic policies: "They always blame America first." Niebuhr could sympathize with her outrage, but he warned us against presuming that American policies are always right. Niebuhr cared less about Americans who always blame America than about those who always equate American history with divine Providence. The American character, so proud in its innocence, so vain in its arrogance, refuses to reflect on its own actions. Niebuhr was always willing to forgive his fellow Americans, but he asked them to be mindful of a question that goes to the heart of ethics and their moral responsibilities: How much evil might America do in attempting to do good?

Section 4

Religion and Justice

Justice: Four Windows

Jane Hirshfield

1. Evolution and Justice

The mineral world stands apart from the axis of justice. A mountain rises and erodes, sandstones form and harden, granite decomposes to grass, rivers change course without the possibility of outrage or protest. What happens cannot be put on the scale of morality, cannot be felt as right or wrong. It is simply what happens.

The vegetable world also seems innocent of justice's negotiations. Light comes and goes from a field. Heat, cold, rain, drought come and go and are, as we say, simply weathered. If the color-changed light cast onto one tree's leaves by the leaves of another shows they are approaching too closely, the branch quite frequently turns away, in a gesture described as "crown shyness." Some experience of suffering may accompany the competition for soil nutrients and water, but if so, it is suffering of a kind beyond human grasp.

Recognizable conceptions of morality and justice begin with the rudiments of a sense of a separate self and of self's "place"; that is, with the social birds, fishes, and mammals. The experience of a correct order, or of dismaying disorder, becomes possible only if order is first present. The whiplash of inequality—its enforcement, its possible correction—becomes possible only when there are compacts of behavior between those who live in the context of a larger whole.

Hierarchy in herd, flock, or troupe is the acquiescence of others, won, maintained, or lost. Discomfort over who eats or mates first, last, or not at all is precursor to our ideals of "inalienable rights," to our feelings that each human being should know freedom of body, spirit, and mind; know security from arbitrary power; know love more than hunger, curiosity and ingenuity more than fear. Among social animals is also the beginning of visible mercy; the body language of submission is a surety that injury will end. Social animals (with a single exception—ourselves) rarely kill their own kind, and among the few species that do, almost never within their home community unless that community is stressed past bearable limits.

Primates, recent experiments show, possess both a sense of fairness and the impulse to collaborate and assist. A capuchin monkey, rewarded for some trained action with a bit of cucumber, sees a neighbor rewarded for the same behavior with a tasty grape and goes on strike, sulks in a corner, refusing clearly inequable wages. The capuchin's ostracism of the experimenter is a communication as telling—and, in the wild, as strongly repercussive—as a bite. Conversely, another recent experiment revealed that both chimpanzees and eighteen-month-old human infants will hurry to bring a dropped item back to the researcher's hand—though if the clothespin or book is deliberately thrown down, it will be left where it landed.

This innate impulse toward helpfulness offers one alternative to the order of punishment and force. Altruism, empathy, and mutual nurturance—the evidence of a basic tenderness between fellow creatures—carry the survival strategies of symbiosis into the social world. Red foxes bring food to other, injured foxes that are not their own young. Elephants bring edible branches to dying elephant elders unable to rise. Scientists have videotaped a humpback whale repeatedly lifting another, dead whale to the surface, the same way a newborn whale is lifted to the surface for its first breath; the whale carried the corpse for five hours before giving up. These acts, which might be rightly named acts of empathy, of compassion, extend interspecies. Traditional stories in many cultures tell of animals adopting and suckling orphaned young of a different kind, including the she-wolf's suckling of Romulus and Remus. One man who attempted suicide from the Golden Gate Bridge in San Francisco was brought to the surface by a seal (a circumstance so unnerving he spoke of it to no one for three years). Newspaper stories, most recently one from Australia, report dolphins forming a circle around human swimmers to protect them from sharks.

These examples may not at first seem to center on issues of justice, yet they underlie our faith in the possibility of a life not ruled entirely by chaos, force, and fear. Simone Weil described the hope for justice in this way: "At the bottom of the heart of every human being, from earliest infancy until the tomb, there is something that goes on indomitably expecting, in the teeth of all experience of crimes committed, suffered, and witnessed, that good and not evil will be done to him. It is this above all that is sacred in every human being."[1]

Weil rooted our most fundamental sense of Tightness in what transcends both personality and the personal, yet is also independent of the changing whims and fashions of collective life. She called this the realm of God, and it seems that in every human culture, the laws of right behavior (the Latin *ius*, "law," underlies the English word *justice*) are first attributed to the divine. Yet given how often divergent ideas of the sacred seem to lead us to bloodshed, it may be a usefully calming corrective to acknowledge the creaturely acts of discipline and kindness that underlie our human sense of justice and injustice, of compassion and ruthless force, and to acknowledge that even among the social animals, the individual matters and is cared for beyond practical exigency, beyond mere usefulness to the group. Civil society is older, and larger of heart, than is generally imagined.

That these concepts are primal in us—innate, pre-verbal, pre-human—explains no small part of the strength of their grip. That the desire for justice is seated in the friction between selves and their differing desires—in communal and not individual life, that is—remains a binding truth. A workable sense and measure of justice bestows on all social animals, including humans, no small part of our basic survival, both of body and spirit.

---

[1]From "La Personnalité humaine, le juste et l'injuste," as translated in "Human Personality," in *Simone Weil: An Anthology,* ed. Sian Miles (New York: Grove Press, 1986).

The failure of justice lacerates because it is, at bottom, an injury to life itself.

2. Aeschylus' Oresteia

I asked a friend—a lawyer who specializes in the final appeals of death penalty cases—what he might have to say on the subject of justice. He answered with a quote from William Gaddis: "Justice?—You get justice in the next world, in this world you have the law."

Justice in animal life is simple—the customs of right behavior don't often change, or do so at the almost unobservable pace of evolution. Nor do they conflict with one another because of different conceptions of the meaning of right. In human life, the complexities tangle and entangle. We recognize injustice by the uprising of outrage within us. Yet those—whether the empowered or the almost powerless—who act in ways universally decried as "inhuman" claim themselves warranted, claim they have no other choice, that their actions are necessary, done for justifiable "reason." Reason: the double-edged sword in our human relationship to justice. Rational mind can harden the heart, strip it of the capacity for compassion, prevent it from reeling back from the commission of horrors; it does this by overpowering the recognition of outrage with manufactured rage or manufactured complacence. Equally though, rational mind can temper the heart's loosed fears and angers, which would equally perpetuate horror, if allowed.

To see the conflict of emotion and ideas in action, we need only read Greek tragedy, a body of work that explores the most difficult collisions of heart and mind and allegiance to conflicting values. Taken as a whole, these plays attempt to work through the question of what it means to act well, to choose well, in a human life amid human straits and dilemmas.

In Sophocles' *Antigone* (circa 440 BCE), the issues and their resolution are both basic and comparatively simple. The king Creon forbids the burial of one of two brothers—the one who attacked rather than defended his city—as punishment for treason. Antigone, sister to both and also betrothed to the king's son, defies the command: to leave a brother unburied defiles an order stronger than any decreeable by kings. By the end of the play, the brother is buried, and the offended gods have stripped Creon of everything he loves: son, wife, and power. Antigone, too, is dead. It is a tragedy of the most straightforward form, in which no one survives intact. But the hierarchy of justice and right behavior is also clear—Antigone defends her desire to bury her brother with a simple statement: "I share my love, not my hate." Forgiveness, fidelity to blood kin, respect for the dead—these are presented as transcendent values, which must be honored.

Aeschylus' slightly earlier trilogy, *The Oresteia* (458 BCE), presents a story both more extended and more complex, one that is also, in no small part, an account of justice's evolution, in the face of irresolvably divergent claims, from private to public realms. That these Greek plays were created in the context of ritual—enactments intended to be repeated—is not accidental. Questions of justice—or any other genuine dilemma—cannot be answered in static or absolute form; they will continually be refound, recreated, renewed, and reformed.

The curse on the House of Atreus precedes both Atreus' own crime and the segment of the story recounted in the three plays. It stems from an alternation of parricide and sacrificed children (more than once then served up to their father as a vengeance-meal) that recedes into the past to the earliest gods. Vestigial from that first world of overthrown gods are the Erinyes, or Furies. Primordial forces of vengeance and the outward embodiment of inescapable inner guilt, they defend "right order" of the most fundamental kind: its roots in the love between kin. The story of their transformation and domestication into the Eumenides, or Kindly Ones—their inclusion, that is, into the world and order of human-centered affairs—is the end point of *The Oresteia*'s tale.

The events explored in Aeschylus' trilogy begin with the sacrifice of a daughter in order to go to war. Then follow the killing of a husband to avenge the daughter, the murder of a mother to avenge the father. The core question of the *Oresteia* plays—a question that continually resurrects itself in new places and forms—is how this succession of vengeance and guilt might ever end. The god Apollo has demanded that Orestes kill his mother, Clytemnestra, who has killed Agamemnon, who has killed Iphigenia, also at the demand of the gods. Orestes does so. But even Apollo cannot then release Orestes from the pursuing Furies, whose cry is that the murder of a mother is a crime so scalding not even a god's command provides excuse.

It is the Furies' role to preserve horror at such an act, both within the community and within the self; their role not to allow the unforgivable to go unnoticed, let alone be forgiven. Orestes himself has played the role of a Fury against his mother, as powerless not to act against her for having killed his father as the Furies are powerless not to act against him. The insolubility of human grief before injustice stands at the center. In the Greek world preceding *The Oresteia*, a primal crime can never be undone or redressed. It can only become a new basis for the current condition of existence. And so there is further murder, for generations.

Northern Ireland, Iraq, Palestine, Darfur, Afghanistan, Argentina, Rwanda, Lebanon, Guantanamo, Bosnia, Chechnya, Haiti, Cambodia, Kashmir, Burma, Korea, East L.A.—loosed Furies move through them all. One religious disciple murders another and a millennium later the act remains a reason for carnage. A people displaced from its homeland displaces another people from its homeland, and a child watches a house bulldozed while his mother weeps. An outspoken daughter is made to disappear without any accounting. A farmer is tortured because someone hid in his barn. A woman gathering wood for cooking is raped and visibly branded as having been raped; she returns home and is killed for shaming her husband. A gang member's young brother is killed; a nation knowingly left to starve. Gift blankets are seeded with smallpox, conquered fields with salt, and suffering leaps from victim to victor as invisibly and inevitably as a plague flea.

The Furies speak for the outraged dead from beyond the grave. They are pure vengeance, creatures beyond placation or reason. They are, themselves, for all who see them, terror.

Yet what *The Oresteia* proposes as a resolution is not the Furies' rejection. Pushed away, they goad harder. It is the courteous acknowledgment of them in the final play that makes possible a remedy beyond the cyclical continuance of bloodshed and revenge. Orestes has been sent by Apollo to Athena, goddess of wisdom, to establish his innocence or guilt. Athena listens to Orestes' story, then listens to that of the Furies. She is the first to treat them with honor, and her offered respect changes them from harrying, outcrying hounds to creatures who speak and explain themselves, who can stand within a broadened circle of communication. There is another step as well: Athena declares the decision of Orestes' fate too difficult for her to make alone. The full community must be drawn into the process. A representative group of citizens will listen and vote, with Athena herself, if necessary, breaking a tie—which she declares in advance will be a vote for mercy.[2]

---

[2]To be thorough, we must also note Athena's use of power as well as courteous invitation: she reminds the Furies that she alone, of all the gods, holds the keys to the place

What we see in this final play, *The Eumenides*, is the invention of what remains recognizably our own system of justice: trial by jury, in which, even today, a hung jury results in retrial or freedom. *The Oresteia* proposes that private daemons can be softened by deeding them over to the realm of the communal—if, at the same time, the community is deeded in turn to the defense of fundamental values. The Furies are promised a decisive place in the fate of every household, and the first portion of every tribute to the gods, in return for entering into the compact of civil adjudication. The trilogy's resolution addresses more than Orestes' personal torment: individual impulse, uncountered by a communal desire for good, is disastrous for all.

From *The Oresteia* come the truth and reconciliation trials of South Africa, the gacaca courts of Rwanda, the opening of the Stasi files of East Germany and of the mass graves of Argentina and Salvador; will come, we know, the opening of the gates and records of Guantánamo Bay. These processes bring the Furies to heel, allow the accumulated history of insurmountable grief and outrage to be spoken fully aloud and acknowledged by the community as a whole. Simple recognition, the admission and dignification of what has been suffered, the inclusion of all participants from every side—the Greeks' insight was to see that these gestures, in themselves, are aeration and healing.

3. Justice without "Justice": An Alternative View

When Aeschylus has Athena arrange the participants of *The Eumenides* story for trial, she

where Zeus' thunderbolt is stored. Yet the thunderbolt need not be interpreted only as literal force-threat—it can also be understood as light, an enlightenment overwhelming the darker and partisan aspects of our nature.

instructs Orestes to stand by the Stone of Outrage, the Furies by the Stone of Mercilessness. The bare, high outcrop where this takes place, overlooking Athens, is a topography mirroring the inner sensations of justice. W. B. Yeats wrote, in "Easter, 1916" (his poem mourning and honoring the leaders of a failed attempt to win Irish independence by force of arms): "Too long a sacrifice / Can make a stone of the heart. / O when may it suffice?" By the time we find ourselves weighing the actions of self or other as right or wrong, we already stand in the hardening that rage and outrage elicit. The visceral awareness of justice, it seems, comes only when actual justice has already failed.

There may be a way to forego the realm of stones entirely. As with the transformation of Furies to Kindly Ones, it may be that justice's rigidities can give way to something more supple and more kind: compassion. Might not the bond and acknowledgment of shared life—the very thing the Furies defend—already suggest the foundation for a coexistence less saturated with suffering? This is the path proposed by Buddhist views of the nonduality of existence, in which selves are not experienced as steeply divided and separate. In this seamless comprehension, harm cannot be inflicted by one on another. To harm anyone is to harm one's own heart.

Most people have had at least a momentary glimpse of what it is to experience the world as undivided—the narrow sense of self drops away, ego and its need to dominate drop away, proprietariness becomes the subject of laughter, as if left hand were stealing from right hand. The threads of one piece of fabric cannot argue with each other, and what happens to any part happens to the whole. The same description is given by mystics of every tradition: a simple falling into right relationship with all that is. Generosity, patience, truthfulness, morality, equanimity, energy, wisdom, and loving-kindness are not felt as exceptional; they are the fundamental qualities of human nature, present in us from the start. Within such a state of being, how can there be justice, how can there be injustice? Each encounter is intimate, each person is mother, child, "Buddha," "Christ," "Allah," self. "Do unto others as you would have them do unto you" becomes tautology, not advice. Yet the experience must not be understood as some sophomoric or saccharine "oneness." "Not one, not two," are the words used to describe it, in Zen.

All spiritual traditions, including Buddhism, possess explicit moral components. Still, justice within classical Buddhism is not so much something imposed from outside as an understanding of cause and effect, operating from within. The Buddhist concept closest to the Western idea of justice is karma, in which the actions of each moment, or lifetime, are seen as influencing the circumstances of the next, in a continual opportunity for readjustment. Good follows good; evil is followed by further suffering. Moral sensibility emerges from self-observation and learning rather than fear of judgment by others.

Buddhism does offer as well guidance for virtuous behavior, in what are known as the ten prohibitory precepts—a person taking these precepts vows not to kill, lie, take what is not given, abuse sexuality, dull the senses by intoxication, and so on. A few of the precepts, however, are less familiar: "A disciple of the Buddha does not possess anything, not even the truth," one translation reads. This nonpossession points back toward the nondual: part of what isn't possessable is self itself. Our sense of "self-worth," "rights," identity itself—each depends on making the distinction that I am I and you are you. Yet if the skin is felt less as barrier than as point of continuity and connection, no distinction between selves can be found. In this way, nonduality and compassion are inextricably linked—the second arises from the first, and the vow to relieve suffering immediately follows.

For practitioners of such Buddhist paths as Zen and Dzogchen, nondual understanding is foundation ground, recognizable at any moment as where we already stand. In most Buddhist traditions, though, time is acknowledged as part of the karmic process—lifetimes may be needed for compassion to take root, for even the best of intentions to reach mature harvest. The intention, and its continual renewal, is what matters. When Gerard Manley Hopkins wrote, "the just man justices," he reminded of justice's perennially elusive nature. Justice is not noun, but adjective, verb—attribute or action. It is either actively ongoing or nonexistent. Folk Buddhism conveys the same comprehension, showing the need for a compassion of continuous reenactment. In the folk tales known as the Jataka stories, the Buddha, during many lifetimes, sacrifices himself for the sake of others. Seeing a hungry tigress with starving cubs, he gives himself to be eaten. Without identification in ego or attachment to a segregate and distinct existence, nothing can be lost. Still, suffering remains perceptible. Even if the fully awakened mind does not feel it as personal injury, an awake person, seeing suffering in others, attempts to end it. This is what Western conceptions of Buddhism as passive before suffering and political injustice miss. Acceptance of momentary conditions as momentary does not mean a failure to engage them.[3]

The Oresteia proposes that the solution to the unredressable lies in collective wisdom and the needs of the community as a whole for peace. Evolution would second this—altruism arises in animals, symbiosis in plants and biological systems, because the good of the whole *is* the good of the part. The Buddhism of nondual awakening

---

[3]The misconception also disregards Buddhism's source: a prince who, having learned the existence of poverty, old age, sickness, and death, could not return to his former life of comfort and palace.

proposes that this can be so fully internalized, in each of us, that every vestige of self-seeking impulse is flooded by a deeper identification. Proposes it possible to say "we" without limit, to mean by "we" nothing less than "all."

4. Kissing the Murderer's Hand: Poetry, Reconciliation, and Justice

When I began assembling these thoughts, I was staying briefly in a seventeenth-century coal-heated cottage in Northumberland. One night— March 26, 2007—I turned on the television. The reception was just clear enough to bring the BBC's report that Ian Paisley and Gerry Adams had, quite remarkably, sat down at a conference table and agreed that the future of Northern Ireland lay in just that: their ability to sit down at a table and speak, not on behalf of the partisan but for the whole country's well-being. This seems to me, as must by now be clear, the single through-line of genuine justice.

A few days later I was at a poetry festival in Dublin, and asked the poet Derek Mahon—born in Belfast, now a resident of the Republic of Ireland—what he might think about justice. He answered, "Justice? In Ireland, there's no justice." And then, "Justice has always got a bit of sadism in it, doesn't it, a taste of the urge to punish." The statement punctures, reminding of the inadequacy of absolutes before the actualities of human histories and lives, reminding that ideals too often endanger.

Good poetry—allergic to the manipulations of slogan and propaganda—can bring to expression things inexpressible in any other mode. As we have seen with *The Oresteia*, it can not only hold the record of justice's inceptions but also help create them. This is why, even now, cultures in trouble turn to their poets, singers, novelists, artists, filmmakers, and playwrights, to find a way out amid conditions seemingly insoluble. Through those whose only allegiance is actuality's discovery and its recording, suffering can first be fully seen and acknowledged, then alchemized into a changed comprehension.[4] Art allows a moving forward because it invites the seemingly fixed to yield. It makes of the unbearable something that can be taken in and grieved, that can be healed by making it, quite simply, both hearable and heard.

Good poetry perforates our hard-shelled realities, allowing the seemingly fixed to yield. This is why it is so useful in times of duress. It complicates and unfastens the conceptual mind's black-and-white words and worlds. It defies the ego's wish for categorical statement and overly certain knowledge. It dissolves vitrification, at times almost unbearably well. If a poem is good, the solvent of compassion will also be in it, whether in visible foreground or as the subterranean murmur of counter thought beneath the uttered words.

Because I have been thinking about both Ireland and classical Greece, of the many poems I looked at to see which might offer something otherwise unavailable here, I've picked a brief work by Michael Longley, another Irish poet who has witnessed the decades of sectarian violence and their grief-price. It describes and reimagines a scene from the *Iliad*, in which the Greek Achilles returns to the Trojan king, Priam, the dragged and dishonored corpse of Priam's son. The poem is a sonnet broken into four parts, whose rhymes are so tactful until the final couplet that they barely hold the balancing closures and reassurance it is rhyme's work to bring.

---

[4] I am thinking here of Akhmatova and Milosz, of Coetzee, Gordimer, and Solzhenitsyn; but in subtler ways, innumerable works of art have changed their cultures: small measures that together work significant effects.

Ceasefire

I

Put in mind of his own father and moved to tears
Achilles took him by the hand and pushed the old king
Gently away, but Priam curled up at his feet and
Wept with him until their sadness filled the building.

II

Taking Hector's corpse into his own hands Achilles
Made sure it was washed and, for the old king's sake,
Laid out in uniform, ready for Priam to carry
Wrapped like a present home to Troy at daybreak.

III

When they had eaten together, it pleased them both
To stare at each other's beauty as lovers might,
Achilles built like a god, Priam good-looking still
And full of conversation, who earlier had sighed:

IV

"I get down on my knees and do what must be done
And kiss Achilles' hand, the killer of my son."[5]

_____

5From *Collected Poems* (London: Jonathan Cape, 2006); used by permission of the author.

Justice is built on admixture: on the optimisms of altruism and awakened compassion mixed with the frictions—often ferocities—of personal and tribal desire for survival and power. Yet what "Ceasefire" (written, Longley has said, on the occasion of an earlier attempt at peace between Catholic and Protestant forces in Northern Ireland, and with his own father strongly in mind) brings into view is not insight into justice, nor anything about justice, really. It presents the pure necessity of actual life, and one possibility for how the unendurable might be endured: by entering it fully. The choice is either madness or softening, either mindless slaughter or replacing the concept of enemy with the knowledge that the father of the person we have killed could have been our own father, that the killed son could have been Achilles as easily as Hector.

The path to Ian Paisley and Gerry Adams sitting together at table, my Irish friends told me, was exhaustion: suffering endured too long. The people, they told me, had simply grown tired of death and hardness. Their leaders could either follow or be left behind.

And the hallmark and signal of this moment? A public act of conversation, of shared speech. An act that finds itself on a spectrum that includes the truth and reconciliation process in South Africa as well as a play written and performed by a group of Turkish and Armenian children; the publication of a diary kept by a woman when the Allied forces entered Berlin, of the poems written in the Japanese American internment camp of Manzanar, of the stories of the "comfort women" of Korea.

The Athenian Furies were put to ground for perhaps fifty years before they rose up again. It may be that no permanent justice can be negotiated among us while we remain unenlightened and human, gripped by the oscillant moods of complacence and partisan passion. It may be that the suffering everywhere around us—from the dispossessed and uncared-for people of New Orleans's Ninth Ward to those of East Timor—is too immediate to wait for awakened compassion. That what I've suggested here as an alternative to the sadisms and fixities of conflictual justice—the cultivation of nondual understanding and kindness—is too rare and hard-come-by to count on, in any foreseeable future, as answer to cruelty, passivity, and strife. It may be that all we can hope for is ordinary law, ordinary justice, and the achievable, moment-by-moment cease-fire of Longley's poem. And to be held by his words' embraced knowledge, that all griefs will visit all hearts.

To see humanness when another person stands before us, to see the deep beauty of those we have wronged past any conceivable conception of forgiveness, the deep beauty of those who have wronged us past any conceivable conception of forgiveness—this is what Michael Longley's poem proposes. It is the most intimate description of what truth and reconciliation look like, lived fully through, between opposing soldiers and peoples, between neighbor and neighbor. The heart shattered, from stone-adamance to open.

* * *

This *essay was written* for the New Symposium, an international gathering of writers held on Paros, Greece, in May 2007, sponsored by the University of Iowa's International Writing Program and the Fulbright Foundation in Greece.

Jane Hirshfield is the author of six collections of poetry, including *After* (HarperCollins, 2006) and Given *Sugar, Given Salt* (HarperCollins, 2001), finalist for the National Book Critics Circle Award. She is also the author of the essay collection *Nine Gates: Entering the Mind of Poetry* (HarperCollins, 1997).

Letter from Birmingham City Jail

Martin Luther King, Jr.

April 16, 1963

My dear Fellow Clergymen,

While confined here in the Birmingham City Jail, I came across your recent statement calling our present activities "unwise and untimely." Seldom, if ever, do I pause to answer criticism of my work and ideas. If I sought to answer all the criticisms that cross my desk, my secretaries would be engaged in little else in the course of the day and I would have no time for constructive work. But since I feel that you are men of genuine goodwill and your criticisms are sincerely set forth, I would like to answer your statement in what I hope will be patient and reasonable terms.

I think I should give the reason for my being in Birmingham, since you have been influenced by the argument of "outsiders coming in." I have the honor of serving as president of the Southern Christian Leadership Conference, an organization operating in every Southern state with headquarters in Atlanta, Georgia. We have some eighty-five affiliate organizations all across the South—one being the Alabama Christian Movement for Human Rights. Whenever necessary and possible we share staff, educational, and financial resources with our affiliates. Several months ago our local affiliate here in Birmingham invited us to be on call to engage in a nonviolent direct action program if such were deemed necessary. We readily consented and when the hour came we lived up to our promises. So I am here, along with several members of my staff, because we were invited here. I am here because I have basic organizational ties here. Beyond this, I am in Birmingham because injustice is here. Just as the eighth century prophets left their little villages and carried their "thus saith the Lord" far beyond the boundaries of their home town, and just as the Apostle Paul left his little village of Tarsus and carried the gospel of Jesus Christ to practically every hamlet and city of the Graeco-Roman world, I too am compelled to carry the gospel of freedom beyond my particular home town. Like Paul, I must constantly respond to the Macedonian call for aid.

Moreover, I am cognizant of the interrelatedness of all communities and states. I cannot sit idly by in Atlanta and not be concerned about what happens in Birmingham. Injustice anywhere is a threat to justice everywhere. We are caught in an inescapable network of mutuality tied in a single garment of destiny. Whatever affects one directly affects all indirectly. Never again can we afford to live with the narrow, provincial "outside agitator" idea. Anyone who lives inside the United States can never be considered an outsider anywhere in this country.

You deplore the demonstrations that are presently taking place in Birmingham. But I am sorry that your statement did not express a similar concern for the conditions that brought the demonstrations into being. I am sure that each of you would want to go beyond the superficial social analyst who looks merely at effects, and does not grapple with underlying causes. I would not hesitate to say that it is unfortunate that so-called demonstrations are taking place in Birmingham at this time, but I would say in more emphatic terms that it is even more unfortunate that the white power structure of this city left the Negro community with no other alternative.

In any nonviolent campaign there are four basic steps: (1) Collection of the facts to determine whether injustices are alive; (2) Negotiation; (3) Self-purification; and (4) Direct action. We have gone through all of these steps in Birmingham. There can be no gainsaying of the fact that racial injustice engulfs this community. Birmingham is probably the most thoroughly segregated city in the United States. Its ugly record of police brutality is known in every section of this country. Its unjust treatment of Negroes in the courts is a notorious reality. There have been more unsolved bombings of Negro homes and churches in Birmingham than any city in this nation. These are the hard, brutal, and unbelievable facts. On the basis of these conditions Negro leaders sought to negotiate with the city fathers. But the political leaders consistently refused to engage in good faith negotiation.

Then came the opportunity last September to talk with some of the leaders of the economic community. In these negotiating sessions certain promises were made by the merchants—such as the promise to remove the humiliating racial signs from the stores. On the basis of these promises Rev. Shuttlesworth and the leaders of the Alabama Christian Movement for Human Rights agreed to call a moratorium on any type of demonstrations. As the weeks and months unfolded we realized that we were the victims of a broken promise. The signs remained. As in so many experiences of the past we were confronted with blasted hopes, and the dark shadow of a deep disappointment settled upon us. So we had no alternative except that of preparing for direct action, whereby we would present our very bodies as a means of laying our case before the conscience of the local and national community. We were not unmindful of the difficulties involved. So we decided to go through a process of self-purification. We started having workshops on nonviolence and repeatedly asked ourselves the questions, "Are you able to accept blows without retaliating?" "Are you able to endure the ordeals of jail?"

We decided to set our direct-action program around the Easter season, realizing that with the exception of Christmas, this was the largest shopping period of the year. Knowing that a strong economic withdrawal program would be the by-product of direct action, we felt that this was the best time to bring pressure on the merchants for the needed changes. Then it occurred to us that the March election was ahead, and so we speedily decided to postpone action until after election day. When we discovered that Mr. Connor was in the run-off, we decided again to postpone action so that the demonstrations could not be used to cloud the issues. At this time we agreed to begin our nonviolent witness the day after the run-off.

This reveals that we did not move irresponsibly into direct action. We too wanted to see Mr. Connor defeated; so we went through postponement after postponement to aid in this community need. After this we felt that direct action could be delayed no longer.

You may well ask, Why direct action? Why sit-ins, marches, etc.? Isn't negotiation a better path?" You are exactly right in your call for negotiation. Indeed, this is the purpose of direct action. Nonviolent direct action seeks to create such a crisis and establish such creative tension that a community that has constantly refused to negotiate is forced to confront the issue. It seeks so to dramatize the issue that it can no longer be ignored. I just referred to the creation of tension as a part of the work of the nonviolent resister. This may sound rather shocking. But I must confess that I am not afraid of the word tension. I have earnestly worked and preached against violent tension, but there is a type of constructive nonviolent tension that is necessary for growth. Just as Socrates felt that it was necessary to create a tension in the mind so that individuals could rise from the bondage of myths and half-truths to the unfettered realm of creative analysis and objective appraisal, we must see the need of having nonviolent gadflies to create the kind of tension in society that will help men rise from the dark depths of prejudice and racism to the majestic heights of understanding and brotherhood. So the purpose of the direct action is to create a situation so crisis-packed that it will inevitably open the door to negotiation. We, therefore, concur with you in your call for negotiation. Too long has our beloved Southland been bogged down in the tragic attempt to live in monologue rather than dialogue.

One of the basic points in your statement is that our acts are untimely. Some have asked, "Why didn't you give the new administration time to act?" The only answer that I can give to this inquiry is that the new administration must be prodded about as much as the outgoing one before it acts. We will be sadly mistaken if we feel that the election of Mr. Boutwell will bring the millennium to Birmingham. While Mr. Boutwell is much more articulate and gentle than Mr. Connor, they are both segregationists dedicated to the task of maintaining the status quo. The hope I see in Mr. Boutwell is that he will be reasonable enough to see the futility of massive resistance to desegregation. But he will not see this without pressure from the devotees of civil rights. My friends, I must say to you that we have not made a single gain in civil rights without determined legal and nonviolent pressure. History is the long and tragic story of the fact that privileged groups seldom give up their privileges voluntarily. Individuals may see the moral light and voluntarily give up their unjust posture; but as Reinhold Niebuhr has reminded us, groups are more immoral than individuals.

We know through painful experience that freedom is never voluntarily given by the oppressor; it must be demanded by the oppressed. Frankly I have never yet engaged in a direct action movement that was "well timed," according to the timetable of those who have not suffered unduly from the disease of segregation. For years now I have heard the word "Wait!" It rings in the ear of every Negro with a piercing familiarity. This "wait" has almost always meant "never." It has been a tranquilizing thalidomide, relieving the emotional stress for a moment, only to give birth to an ill-formed infant of frustration. We must come to see with the distinguished jurist of yesterday that "justice too long delayed is justice denied." We have waited for more than three hundred and forty years for our constitutional and God-given rights. The nations of Asia and Africa are moving with jet-like speed toward the goal of political independence, and we still creep at horse and buggy pace toward the gaining of a cup of coffee at a lunch counter.

I guess it is easy for those who have never felt the stinging darts of segregation to say wait. But when you have seen vicious mobs lynch your mothers and fathers at will and drown your sisters and brothers at whim; when you have seen hate filled policemen curse, kick, brutalize, and even kill your black brothers and sisters with impunity; when you see the vast majority of your twenty million Negro brothers smothering in an air-tight cage of poverty in the midst of an affluent society; when you suddenly find your tongue twisted and your speech stammering as you seek to explain to your six-year-old daughter why she can't go to the public amusement park that has just been advertised on television, and see tears welling up in her little eyes when she is told that Funtown is closed to colored children, and see the depressing clouds of inferiority begin to form in her little mental sky, and see her begin to distort her little personality by unconsciously developing a bitterness toward white people; when you have to concoct an answer for a five-year-old son asking in agonizing pathos: "Daddy, why do white people treat colored people so mean?"; when you take a cross-country drive and find it necessary to sleep night after night in the uncomfortable corners of your automobile because no motel will accept you; when you are humiliated day in and day out by nagging signs reading "white" men and "colored"; when your first name becomes "nigger" and your middle name becomes "boy" (however old you are) and your last name becomes "John," and when your wife and mother are never given the respected title "Mrs."; when you are harried by day and haunted by night by the fact that you are a Negro, living constantly at tip-toe stance never quite knowing what to expect next, and plagued with inner fears and outer resentments; when you are forever fighting a degenerating sense of "nobodiness"—then you will understand why we find it difficult to wait. There comes a time when the cup of endurance runs over, and men are no longer willing to be plunged into an abyss of injustice where they experience the bleakness of corroding despair. I

hope, sirs, you can understand our legitimate and unavoidable impatience.

You express a great deal of anxiety over our willingness to break laws. This is certainly a legitimate concern. Since we so diligently urge people to obey the Supreme Court's decision of 1954 outlawing segregation in the public schools, it is rather strange and paradoxical to find us consciously breaking laws. One may well ask: "How can you advocate breaking some laws and obeying others?" The answer is found in the fact that there are two types of laws: There are just laws and there are unjust laws. I would be the first to advocate obeying just laws. One has not only a legal but moral responsibility to obey just laws. Conversely, one has a moral responsibility to disobey unjust laws. I would agree with Saint Augustine that "An unjust law is no law at all."

Now what is the difference between the two? How does one determine when a law is just or unjust? A just law is a man-made code that squares with the moral law or the law of God. An unjust law is a code that is out of harmony with the moral law. To put it in the terms of Saint Thomas Aquinas, an unjust law is a human law that is not rooted in eternal and natural law. Any law that uplifts human personality is just. Any law that degrades human personality is unjust. All segregation statutes are unjust because segregation distorts the soul and damages the personality. It gives the segregator a false sense of superiority and the segregated a false sense of inferiority. To use the words of Martin Buber, the great Jewish philosopher, segregation substitutes an "I-it" relationship for an "I-thou" relationship, and ends up relegating persons to the status of things. So segregation is not only politically, economically, and sociologically unsound, but it is morally wrong and sinful. Paul Tillich has said that sin is separation. Isn't segregation an existential expression of man's tragic separation, an expression of his awful estrangement, his terrible sinfulness? So

I can urge men to obey the 1954 decision of the Supreme Court because it is morally right, and I can urge them to disobey segregation ordinances because they are morally wrong.

Let us turn to a more concrete example of just and unjust laws. An unjust law is a code that a majority inflicts on a minority that is not binding on itself. This is difference made legal. On the other hand a just law is a code that a majority compels a minority to follow that it is willing to follow itself. This is sameness made legal.

Let me give another explanation. An unjust law is a code inflicted upon a minority which that minority had no part in enacting or creating because they did not have the unhampered right to vote. Who can say that the legislature of Alabama which set up the segregation laws was democratically elected? Throughout the state of Alabama all types of conniving methods are used to prevent Negroes from becoming registered voters and there are some counties without a single Negro registered to vote despite the fact that the Negro constitutes a majority of the population. Can any law set up in such a state be considered democratically structured?

These are just a few examples of unjust and just laws. There are some instances when a law is just on its face but unjust in its application. For instance, I was arrested Friday on a charge of parading without a permit. Now there is nothing wrong with an ordinance which requires a permit for a parade, but when the ordinance is used to preserve segregation and to deny citizens the First Amendment privilege of peaceful assembly and peaceful protest, then it becomes unjust.

I hope you can see the distinction I am trying to point out. In no sense do I advocate evading or defying the law as the rabid segregationist would do. This would lead to anarchy. One who breaks an unjust law must do it openly, lovingly (not hatefully as the white mothers did in New Orleans when they were seen on television screaming "nigger, nigger, nigger") and with a willingness to accept the penalty. I submit that an individual who breaks a law that conscience tells him is unjust, and willingly accepts the penalty by staying in jail to arouse the conscience of the community over its injustice, is in reality expressing the very highest respect for law.

Of course there is nothing new about this kind of civil disobedience. It was seen sublimely in the refusal of Shadrach, Meshach, and Abednego to obey the laws of Nebuchadnezzar because a higher moral law was involved. It was practiced superbly by the early Christians who were willing to face hungry lions and the excruciating pain of chopping blocks, before submitting to certain unjust laws of the Roman Empire. To a degree academic freedom is a reality today because Socrates practiced civil disobedience.

We can never forget that everything Hitler did in Germany was "legal" and everything the Hungarian freedom fighters did in Hungary was "illegal." It was "illegal" to aid and comfort a Jew in Hitler's Germany. But I am sure that, if I had lived in Germany during that time, I would have aided and comforted my Jewish brothers even though it was illegal. If I lived in a communist country today where certain principles dear to the Christian faith are suppressed, I believe I would openly advocate disobeying these anti-religious laws.

I must make two honest confessions to you, my Christian and Jewish brothers. First, I must confess that over the last few years I have been gravely disappointed with the white moderate. I have almost reached the regrettable conclusion that the Negroes' great stumbling block in the stride toward freedom is not the White Citizen's "Counciler" or the Ku Klux Klanner, but the white moderate who is more devoted to "order" than to justice; who prefers a negative peace which is the absence of tension to a positive peace which is the presence of justice; who constantly says "I agree with you in the goal you seek, but I can't agree with your methods of direct action"; who paternalistically feels that he can set the timetable for another man's freedom; who lives by the myth of time and who constantly advises the Negro to wait until a "more convenient season." Shallow understanding from people of good will is more frustrating than absolute misunderstanding from people of ill will. Lukewarm acceptance is much more bewildering than outright rejection.

I had hoped that the white moderate would understand that law and order exist for the purpose of establishing justice, and that when they fail to do this they become dangerously structured dams that block the flow of social progress. I had hoped that the white moderate would understand that the present tension in the South is merely a necessary phase of the transition from an obnoxious negative peace, where the Negro passively accepted his unjust plight, to a substance-filled positive peace, where all men will respect the dignity and worth of human personality. Actually, we who engage in nonviolent direct action are not the creators of tension. We merely bring to the surface the hidden tension that is already alive. We bring it out in the open where it can be seen and dealt with. Like a boil that can never be cured as long as it is covered up but must be opened with all its pus-flowing ugliness to the natural medicines of air and light, injustice must likewise be exposed, with all of the tension its exposing creates, to the light of human conscience and the air of national opinion before it can be cured.

In your statement you asserted that our actions, even though peaceful, must be condemned because they precipitate violence. But can this assertion be logically made? Isn't this like condemning the robbed man because his possession of money precipitated the evil act of robbery? Isn't this like condemning Socrates because his unswerving commitment to truth and his philosophical delvings precipitated the misguided popular mind

to make him drink the hemlock? Isn't this like condemning Jesus because His unique God consciousness and never-ceasing devotion to His will precipitated the evil act of crucifixion? We must come to see, as federal courts have consistently affirmed, that it is immoral to urge an individual to withdraw his efforts to gain his basic constitutional rights because the quest precipitates violence. Society must protect the robbed and punish the robber.

I had also hoped that the white moderate would reject the myth of time. I received a letter this morning from a white brother in Texas which said: "All Christians know that the colored people will receive equal rights eventually, but is it possible that you are in too great of a religious hurry? It has taken Christianity almost 2,000 years to accomplish what it has. The teachings of Christ take time to come to earth." All that is said here grows out of a tragic misconception of time. It is the strangely irrational notion that there is something in the very flow of time that will inevitably cure all ills. Actually time is neutral. It can be used either destructively or constructively. I am coming to feel that the people of ill will have used time much more effectively than the people of good will. We will have to repent in this generation not merely for the vitriolic words and actions of the bad people, but for the appalling silence of the good people. We must come to see that human progress never rolls in on wheels of inevitability. It comes through the tireless efforts and persistent work of men willing to be co-workers with God, and without this hard work time itself becomes an ally of the forces of social stagnation.

We must use time creatively, and forever realize that the time is always ripe to do right. Now is the time to make real the promise of democracy, and transform our pending national elegy into a creative psalm of brotherhood. Now is the time to lift our national policy from the quicksand of racial injustice to the solid rock of human dignity.

You spoke of our activity in Birmingham as extreme. At first I was rather disappointed that fellow clergymen would see my nonviolent efforts as those of the extremist. I started thinking about the fact that I stand in the middle of two opposing forces in the Negro community. One is a force of complacency made up of Negroes who, as a result of long years of oppression, have been so completely drained of self-respect and a sense of "somebodiness" that they have adjusted to segregation, and of a few Negroes in the middle class who, because of a degree of academic and economic security, and because at points they profit by segregation, have unconsciously become insensitive to the problems of the masses. The other force is one of bitterness and hatred and comes perilously close to advocating violence. It is expressed in the various black nationalist groups that are springing up over the nation, the largest and best known being Elijah Muhammad's Muslim movement. This movement is nourished by the contemporary frustration over the continued existence of racial discrimination. It is made up of people who have lost faith in America, who have absolutely repudiated Christianity, and who have concluded that the white man is an incurable "devil." I have tried to stand between these two forces saying that we need not follow the "do-nothingism" of the complacent or the hatred and despair of the black nationalist. There is the more excellent way of love and nonviolent protest. I'm grateful to God that, through the Negro church, the dimension of nonviolence entered our struggle. If this philosophy had not emerged I am convinced that by now many streets of the South would be flowing with floods of blood. And I am further convinced that if our white brothers dismiss us as "rabble rousers" and "outside agitators"—those of us who are working through the channels of nonviolent direct action—and refuse to support our nonviolent efforts, millions of Negroes, out of frustration and despair, will seek solace and security in black-nationalist ideologies, a development that will lead inevitably to a frightening racial nightmare.

Oppressed people cannot remain oppressed forever. The urge for freedom will eventually come. This is what has happened to the American Negro. Something within has reminded him of his birthright of freedom; something without has reminded him that he can gain it. Consciously and unconsciously, he has been swept in by what the Germans call the Zeitgeist, and with his black brothers of Africa, and his brown and yellow brothers of Asia, South America, and the Caribbean, he is moving with a sense of cosmic urgency toward the promised land of racial justice. Recognizing this vital urge that has engulfed the Negro community, one should readily understand public demonstrations. The Negro has many pent-up resentments and latent frustrations. He has to get them out. So let him march sometime; let him have his prayer pilgrimages to the city hall; understand why he must have sit-ins and freedom rides. If his repressed emotions do not come out in these nonviolent ways, they will come out in ominous expressions of violence. This is not a threat; it is a fact of history. So I have not said to my people, "Get rid of your discontent." But I have tried to say that this normal and healthy discontent can be channeled through the creative outlet of nonviolent direct action. Now this approach is being dismissed as extremist. I must admit that I was initially disappointed in being so categorized.

But as I continued to think about the matter I gradually gained a bit of satisfaction from being considered an extremist. Was not Jesus an extremist in love? "Love your enemies, bless them that curse you, pray for them that despitefully use you." Was not Amos an extremist for justice—"Let justice roll down like waters and righteousness like a mighty stream." Was not Paul an extremist for the gospel of Jesus Christ—"I bear in my body the marks of the Lord Jesus." Was not Martin Luther an extremist—"Here I stand; I can do none other so help me God." Was not John Bunyan an extremist— "I will stay in jail to the end of my days before I make a butchery of my conscience." Was not Abraham Lincoln an extremist—"This nation cannot survive half slave and half free." Was not Thomas Jefferson an extremist—"We hold these truths to be self-evident, that all men are created equal." So the question is not whether we will be extremist but what kind of extremist will we be. Will we be extremists for hate or will we be extremists for love? Will we be extremists for the preservation of injustice—or will we be extremists for the cause of justice? In that dramatic scene on Calvary's hill three men were crucified. We must never forget that all three were crucified for the same crime—the crime of extremism. Two were extremists for immorality, and thus fell below their environment. The other, Jesus Christ, was an extremist for love, truth, and goodness, and thereby rose above His environment. So, after all, maybe the South, the nation, and the world are in dire need of creative extremists.

I had hoped that the white moderate would see this. Maybe I was too optimistic. Maybe I expected too much. I guess I should have realized that few members of a race that has oppressed another race can understand or appreciate the deep groans and passionate yearnings of those that have been oppressed, and still fewer have the vision to see that injustice must be rooted out by strong, persistent, and determined action. I am thankful, however, that some of our white brothers have grasped the meaning of this social revolution and committed themselves to it. They are still all too small in quantity, but they are big in quality. Some like Ralph McGill, Lillian Smith, Harry Golden, and James Dabbs have written about our struggle in eloquent, prophetic, and understanding terms. Others have marched with us down nameless streets of the South. They have

languished in filthy, roach-infested jails, suffering the abuse and brutality of angry policemen who see them as "dirty nigger lovers." They, unlike so many of their moderate brothers and sisters, have recognized the urgency of the moment and sensed the need for powerful "action" antidotes to combat the disease of segregation.

Let me rush on to mention my other disappointment. I have been so greatly disappointed with the white Church and its leadership. Of course there are some notable exceptions. I am not unmindful of the fact that each of you has taken some significant stands on this issue. I commend you, Rev. Stallings, for your Christian stand on this past Sunday, in welcoming Negroes to your worship service on a non-segregated basis. I commend the Catholic leaders of this state for integrating Spring Hill College several years ago.

But despite these notable exceptions I must honestly reiterate that I have been disappointed with the Church. I do not say that as one of those negative critics who can always find something wrong with the Church. I say it as a minister of the gospel, who loves the Church; who was nurtured in its bosom; who has been sustained by its spiritual blessings and who will remain true to it as long as the cord of life shall lengthen.

I had the strange feeling when I was suddenly catapulted into the leadership of the bus protest in Montgomery several years ago that we would have the support of the white Church. I felt that the white ministers, priests, and rabbis of the South would be some of our strongest allies. Instead, some have been outright opponents, refusing to understand the freedom movement and misrepresenting its leaders; all too many others have been more cautious than courageous and have remained silent behind the anesthetizing security of the stained glass windows.

In spite of my shattered dreams of the past, I came to Birmingham with the hope that the white religious leadership of this community would see the justice of our cause and with deep moral concern, serve as the channel through which our just grievances could get to the power structure. I had hoped that each of you would understand. But again I have been disappointed.

I have heard numerous religious leaders of the South call upon their worshippers to comply with a desegregation decision because it is the law, but I have longed to hear white ministers say follow this decree because integration is morally right and the Negro is your brother. In the midst of blatant injustices inflicted upon the Negro, I have watched white churches stand on the sideline and merely mouth pious irrelevancies and sanctimonious trivialities. In the midst of a mighty struggle to rid our nation of racial and economic injustice, I have heard so many ministers say, "Those are social issues with which the gospel has no real concern," and I have watched so many churches commit themselves to a completely other-worldly religion which made a strange distinction between body and soul, the sacred and the secular.

So here we are moving toward the exit of the twentieth century with a religious community largely adjusted to the status quo, standing as a tail-light behind other community agencies rather than a headlight leading men to higher levels of justice.

I have travelled the length and breadth of Alabama, Mississippi and all the other southern states. On sweltering summer days and crisp autumn mornings I have looked at her beautiful churches with their spires pointing heavenward. I have beheld the impressive outlay of her massive religious education buildings. Over and over again I have found myself asking: "Who worships here? Who is their God? Where were their voices when the lips of Governor Barnett dripped with words of interposition and nullification? Where were they when Governor Wallace gave the clarion call for defiance and hatred? Where were their voices of support when tired, bruised, and weary Negro men and women decided to rise from the dark dungeons of complacency to the bright hills of creative protest?"

Yes, these questions are still in my mind. In deep disappointment, I have wept over the laxity of the church. But be assured that my tears have been tears of love. There can be no deep disappointment where there is not deep love. Yes, I love the Church; I love her sacred walls. How could I do otherwise? I am in the rather unique position of being the son, the grandson, and the great-grandson of preachers. Yes, I see the Church as the body of Christ. But, oh! How we have blemished and scarred that body through social neglect and fear of being nonconformist.

There was a time when the Church was very powerful. It was during that period when the early Christians rejoiced when they were deemed worthy to suffer for what they believed. In those days the Church was not merely a thermometer that recorded the ideas and principles of popular opinion; it was a thermostat that transformed the mores of society. Wherever the early Christians entered a town the power structure got disturbed and immediately sought to convict them for being "disturbers of the peace" and "outside agitators." But they went on with the conviction that they were "a colony of heaven" and had to obey God rather than man. They were small in number but big in commitment. They were too God-intoxicated to be "astronomically intimidated." They brought an end to such ancient evils as infanticide and gladiatorial contest.

Things are different now. The contemporary Church is so often a weak, ineffectual voice with an uncertain sound. It is so often the arch-supporter of the status quo. Far from being disturbed by the presence of the Church, the power structure of the average community is consoled by the Church's silent and often vocal sanction of things as they are.

But the judgment of God is upon the Church as never before. If the Church of today does not recapture the sacrificial spirit of the early Church, it will lose its authentic ring, forfeit the loyalty of millions, and be dismissed as an irrelevant social club with no meaning for the twentieth century. I am meeting young people every day whose disappointment with the Church has risen to outright disgust.

Maybe again I have been too optimistic. Is organized religion too inextricably bound to the status quo to save our nation and the world? Maybe I must turn my faith to the inner spiritual Church, the church within the Church, as the true ecclesia and the hope of the world. But again I am thankful to God that some noble souls from the ranks of organized religion have broken loose from the paralyzing chains of conformity and joined us as active partners in the struggle for freedom. They have left their secure congregations and walked the streets of Albany, Georgia, with us. They have gone through the highways of the South on torturous rides for freedom. Yes, they have gone to jail with us. Some have been kicked out of their churches and lost the support of their bishops and fellow ministers. But they have gone with the faith that right defeated is stronger than evil triumphant. These men have been the leaven in the lump of the race. Their witness has been the spiritual salt that has preserved the true meaning of the Gospel in these troubled times. They have carved a tunnel of hope through the dark mountain of disappointment.

I hope the Church as a whole will meet the challenge of this decisive hour. But even if the Church does not come to the aid of justice, I have no despair about the future. I have no fear about the outcome of our struggle in Birmingham, even if our motives are presently misunderstood. We will reach the goal of freedom in Birmingham and all over the nation, because the goal of America is freedom. Abused and scorned though we may be,

our destiny is tied up with the destiny of America. Before the pilgrims landed at Plymouth, we were here. Before the pen of Jefferson etched across the pages of history the majestic words of the Declaration of Independence, we were here. For more than two centuries our foreparents labored in this country without wages; they made cotton "king"; and they built the homes of their masters in the midst of brutal injustice and shameful humiliation—and yet out of a bottomless vitality they continued to thrive and develop. If the inexpressible cruelties of slavery could not stop us, the opposition we now face will surely fail. We will win our freedom because the sacred heritage of our nation and the eternal will of God are embodied in our echoing demands.

I must close now. But before closing I am impelled to mention one other point in your statement that troubled me profoundly. You warmly commend the Birmingham police force for keeping "order" and "preventing violence." I don't believe you would have so warmly commended the police force if you had seen its angry violent dogs literally biting six unarmed, nonviolent Negroes. I don't believe you would so quickly commend the policemen if you would observe their ugly and inhuman treatment of Negroes here in the city jail; if you would watch them push and curse old Negro women and young Negro girls; if you would see them slap and kick old Negro men and young Negro boys; if you will observe them, as they did on two occasions, refuse to give us food because we wanted to sing our grace together. I'm sorry that I can't join you in your praise for the police department.

It is true that they have been rather disciplined in their public handling of the demonstrators. In this sense they have been rather publicly "nonviolent." But for what purpose? To preserve the evil system of segregation. Over the last few years I have consistently preached that nonviolence demands the means we use must be as pure as the ends we seek. So I have tried to make it clear that it is wrong to use immoral means to attain moral ends. But now I must affirm that it is just as wrong or even more so to use moral means to preserve immoral ends. Maybe Mr. Connor and his policemen have been rather publicly nonviolent, as Chief Pritchett was in Albany, Georgia, but they have used the moral means of nonviolence to maintain the immoral end of flagrant injustice. T. S. Eliot has said that there is no greater treason than to do the right deed for the wrong reason.

I wish you had commended the Negro sit-inners and demonstrators of Birmingham for their sublime courage, their willingness to suffer, and their amazing discipline in the midst of the most inhuman provocation. One day the South will recognize its real heroes. They will be the James Merediths, courageously and with a majestic sense of purpose, facing jeering and hostile mobs and the agonizing loneliness that characterizes the life of the pioneer. They will be old, oppressed, battered Negro women, symbolized in a seventy-two year old woman of Montgomery, Alabama, who rose up with a sense of dignity and with her people decided not to ride the segregated buses, and responded to one who inquired about her tiredness with ungrammatical profundity: "My feets is tired, but my soul is rested." They will be the young high school and college students, young ministers of the gospel and a host of their elders courageously and nonviolently sitting-in at lunch counters and willingly going to jail for conscience sake. One day the South will know that when these disinherited children of God sat down at lunch counters they were in reality standing up for the best in the American dream and the most sacred values in our Judaeo-Christian heritage, and thus carrying our whole nation back to great wells of democracy which were dug deep by the founding fathers in the formulation of the Constitution and the Declaration of Independence.

Never before have I written a letter this long (or should I say a book?). I'm afraid it is much too long to take your precious time. I can assure you that it would have been much shorter if I had been writing from a comfortable desk, but what else is there to do when you are alone for days in the dull monotony of a narrow jail cell other than write long letters, think strange thoughts, and pray long prayers?

If I have said anything in this letter that is an overstatement of the truth and is indicative of an unreasonable impatience, I beg you to forgive me. If I have said anything in this letter that is an understatement of the truth and is indicative of my having a patience that makes me patient with anything less than brotherhood, I beg God to forgive me.

I hope this letter finds you strong in the faith. I also hope that circumstances will soon make it possible for me to meet each of you, not as an integrationist or a civil rights leader, but as a fellow clergyman and a Christian brother. Let us all hope that the dark clouds of racial prejudice will soon pass away and the deep fog of misunderstanding will be lifted from our fear-drenched communities and in some not too distant tomorrow the radiant stars of love and brotherhood will shine over our great nation with all their scintillating beauty.

Yours for the cause of
Peace and Brotherhood,
Martin Luther King, Jr.

Who Is My Neighbor?

Naim Ateek

When examined in light of the Israeli-Palestinian conflict, the term "neighbor" raises questions of exclusivity and inclusivity, one's understanding of God, and responsibility toward the "Other."

The question posed by the young lawyer to Jesus, "Who is my neighbor?" (Luke 10:29), is as relevant today as it was two thousand years ago. So long as we define the neighbor negatively as a person who is foreign and alien, our humanity is in jeopardy. So long as we divide the world and our own communities into friends and enemies, neighbors and strangers, we feel no moral obligation towards those whom we have already designated as outsiders. This distinction between "us" and "them" creates a binary society that shuts the door on viewing the "Other" as a neighbor that deserves to be loved. Such a view, as Chris Hedges describes, "fosters rigidity, conformity, and intolerance."[1]

---

[1]Chris Hedges, *American Fascists* (New York: Free Press, 2006), 150-151

Tragically, we find people within the Christian church that espouse such beliefs:

> ...they are incapable of seeing others as anything more than inverted reflections of themselves. If they seek to destroy nonbelievers to create a Christian America, then nonbelievers must be seeking to destroy them. This belief system negates the possibility of the ethical life. It fails to grasp that goodness must be sought outside the self and that the best defense against evil is to seek it within. When people come to believe that they are immune from evil, that there is no resemblance between themselves and those they define as the enemy, they will inevitably grow to embody the evil they claim to fight. It is only by grasping our own capacity for evil, our own darkness, that we hold our own capacity for evil at bay. When evil is always external, then moral purification always entails the eradication of others.

Naim Ateek, "Who Is My Neighbor?," *Interpretation*, vol. 62, no. 2, pp. 156-165, 122. Copyright © 2008 by Union Presbyterian Seminary. Reprinted with permission. Provided by ProQuest LLc

This rhetoric of depersonalization creates a frightening moral fragmentation, an ability to act with compassion and justice toward those within the closed, Christian circle yet allow others outside the circle to be abused, silenced and stripped of their rights.... Extremists never begin as extremists. They become extremists gradually. They move gingerly forward in an open society. They advance only so far as they fail to meet resistance. And no society is immune from this moral catastrophe.[2]

These words do not apply only to fundamentalist groups in America; they can apply to Israeli Jews, to Palestinians, and many others as well. Therefore, in the Israel-Palestine conflict, the question "Who is my neighbor?" is not only at the heart of the human quest for meaningful relationships, it is also at the heart of our quest for peace and reconciliation. Indeed, the very answer we give to the question determines where we stand on issues of peace as well as whether we believe in the possibility of a resolution of the conflict between the two conflicting groups.

There is another important dimension that must be considered. Since religion has come to play such a critical role in the Israel-Palestine conflict, it has become impossible to explore the question "Who is my neighbor?" without first exploring the question "Who is my God?" In other words, questions of God and neighbor have become intrinsically connected. Extremists among religious Jews and Muslims as well as millions of western fundamentalist Christians, who take the words of their Scriptures literally and infallibly, arrive at the answer to the question of neighbor through what they have come to believe about God. If they believe in an exclusive God,

then automatically their answer about the neighbor is equally exclusive. They define neighbor in a narrow and exclusive way because they believe in an exclusive God.

Sadly, in most cases, we are not dealing with a concept of God as one who embraces all of us as a loving creator and before whom we all stand on an equal basis—the God of justice, mercy, and love. The dominant view of God among many Israeli Jews and Palestinians is very narrow. Even if they give lip service to the belief in one God, they are convinced that their God favors them over others and has especially chosen them. If they are on the top politically, it is because God is with them. If they are at the bottom, it is because they are being tested by God, and they must repent and return to the precepts of God. They believe that eventually the time will come when they will triumph over others. Such a view of God negates and undermines the "Other." The quest for the neighbor is, therefore, one of the most crucial questions that faces human beings in their journey through life.

The candor expressed by the writer of the first letter of John in the NT becomes absolutely essential to our present discussion and must be clearly lifted up and emphasized:

> Those who say, "I love God" and hate their brothers or sisters, are liars; for those who do not love a brother or sister whom they have seen, cannot love God whom they have not seen. The commandment we have from him is this: those who love God must love their brothers and sisters also. (1 John 4:20-21)

Etymology And Linguistic Comparisons

The translation of the Hebrew word *ra'* as "neighbor" is not precise. A more correct rendering

---

[2]Ibid.

would be "friend, fellow, or companion." In Arabic, the word that is translated neighbor is *Qareeb* (in the masculine form) and carries multiple meanings. *Qareeb* can be a blood relative or one who is near or close. There is a famous saying in Arabic: "A close neighbor is better (or more valuable) than a far away brother or sister."

In English, the word "neighbor" carries the meaning of one who lives next door. According to *Webster's Dictionary*, the word means a nigh dweller that could be near in place, time, relationship, likeness, or course of events. In both Arabic and Hebrew, there are specific words for neighbor: *Jar* and *shakhain*, respectively. Yet the question that was asked, "Who is my neighbor," was not intended to mean, "who is your next door neighbor," i.e., who is your *Jar* or *shakhain*, but to whom should you act in a neighborly way, or to whom should you feel close or near. The obvious answer according to the story is, all those who need my help and my compassion. In this sense, the whole world becomes one neighborhood, yet what counts is not neighborhood, but neighborliness.

The same love and help that we extend to those who are our friends and close relatives we should extend to all those who are in need. Conversely, those who are in need have a claim on our love. We need to consider them as our neighbors, our *Qareeb*. This is the lesson Jesus was trying to teach the lawyer. It was a revolutionary message, which Jesus articulated through the beautiful story of the Good Samaritan. With this background, let us look at two primary texts regarding the neighbor in Leviticus and Luke.

The Leviticus Text

You shall not go around as a slanderer among *your people,* and you shall not profit by the blood of *your neighbor,*

I am the Lord. You shall not hate in your heart anyone of *your kin,* you shall reprove *your neighbor,* or you will incur guilt yourself. You shall not take vengeance or bear a grudge against any of *your people,* but you shall love *your neighbor* as yourself: I am the LORD. (Lev 19:16-18, emphasis added)

In classical Judaism, and among present day Orthodox Jews, the injunction to love *re' aka* ("your fellow") as you love yourself still means to love one's fellow Jew.[3] This parochial understanding is implied in the text (see the emphasis above). Generally speaking, the Leviticus text reflects our common human nature. It expresses our natural inclination to love those who are close to us and not outsiders. In order to maintain peace and order within the tribal family and community, it was essential that people who were related maintain strong bonds of love towards each other. Such a practice ensured not only the peace but also the unity, solidarity, and strength of the community.

Such laws must have evolved as a result of the daily experience of people in their relationships with one another. They were not peculiar to the ancient Israelites. Scholars have identified many parallels between the ancient Amorite laws and those we find in the Torah.[4]

The text in Lev 19:18 carries within it a specific injunction, "You shall not take vengeance or bear a grudge against any of your people, but you shall love your neighbor as yourself: I am the LORD." To love the "Other" as oneself is an ethic that is inherently logical, so long as it is confined within a close circle of friends and relatives. That is why Jesus expressed its ordinary nature and

---

[3]Israel Shahak, *Jewish History, Jewish Religion* (London: Pluto Press, 1994), 37.

[4]George E. Mendenhall, *Ancient Israel's Faith and History* (Louisville: Westminster John Knox, 2001), 25.

unimpressive value. "For if you love those who love you, what reward do you have? Do not even tax collectors do the same?...do not even the Gentiles do the same?" (Matt 5:46, 47).

In other words, loving one's neighbor as oneself presupposes a certain affiliation with that neighbor. But if no bond exists, the commandment on the natural level, for many people, becomes absurd. It is interesting to note Freud's comment in this regard, "If this grandiose commandment had run 'love thy neighbor as thy neighbor loves thee,' I should not take exception to it," he wrote. Loving a stranger, Freud said, is counter to human nature: "If he is a stranger to me ... it will be hard for me to love him."[5] Such a situation creates a psychological barrier with the "stranger" who is outside the circle of kinship.

I believe that the ethical and theological value lies not in the first part of the text but in the verses that follow:

> When an alien resides with you *in your land*, you shall not oppress the alien. The alien who resides with you shall be to you as the citizen among you; you shall love the alien as yourself, for you were aliens in the land of Egypt: I am the Lord your God. (Lev 19:33-34, emphasis added)

This commandment transcends the natural propensity of humans, and recognizes the humanity of others, and reaches out in love to them. Undoubtedly, this commandment reflects a very progressive view when comprehended against its own historical and environmental context. One can only applaud its deeper and more enlightened religious insights. The understanding of neighbor has been broadened, and the circle has been enlarged to include the resident alien.

Indeed, this commandment lifts up an ordinary human injunction to a higher moral level but, unfortunately, it stops short of giving the aliens full equality. There is no mention that aliens can enjoy an equal share of the land. The aliens can become "citizens" and are entitled to the protection of their human rights—"You shall not oppress the alien"—but they remain resident aliens. The basic assumption, and in fact the major premise, is that the land belongs only to the Israelites and, therefore, all others who are in the land, regardless of how long they have lived there, are designated as aliens. They cannot be rooted in the land, because the land, *a priori*, does not belong to them.[6]

At this point, it is important to compare the Leviticus text with that of Ezekiel. Apparently, the book of Leviticus was edited during the exile and scholars believe that it shares many of the same interests as the book of Ezekiel.[7]

> So you shall divide this land among you according to the tribes of Israel. You shall allot it as an inheritance for yourselves and for the aliens who reside among you and have begotten children among you. They shall be to you as citizens of Israel; with you they shall be allotted an inheritance among the

---

[5]Quoted in Hedges, *American Fascists*, 151.

[6]In the conflict over Palestine, the Palestinians do not consider themselves as resident aliens. They are the indigenous people of the land. Yet this is precisely the way religious settlers and Orthodox Jews consider them. Obviously, Palestinians reject such an absurdity. However, even if some Jews see the Palestinians as aliens, they need to implement the demands of God by giving "the aliens" their human rights and equal treatment, as the Leviticus law prescribes. By oppressing the Palestinians, they are in fact contravening their own Scriptures.

[7]Bernhard W. Anderson with Steven Bishop and Judith H. Newman, *Understanding the Old Testament* (5th ed.; Englewood Cliffs, N.J.: Prentice Hall, 2007), 93.

tribes of Israel. In whatever tribe aliens reside, there you shall assign them their inheritance, says the Lord God. (Ezek 47:21-23)

I believe that the significance of the Ezekiel text is that it raises the standard demanded by God by eliminating the basic discrimination regarding the land. Ezekiel recognizes that one of the most fundamental problems after the exile was that of the land. As some of the Judean exiled returned, they did not find the land empty; it was inhabited by many other people. This constituted a major problem. Leviticus was willing to be tolerant to the "aliens," to accept them as resident aliens, but it does not concede to them the full sharing of the land. The authors of the Leviticus text believed that the land was bequeathed only to their fellow Israelites by God. Admittedly, Ezekiel also believed that.[8] His theology, however, was not static. God is a living and dynamic God who continues to stretch our narrow theologies and force us to look beyond ourselves and confront the immediate challenges that face us.

Ezekiel articulates a more pragmatic theology for the returning exiles. With God's authority, he declares that the land must be shared by all its inhabitants. Although both the Leviticus and Ezekiel texts consider the non-Israelite inhabitants "aliens," the latter gives the aliens equal justice. In other words, all the people must enjoy human and political rights as equal citizens and share the land on an equal basis. Without this full and comprehensive view that accepts others and recognizes their rights, any commandment that talks about loving the neighbor as oneself is merely a farce.

The Ezekiel passage is very significant in addressing the contemporary scene in Israel-Palestine. Both of these areas have a direct relationship with the question of neighbor. In Israel today, more than 1.3 million Palestinians are known as Israeli Arabs and are Israeli citizens. Yet because they are not Jewish, they cannot be considered nationals. The distinction between citizenship and nationality is one of the most contested issues within Israel. Jews are citizens and nationals, but the Israeli Arabs can only be citizens. I believe that at the root of this problem, consciously or unconsciously, is the way Israel interprets the Leviticus text.

Under the Israeli occupation of the West Bank and the Gaza Strip live over three million Palestinians. Since 1967, the government of Israel has been confiscating their land, building set- dements, denying their rights, and oppressing them. The premise behind this goes back to an exclusive interpretation of Leviticus and other texts, i.e., that the land belongs to the Jewish people only and the Palestinians have no rights to it. They are considered "resident aliens," and Israel refuses to implement international law, end its occupation, and give the Palestinians their freedom and independence. Again, it is Ezekiel versus Leviticus.

Under the Leviticus text, which for religious Jews is more binding because it comes from the heart of the Torah, loving one's neighbor as oneself has no chance of being achieved unless the government of Israel enacts new legislation that eliminates the basic injustice. Martin Luther King, Jr., recognized in the civil rights struggle in the United States the importance of legislation and judicial decrees. He said,

> Morality cannot be legislated, but behavior can be regulated. Judicial decrees may not change the heart, but they restrain the heartless. The law cannot make an employer love an employee, but it can prevent him from refusing to hire me because of the color of my skin.

---

[8] There are many references throughout Ezekiel. For example, see chs. 20, 28, 34, 36, 37.

The habits, if not the hearts, of people have been and are being altered every day by legislative acts, judicial decision, and executive orders. Let us not be mis-led by those who argue that segregation cannot be ended by the force of law.[9]

Discrimination is confronted when we stop viewing the world in a binary way. It is comfortable for bigots to keep dividing the world into Jew and Gentile, friends and enemies, kin and strangers. The change happens when people stop thinking within the box, and the door is open to the "Other."

The Good Samaritan Text

In many ways, we are indebted to the young lawyer who asked Jesus, "Who is my neighbor?" Jesus replied by telling the story of the Good Samaritan[10] and left the interlocutor to deduce the answer:

A man was going down from Jerusalem to Jericho, and fell into the hands of rob-bers, who stripped him, beat him, and went away, leaving him half dead. Now by chances a priest was going down that road, and when he saw him, he passed by on the other side. So likewise a Levite, when he came to the place and saw him, passed by on the side. But a Samaritan while traveling came near him and when he saw him, he was moved with pity. He went to him and bandaged his wounds, having poured oil and wine on them. Then he put him on his own animal, brought him to an inn, and took care of him. The next day he took out two denarii, gave them to the innkeeper, and said, 'Take care of him, and when I come back, I will repay you whatever more you spend.' Which of these three, do you think, was a neighbor to the man who fell into the hands of the robbers?" He said, "The one who showed him mercy." Jesus said to him, "Go and do likewise." (Luke 10:30-37)

This story presents three possible answers to the question "Who is my neighbor?" The first is that of the robbers. For the robbers, any person outside their immediate family and friends was not a neighbor but a target and an object from which they can extort a profit. This was their philosophy of life, and they were willing to use force to achieve their goals. Their philosophy did not lend itself to compassion or mercy. When they robbed, they were not worried about the consequences of their actions on their victims. The robbers did not live by the commandments. They lived by their own laws.

John Powell wrote, "Human life has its own laws. One of these basically says that human beings need to love people and use things, not to love things and use people."[11] Whenever we use people and love things, we are exercising the

---

[9]Martin Luther King, Jr., *Strength to Love* (Philadelphia: Fortress, 1981), 37.

[10]The name that people have given to this parable, that of the "Good Samaritan," is not part of the Lukan text. In light of the political conflict in Israel-Palestine, the implication of such a name can be disturbing. If the "Good" Samaritan is an exception—precisely as when people today refer to "a good Palestinian" or "a good Jew," it could imply a racist statement, since it negates the many and only discovers one "good" exception.

[11]John Powell, *Why Am I Afraid to Tell You Who I Am?* (trans. Paul Sayyah and Dar Almashirq; Beirut: Lebanon, 1992), 44.

philosophy of the robbers. In this case, all of us have fallen short of what God intends for us to be. The robbers in the Good Samaritan story did not see a person, they saw an object of profit, and they were ready to attack.

In one form or another, this philosophy has been practiced by many people throughout history. Many people of power have lived by it when they robbed and exploited the poor and needy. They, too, did not have any fear of God in their hearts. History is full of stories of all ranks of society—from heads of state to minor officials—who have lived by the philosophy of the robbers. They did not stop to ask, "Who is my neighbor?" From a Palestinian perspective, the Zionists practiced the same philosophy in 1948 when they ethnically cleansed Palestine by driving out three quarters of a million of its Palestinian inhabitants. Defying many United Nations resolutions, they took their land and denied them the right to return to their villages and towns. Similarly, many of us are guilty of living by a philosophy, and even a theology, that is devoid of kindness and compassion and robs others of their dignity and humanity. Such behavior does not take into consideration the question of neighbor. We use people and love things. Someone wrote, "When a pickpocket meets a saint, all he sees are pockets."[12] The writer of the Book of Proverbs considered such acts abominable. "Those who oppress the poor insult their Maker" (Prov 14:31).

When we are dealing with the theology of robbers, we must intensify our efforts to work for justice. As Walter Brueggemann said, "Justice is to sort out what belongs to whom, and to return it to them."[13] To do justice is to be involved in the issues of the neighbors and to intervene on their behalf, "... as did Moses in Pharaoh's court when he insisted on freedom for the Hebrew slaves; as did Nathan in David's court when he protested the king's rapacious action against Uriah the Hittite; as did Elijah when he thundered against Ahab and Jezebel for having done in Naboth in order to take his land."[14]

The philosophy of the robbers does not surprise us. After all, they are robbers. The tragedy in the story lies in the behavior of the priest and the Levite, who represent two other possible answers to the question, "Who is my neighbor?" They, too, had a theology that guided their behavior toward others. When they saw the injured and beaten victim on the road, they were frightened, and they could only think of their own well-being. How can they avoid having the same fate? What if the victim is dead? If they touched the corpse, they would risk being defiled and unclean for seven days (Num 19:11). They would not be able to exercise their duties in the temple. At that moment all their religious beliefs were severely tested. Fear for their life as well as fear and anxiety about being contaminated placed the claims of religious duty above the demands of love. Martin Luther King, Jr., wrote, "The ultimate measure of a man [or woman] is not where he [or she] stands in moments of comfort and convenience, but where he [or she] stands at times of challenge and controversy."[15]

Most of us probably find ourselves within the category of the priest or the Levite. And it is on this level that we most often fail. One of the main reasons for our lack of response is fear. It is fear that freezes and cripples us, and our response to the question of who is my neighbor takes on a very selfish form. Fear is one of our greatest enemies. Many times we do not act because we are afraid. It is not that we do not know what we need

---

[12]From the oral teachings of Neem Karoli Baba.

[13]Walter Brueggemann, quoted without attribution in William Sloane Coffin, Credo (Louisville: Westminster John Knox, 2004), 63.

[14]William Sloane Coffin, Credo, 63.

[15]King, Strength to Love, 35.

to do or lack the ability to distinguish between right and wrong, justice and injustice, morality and immorality, compassion and callousness. It is fear that stifles and paralyses us and prevents us from taking risks. This is the malaise of human beings, no matter who they are or where they live. In this sense, the opposite of love is not hate but fear. When there is love, fear disappears, and we are able to have the courage to speak out and take risks. As John wrote, "There is no fear in love, but perfect love casts out fear" (1 John 4:18).[16]

The fact that Jesus used a priest and a Levite to describe the second category is a stroke of genius. Clergy of all religions are generally seen as models of faith. They know God's requirement of justice and compassion (Mic 6:8). The fact that they had nothing to say to the dying victim shows in essence the failure of religion to take people's needs seriously. That is why Jesus was very critical of them (Matt 23).

The radical twist in the story, however, is in the fact that Jesus chooses a Samaritan as the hero. From the perspective of Jews, the Samaritans were the despised enemies. Yet, it was the Samaritan who acted as neighbor to the victim by stopping to take the risk and come to his rescue. By doing this, Jesus forever revolutionized the interpretation of the Leviticus text. The neighbor is no longer defined exclusively. The door is now flung open to embrace all people, even one's enemies. With such a fresh and innovative interpretation, Jesus lifted humanity to a higher level and challenged all the traditional religious teachings that restricted the love of neighbor to people's kin. Jesus stripped the religious, economic, political, and social labels that divided humanity and confronted racism squarely.

The lesson that the story of the Good Samaritan teaches is repeated in different forms by Jesus and

is finally practiced by him on the cross when he offered forgiveness to his crucifiers.

> You have heard that it was said, "You shall love your neighbor and hate your enemy." But I say to you, Love your enemies and pray for those who persecute you, so that you may be children of your Father in heaven; for he makes his sun rise on the evil and on the good, and sends rain on the righteous and on the unrighteous. (Matt 5:43-5)

It is clear from Jesus' point that there is nothing new or impressive about hating or killing an enemy. To love and be merciful to an enemy is the truly radical behavior, because this lifts the person to the level of the truly human. Any time we do not live by this ideal, we are falling short of the standard of Christ. For Paul, loving one's neighbor as oneself is a debt that we have towards others (Rom 13:8-10).

In today's conflict over Palestine, if we were telling the story of the Good Samaritan to a Jewish audience, instead of a Samaritan, we would choose a Palestinian as the hero. Conversely, if we were to challenge a Palestinian audience, we would use an Israeli Jew. Indeed, in the midst of the conflict, such stories are not totally foreign in Israel-Palestine today. People often relate stories in which an Israeli Jew acted as a good "neighbor" toward a Palestinian in a way that far exceeds the behavior of fellow Palestinians, and the reverse is also true. It is truly refreshing to see people from the various religious communities of the land, whether Muslim, Jew, Druze, or Christian, who in times of crisis and need are able to transcend their racial or religious prejudices and reach out to the "Other" as a fellow human being.

The story of the Good Samaritan challenges us to enlarge the circle of love to include even our enemies. Since it is already difficult to love others

---

[16] 1 John 4:18; see also Coffin, Credo, 27.

as we love ourselves, to love our enemies seems to be an impossibility. The challenge before the Christian, therefore, is to love others, including one's enemies, as God in Christ loves us. This is where faith comes to our rescue. We cannot do it alone. It is our love of, and faith in, God that helps us overcome any feelings of hate and resentment towards the enemy. The NT uses the word "agape" to express Christ's unconditional love.

Agape love is courageous and is not afraid to take risks and to stand for what is right. It refuses to be biased and prejudiced. It detests discrimination and all form of racism. It is a love that is all-inclusive. There are no outcasts in this love. It is a love that is committed to truth and expresses itself in justice and fairness. At the same time, it is a compassionate and merciful love. Agape love refuses to give in to hate. It is love that we can practice because we have experienced the love of God shown to us in Jesus Christ.

I believe that one of the most important ways of enacting such love is to commit ourselves to the practice of nonviolence. To love the neighbor or even the enemy does not mean to approve or condone injustice. It means to takes a stand and, if need be, to reprove the neighbor, as the Leviticus text suggests. Love implies resistance to injustice by using nonviolent methods. It is done not out of hate or in order to crush or destroy the enemy, but in order to force the perpetrators of injustice to undo what is wrong and commit themselves to doing what is just and right.

The case in point is our struggle against the Israeli occupation of the Palestinian territories, i.e., the West Bank including East Jerusalem and the Gaza Strip. According to international law, the occupation is illegal and must end, but Israel refuses to do that and continues in its oppressive domination. Love demands resisting the occupation through nonviolent methods. People need to take risks for peace, even if it involves personal sacrifice. At the same time, it is important not to despair or lose hope but to continue the nonviolent resistance until justice is achieved.[17]

As Christians living in the midst of this political quagmire, it is our responsibility to keep lifting up a comprehensive and inclusive interpretation of the neighbor. Ultimately, instead of wasting precious time in verbal arguments about loving the neighbor, it is much better to practice it. As C.S. Lewis said, "Do not waste your time bothering whether you 'love' your neighbor; act as if you did!"[18]

Ultimately, it is love that makes a difference in the world. In the words of John Powell,

> The size of a person's world is the size of his or her heart. We can be at home in the world of reality only to the extent that we have learned to love it....People who love learn to move the focus of their attention and concern from themselves out to others. They care deeply about others...Our care and concern for others must be genuine, or our love means nothing. This much is certain: there is no learning to live without learning to love."[19]

About the Author

NAIM ATEEK is Director of Sabeel Ecumenical Liberation Theology Center in Jerusalem. His

[17]One such strategy is expressed in the Sabeel document: "A Call for Morally Responsible Investment" (Second Printing, Jerusalem, Israel: Sabeel Ecumenical Liberation Theology Center, May 2005); also available online at http://www.sabeel.org/pdfs/mri.htm.

[18]C.S. Lewis, *Mere Christianity* (New York: McMillan, 1952), 86.

[19]John Powell, *Fully Human Fully Alive* (Allen, Tex.: Thomas More, 1976), 16.

book *Justice and Only Justice: A Palestinian Liberation Theology* (Orbis, 1989) laid the ground-work for application of liberation theology for displaced Palestinians. He is an Anglican priest. Ateek was the recipient of the 2006 Episcopal Peace Fellowship Sayre Award.

Section 5

Religion and Gender

Interpretive Intervention

Religion, Gender, and Boundaries

Bandana Purkayastha

Where the world has not been broken up into fragments by narrow domestic walls. . . . (Tagore 1913b)

The preceding chapters, and the ones following this interpretive intervention, provide detailed discussions about Hinduism and Islam in South Asia and the United States. The authors describe their beliefs and practices, the kinds of opportunities they have had to practice their religions, and the boundaries—especially the social and ideological boundaries—they have encountered. In this chapter we link some of the descriptions in the essays to discussions in academic literature on religion, and gender and religion. We focus primarily on social and ideological boundaries, examining the notions about dual spheres and the conceptual boundaries that make it difficult to study religion in more holistic, inclusive ways. We use the idea of "boundaries as complex structures—physical, social, ideological, and psychological—which establish differences and commonalties between men and women, among women, and among men" (Gerson and

Peiss 1985, 317). We do not provide an exhaustive review of these debates, simply some indication of the ways in which the views of the authors (in this book) contribute to supporting or challenging existing knowledge.

One of our key theoretical arguments in the introduction was about the definition of religion. We argued that most definitions take Christianity as the norm and this affects how gender and religion are studied. In this book, what emerged from the chapters was a picture of religion that is "non-monolithic and operationally plural" (Nandy 1999, 322). Neither the older functionalist idea of religion, which emphasizes shared values and rituals that lead to group cohesion, or religious activities that explicitly draw on the notion of the supernatural source of values (Wilson 1979), or the idea that religions are accompanied by powerful institutions that attempt to spread their influence (Mitchell 2006), are able to capture what is being described here. Nor does Gans' (1979) concept of "symbolic religiosity," which refers to a religious culture that does not involve regular participation in its rituals or organization, or Demerath's cultural religion, which means "an identification with a religious heritage without any religious participation or a sense of personal involvement per se" (2001, 59) capture the descriptions in these chapters. The authors describe religion as a way of life, a "confederation of a number of ways of life," linked by shared values and de-linked from institutions seeking to spread their influence (and to draw boundaries between the groups that belong and those that do not). The authors describe fluid and heterogeneous practices that keep the boundaries between religions blurred, emphasizing connections between people instead of ways of fragmenting them into distinctive groups.

In the accounts by Bandana Purkayastha, Selina Jamil, Bidya Ranjeet, Neela Bhattacharya Saxena, Parveen Talpur, Salma Kamal, and Monoswita Saha, religion spills out of the boundaries of "religion," "symbolic religion," and "cultural religion" so that it becomes difficult, in the conventional sense, to separate culture from religion, and religion from spirituality. Many authors acknowledge drawing from more than one religious tradition. Neela Bhattacharya Saxena presents a "conventional" Hindu puja that ends with a call to Amin, an invocation of an Islamic pir, showing how blurred boundaries can coexist with the formally acknowledged religious "differences." Bidya Ranjeet points out that she is both Hindu and Buddhist, so it is a constant challenge for her to identify herself in one category. Trying to fit these religious beliefs and practices into narrow compartments contribute to the racialization and gendering of the spirit (Ahmed 2002).

Much of the discussion on religion is based on the idea that religions are separate from public worlds in secular societies (Bhargava 1999; Bush 2007). The chapters in this book show that the two spheres intersect. Indeed, the authors point out the lack of holidays or space for religio-cultural events (e.g., Bandana Purkayastha, Bidya Ranjeet, and Salma Kamal) and racial profiling (e.g., Parveen Talpur, also Aysha Saeed and Rafia Zakaria in the next section) as examples of institutionalized ways of ascribing boundaries on minority religions. The authors discuss the ways in which the stereotypes about their religions carry over to other aspects of their lives. Neela Bhattacharya Saxena and Selina Jamil, and in the next section Elora Halim Chowdhury, show how their authority as academics are constantly challenged (and co-opted) by their colleagues; their knowledge and expertise is marginalized as "ethnic knowledge" in academic enterprises. The accounts by Salma Kamal and Monoswita Saha depict their struggles to overcome the boundaries that exclude them from full membership into the category "American" because of their phenotypes and their religion. Regardless of the actual difference of their religious beliefs from mainstream beliefs, the politicization of religious boundaries by the mainstream lead to unequal freedom for them to practice their religion. The chapters by Parveen Talpur in this section, and Aysha Saeed and Rafia Zakaria in the next section, illustrate the overlap between the sacred and secular spheres as well.

Just as there is an ongoing belief about the separateness of the secular and sacred spheres, a private-public binary has been used, historically, to relegate women to the private sphere. This ideology is vigorously challenged by feminist scholars who have shown how it negatively affects women's freedoms, citizenship status, ability to travel, work, claim just wages, access healthcare, own property, marry whom they choose, and other aspects of their lives. But, as we pointed out in the introduction, much of the "W"estern feminist discussions assume ethnic women are mostly shaped (subordinated) by their religions, so that despite the scholarship that insists on getting beyond dual spheres, ethnic women are only seen as victims of their religions and cultures within the private, non-secular sphere. Indeed, in arguing that multiculturalism is bad for women, Okin states, "[minority women] *might* be better off if the cultures into which they were born were either to become extinct (so that its members would become integrated into the less sexist surrounding culture) or be encouraged to alter itself so as to reinforce the equality of women—at least to the degree to which this value is upheld in majority society" (1999, 22-23). The authors show that, contrary to such "Western feminist arguments, some of the most significant boundaries they encounter arise out of *mainstream* institutional and ideological structures that restrict their lives as minority women.

A great deal of feminist scholarship has described how women are ideologically excluded from religions. Much of this scholarship has been based on notions of Adam and Eve, the concept of original sin, and the need for the priest to resemble Christ. Such ideological barriers have been translated into organizational practice in Christianity, and despite the attempts of a few groups like the Shakers to break away from such gendered organizational forms, women typically have been second-class participants in church hierarchy. Christian women have, therefore, engaged in a range of organized effort to create a space for themselves in church (e.g., Katzenstein 1996). In contrast, Saxena (along with Bandana Purkayastha, Monoswita Saha, Shobha Hamal Gurung, and Anjana Narayan) discusses the continuing importance of the feminine (gynocentric) principle in Hinduism. In fact, Bandana Purkayastha and Neela Bhattacharya Saxena (and later Anjana Narayan) point out that the concept of ardhanariswara does not create gender hierarchies in the ways that the Adam and Eve stories do. Many authors in this book indicate that the feminist discussions about the need to develop feminist frames to challenge male-dominated ideologies in religions effectively silences the centuries-long, ongoing importance of the female—Durga, Kali, Sarawati, and Lakshmi—and feminine principles in religions like Hinduism. Similarly, Talpur and Jamil (and later, Elora Halim Chowdhury and Aysha Saeed) point out that Islam offers many humane, gender-neutral paths of religious practice that are not mediated by a male priestly hierarchy. But these views are often silenced because there is a predetermined framework of religion and gender-subordination that is used to discuss minority religions. While many Western scholars claim that feminism has contributed to "new" perspectives inspired by feminist spirituality and theology, the authors here, especially Saxena, show that these are not "new" perspectives. Bidya Ranjeet and Shobha Hamal Gurung's descriptions of women's roles in home-based rituals, even when these sustain gender-segregated activity, serve as an important acknowledged role in family and community life that differ in ways that women are excluded from churches. The roles of these mothers and grandmothers are acknowledged in almost reverential terms (also see Monoswita Saha's account of her grandmother).

The authors point out that there is no linear progression from tradition to modernity in the sense of a move toward a more progressive position. Instead, the pressure to give up decentralized forms of practice in the United States reinscribes new gendered boundaries. As Purkayastha describes, a series of laws that require centralized authority structures and unitary memberships in congregations invariably marginalize women. Practicing religion in a variety of spaces and settings provides much more opportunity to blur religious boundaries and uphold women's central role in religions (e.g., Bidya Ranjeet and Shobha Hamal Gurung). So the gendered boundaries the authors describe are a reflection of sets of intersecting mainstream and ethnic-community factors that contribute to the altered organization of these religions.

While none of the first-generation authors—Bandana Purkayastha, Selina Jamil, Parveen Talpur, and Neela Bhattacharya Saxena—are deeply invested in any congregation, they all describe within-group boundaries that disadvantage women. In spite of describing various ways in which their lives have been enriched by gender-neutral symbolism, religious coexistence, and blurring of religious boundaries through everyday practice, the authors do not romanticize the lives of women. They strongly criticize fundamentalists of their ethnic communities, and offer strong conceptual challenges to the fundamentalist reconstructions of history and religious interpretations. And as Anjana Narayan, Rafia Zakaria, Shanthi Rao, and Aysha Saeed show in the next section, the authors also identify the complicity of a larger group of people who appear to be persuaded by the fundamentalists' ethnocentric ideologies.

In effect, these narratives offer a new way of thinking about religion/spirituality that take these women's understanding and experiences as central to understanding the endeavor of living religions.

Subversive Promises and the Creation of a Parallel Sphere

Divine Encounters with Hagar and Rebekah

Hemchand Gossai

Introduction

I propose the following discussion proceeding from the perspective of one who has been shaped by different religious and cultural environments. My great grand parents came from India to work as indentured servants in the British colony of British Guyana. My formative years were spent in an Hindu environment in British Guyana and then in the independent state of Guyana; my latter years as a Christian were spent living and studying in the United States and Europe. My interest in issues of marginality within the biblical material is directly connected to these experiences.

Is there a place for an exile within a land of the chosen? Will an exile always remain an exile and always be identified as an exile? Is there a future for one who dwells in the shadows? Can divine promises be given to those who do not only function away from the center but in fact are in conflict with the center?

There is a clear sense that the God of primeval history within the opening chapters of Genesis is also the God who seeks and promises a future to the exile or slave, to the one who challenges societal conventions. Those on the margin are not ultimately allowed to languish on the outside without a future, without a promise. Even one like Hagar who is doubly victimized is granted a promise, a spoken word which announces a radical future hitherto unimagined. Rebekah, concerned about her pregnancy, takes up the matter directly with God and the particularity of her internal struggle, which only she, and not Isaac, can fully appreciate is heard by God and placed within a larger universal context. Rebekah understands. The promises which are thus given to Hagar and Rebekah are for generations, one which will in fact shape the future. In neither the encounters of Hagar and Rebekah is there a moral judgement as to which of the futures will be better. There is a clear indication that the covenant established with the one in the center does not in any way exhaust the possibilities of additional relationships beyond the center. When we hear of the divine message given to Rebekah, immediately the reader is led to think in a certain direction.

Hemchand Gossai; Fernando F. Segovia, ed., "Subversive Promises: Divine Encounters with Rebekah and Hagar," *Interpreting Beyond Borders*, pp. 146-160. Copyright © 2000 by Hemchand Gossai. Reprinted with permission.

To be sure the message is given to Rebekah and concerns Jacob and Esau, but the interest is on a grander scale. It is not only a familial story, but one of two nations, two people.

In this paper I propose that as divine promises are pronounced in these ancestral narratives of Genesis, there is a distinct and intentional establishment of provisions for concurrent and seemingly conflictual stories. At one level, it would appear that God is subverting the very thing that God sets out to establish. As if the journeys of Abraham and Sarah; Isaac and Rebekah are not challenging enough in and of themselves, parallel journeys of conflict are also created and they must be reckoned with. That is, the promises made to Abraham and Sarah and carried on through their descendants are assumed to be and established as the central promises. There is, however, nothing within the text that preempts other promises being made which would parallel the ones at the center. What is striking about the parallel sets of promises is that inherently the bearers and descendants of the promises are in conflict. This conflict is established at the outset by God, and there is no textual indication that the conflicts are designed to determine winners and losers, but an indication that people who live together with varying degrees of power, often function in conflict.

It is not so much that the text indicates the moral value of conflict or the relative goodness of the promises. Certainly there is much evidence to suggest that the central promise bearers are flawed characters. The characters, Abraham, Sarah, Isaac, Jacob, Hagar or Ishmael are not in themselves evil or good and the promises which they bear are not predicated on their characteristics.

The Genesis narratives have provided for us a tapestry of human and divine relations which are woven and interwoven in complex, delicate and sometimes inseparable ways. These narratives do not allow us to rest easily and they are far from being linear and straightforward without any semblance of being one dimensional. Even though the focus of this paper will be on Hagar and Rebekah, Ishmael and Jacob, we must also reckon with Esau and Isaac, Abraham and Sarah and the other players within the story. At least within this discussion, there are no villains and evil characters. We cannot overlook the agony of Sarah and Abraham; we cannot overlook the pain of Isaac and Esau. Human stories are complex. For societal conventions such as the role of the primogeniture to be challenged, it is not necessary to cast Esau as the primogeniture in an evil or for that matter even in an unfavorable light.

Let me illustrate what I am talking about. What do we do with Esau? For the direction which I am proposing, it is not necessary to destroy Esau and characterize him as evil or bad or any such. I suggest not. Janzen suggests, "it is that Esau is a non reflective sort, given to action—one who likes to hunt, eat and move on, as in the present instance: 'he ate, he drank, he rose, he went his way, he despised his birthright.' He lacks the patience for delayed satisfactions that is to be a quality of spiritual characteristic of the new people that Yahweh is in the process of fashioning." (p. 96) There is little that one could find to support the notion that delayed satisfaction is a moral quality necessary for spiritual leadership. As we are able to see throughout the biblical tradition, many who would be leaders and promise bearers are anything but patient. Or, as Burton Visotzky concludes, "Esau does not exactly savor his meal. Rather Genesis reports with four brief Hebrew words, 'he ate, drank, rose, left.'" (p. 138) Even though these verbs might remind one of "veni, vidi, vici" in terms of the unreflectiveness, it cannot be dismissed simply on the basis of the convention or the possibility that it does not fit the hermeneutical direction we have chosen. Whatever one might say about the savoring of a meal and all of the sensual overtones of a meal eaten deliberately, and there is certainly a place for that, the fact is, "three martini lunches" are not for the starving and hungry. The very text and the staccato expression underline the fundamental difference between the basic situation of hunger and the sensual joy of lingering over a meal. For Esau, urgency and immediacy of hunger and the extended consequences have taken precedence over the role of the birthright and the future possibilities therein. Hunger as an expression of weakness and poverty is the occasion for the exchange of the birthright. As a systemic issue, hunger is expressly in the domain of the poor and marginalized. Relative importance of wealth, power, or birthright is relegated to a secondary status in the face of hunger or famine.

These Genesis narratives are received by the reader in a variety of ways. They cannot be read and received in a vacuum. The reader, particularly the reader whose experience might be one of slavery or exile or refugee or disenfranchised or marginalized brings to the text a different, and I submit a perfectly legitimate perspective. Commenting on the use of Hagar by Sarah, and the deafening silence of Hagar, Bharati Mukherjee, voices with existential integrity what many experience, and thus must bring to the reading of these narratives. "Those of us who have experienced class prejudice and colonialism can be forgiven for reading into this omission the sad, silenced issues of disenfranchisement." (p. 101)

Historically, research and scholarly attention have been focused on the characters who constitute the main plot and the central themes in these narratives. The principal focus has been on the patriarchs, Abraham, Isaac and Jacob. Feminist scholarship particularly in the last two decades have forged new and significant directions in terms of the multi layered fabric of the narratives and the essential role of the women. Among others, Hagar and Rebekah have been given much needed attention. Yet, even here there

has been a reluctance or perhaps more accurately, an inability to give to their persons and their roles the radically new directions which are essential. Somehow there has been the notion that one cannot speak well of Hagar or Rebekah without soiling the conventions. There has been a timidity in assigning blame to Sarah and having her be responsible along with Abraham for the plight of Hagar. Or for that matter Rebekah is consistently viewed as one who shows favoritism and is deceitful.

On the other hand one might read these texts with great integrity and see clearly that Rebekah was doing precisely what was expected of her, given what was entrusted to her from God. As was the social custom, and believing Esau to be the firstborn, and thus the recipient of the family's birthright, the aged Isaac seeks to pass on the all important blessing from father to son. Equally important, Rebekah, the sole recipient of another promise, told in secrecy, which will challenge and undermine the social convention, must ensure that she does what is necessary and through whatever means at her disposal. In many respects, her "chosenness" brings with it a great deal of agony. Ultimately, at the risk of sounding utilitarian, I would suggest that she makes excruciating sacrifices for the sake of what is known only to her, and for the greater good.

In doing what she must do, Rebekah acts contrary to her maternal instinct. It is not a matter of favoritism. Challenging the status quo and the societal convention and disrupting the comfort zone for the sake of divine promise keeping is not favoritism. Indeed, one of the factors which is frequently neglected in most discussions about Rebekah is her self sacrifice. At the very core of her being, through divine initiative she is made to choose between her sons and she is given no choice. She sacrifices what is at the very core of a mother's being, that is, her instinctive, even fiercely protective love of her children. Rebekah stands to gain nothing from doing what she does. In many respects, she is the embodiment of sacrifice. Those readers who see Rebekah as having ulterior motives, I submit miss the radicality of what is at work. Naomi Sternberg suggests that, "…Rebekah already knows that Jacob will dominate his brother Esau. Thus she intends to secure the loyalty of Jacob in order that he will use his future power to her benefit." (p. 91) This sort of view is textually untenable, as in no way is Rebekah a beneficiary. What the promise to Rebekah entails and what Rebekah does is simply to call into question the manner in which power within society is distributed and executed. Rebekah's actions in halting the convention, not so much established a new custom, but rather gives shape to a new dimension of the status quo. The promise of the ancestors will continue, but not as expected or designed. Those who would fall back on the notion that "this is the way it has always been" will now have to reckon with new realities.

Much has been written on these narratives and within this important framework additional hermeneutical strands have emerged. These narratives continue to provide for us a rich and virtually inexhaustible source of meaning for contemporary circumstances. I would submit that these narratives have redemptive value for contemporary society, though they do not make for an easy interpretive task given all of the social prisms through which we view them. Yet, responsibility dictates that we must seek. There is a triumph of grace in these stories, for the outsiders are allowed to shape their futures to some degree. Despite the roles of Abraham and Sarah and the status of the first born, God protects and grants a future.

Both Hagar and Rebekah are the recipients of what might be termed divine secrets, and while there is some evidence that Hagar and God spoke with Abraham regarding Ishmael, in the case of Rebekah she is the sole bearer of the pronouncement, "Two nations are in your womb, and two peoples born of you shall be divided, the one shall be stronger than the other, the elder shall serve the younger." (Gen. 25:23) In both instances, promises are given which appear to undermine the ongoing central promise. These two women did not seek out God with these promises in mind, nor for that matter did they have any other specific promise in mind. They are taken unawares by what God says and the promises are accepted without argument or discussion. Both know that what has transpired will not be fulfilled routinely. There will be hardships; Hagar will return to the very household where she was brutalized and Rebekah will take whatever curse comes with Jacob, and she will embrace whatever sacrifice. Neither Hagar nor Rebekah speaks much, indeed in the case of Hagar, as reflective of her status, she is not allowed a voice. Yet, when both she and Rebekah speak, what they have to say is enough to confirm the fact that they are both God's chosen also. Both will face daunting challenges and both will proceed with courage.

One also must note that while both Hagar and Rebekah function away from the center, their experiences are clearly not uniformly the same. The experiences of exiles, slaves, marginalized persons cannot be engaged with as if they are uniformly the same. Each person brings his or her experiences and circumstances to bear and gives shape to their own narrative within the framework of the marginalized. Hagar and Rebekah are given two very different promises and what eventuates with Ishmael and Jacob reflects this difference. "For a time Sarah is upstaged by her auxiliary; the pregnant Hagar displaces her mistress." (Pitzele, p. 108) Yet, there is no real displacement here. Hagar never did take the place, or could ever take the place of Sarah. Her importance is not to be understood in displacement. While it was Sarah's idea to use Hagar as a surrogate, there is no textual evidence to suggest or support the notion that the surrogate displaces the mistress.

Power, Identity and Conflict

The narrative in Genesis 16 begins with the naming of three characters, Sarah, Abram, and Hagar. With immediacy in the first two verses, the problem is named, responsibility for Sarai's barrenness is ascribed to Yahweh, and the solution is sought in the person of Hagar, the fertile Egyptian slave woman. Within the continuum of powerlessness Sarah represents the center of oppressed people, while it might be said that Hagar represents those who are on the periphery. One of the very troubling features of this type of gradation is that the oppressed at one level above others begin to treat the oppressed at a more marginalized level, with the same concomitant disdain and contempt as they received. In the eyes of Sarah, Hagar simply provides for her something missing in her own life over which she has no control. In the estimation of Sarah, the One who *does* have control, has chosen not to exercise that control by granting her the fulfillment she seeks in the time line *she* has decided on. There is no inkling in Sarah's plan that Hagar's identity will be any different from its present status, and certainly nothing hints that there will be a fundamental transformation in Hagar after conception. Certainly there is no entertainment of the idea that Sarah's God, who is yet to fulfill his promise to Sarah and Abraham, would make promises to this slave woman. Moreover, Sarah's one-dimensional plan clearly leaves no room for the possibility of a new future with a transformed Hagar. There is little doubt that it never crossed Sarah's mind that Yahweh, her and Abraham's God will seek out Hagar and bestow on her a future apart from Sarah and Abraham.

It is assumed that Hagar, as a slave, is entirely at the disposal of her mistress. Sarah was demonstrating that she was capable of achieving that which Yahweh had naturally prevented her from doing (v. 2a). Like Sarah, Hagar surely understands the importance of an heir. However, given her status as slave, with no framework for an opportunity for offspring, she holds tightly to the chance which she has at her disposal. Even though the act against Hagar treats her as a non-entity, the occasion opens for her a dream which she dared not have dreamt before: the unthinkable becomes thinkable and the impossible appears possible. Hagar does not have the power to challenge the convention, though unwittingly through Sarah's actions she will do precisely that. While Sarah considers the occasion a way of building herself up, she fails to consider that the slave woman might also have such daring hopes for herself. That Hagar would want to build herself up is simply never entertained. This view says as much about the representatives at the center, and about the limitations placed upon God.

While Sarah is fearful of the newly transformed Hagar, she is not willing to recognize fully her own initiative in the matter. The issue is no longer the longing for a child, but a challenge to the status quo and those who constitute the status quo. Some recognize the power in Hagar, which is absent in Sarah, and at this point in her life beyond the latter's reach. Sarah's interest in an offspring now assumes a secondary role as is displayed by her willingness and interest in banishing Hagar and the unborn child. Challenge of power becomes the crux at this point in the narrative.

Abraham assures Sarah that she has the power to do that which is *good in her eyes*. This is essentially a *carte blanche* statement to use one's power. With Hagar in a powerless state and cast into the role of instigator, she is left without recourse. Abraham must be saddled with responsibility here, as he is aware of the fear and anger of Sarah, and still he suggests that she determine the nature of the punishment, on the basis of what she considers good! Essentially Abraham washes his hands of the matter and allows Sarah to be the one to have "hands stained with blood." Sarah, like Lady Macbeth, began this scenario with a plan in mind, and as the plot disintegrates, it is Sarah who has blood-stained hands. On the other hand, Abraham like Pilate attempts to "wash his hands" of the matter, though by not acting with his inherent power, he is deeply embroiled in the episode and is himself responsible. Even before witnessing the result of Sarah's actions, one is placed on alert by Sarah's previous action in inviting Abraham to lie with Hagar. We are aware that she might be incapable of dealing wisely and fairly with Hagar. Whatever else one might think of Sarah in this context, she is not in a position to make a good judgment. As a slave, it is clear that Hagar was not Sarah's equal, and the first remote sign of equal status between the two created an overtly adversarial atmosphere.

While the immediate issue at stake in the Hagar narrative is centered on the quest for a son, and the degree to which Sarah pursued this, a larger matter calls us to recognize the fact that the "outsider" is used to fulfill the needs and desires of the "insider." The use of Hagar goes beyond surrogacy, beyond ethnicity and tradition. So strong is Sarah's urge for a child that she is willing to overlook any such issue regarding Hagar. Moreover, to be a slave is to be fully owned. There is, in reality, no component in a slave's life which belongs exclusively to the slave. The entire being of the slave is at the disposal of the owner. More than anything, Hagar as an "outsider" needed hospitality from the community in general, and Sarah and Abraham in particular. As if being a slave were not demeaning enough, Hagar is the object of additional hostility by her mistress.

The indifference to Hagar as a person in her own right is seen throughout the narrative. Even though Sarah is the one who initiates the plan, she never refers to Hagar by name. Indeed Sarah only refers to Hagar and Ishmael by their social status, not by name. Hagar is never considered another woman. It is the narrator who names Hagar. Thus,

right from the start, Hagar's identity is made incomplete through the absence of her name by Sarah. The name is at the heart and soul of the person. Naming identifies a person and allows us to know and experience him/her. The naming of Ishmael might very well have embodied the greatest promise. The particularity of Ishmael's name bears a universal promise to all who cry to God. In the midst of the circumstances of life, *God hears* (Ishmael) is a real promise.

Yet, this is a hope which must exist in the realm of conventional human power structures. The promise is not eliminating the sources of power (imperial, economic, political, etc.) but functioning confidently within these structures. There is nothing facile about the promise. It will, in fact, necessitate courage. In this way, there continues to be a tension between suffering and hope. The stark and telling difference between human and divine recognition of one's personhood is seen in 16:8, where Hagar is addressed by name by the angel of Yahweh. Even as a slave, an outsider, an oppressed person, a wilderness refugee, Hagar has an identity which is divinely given. She is not allowed to cry out against the double injustice of concubinage and slavery done to her; she is muted by the two sources of power between whom she is caught. The reality is that she is without voice, unable to speak a language of power and domination, and without human advocacy. The oppressed is left voiceless. The only voice in these opening verses is that of Sarah, and she orders Abraham to act. Abraham, who is clearly in a position to decide justly what is right and wrong, listens to the voice of power and proceeds from that point. Clearly the issue of Hagar's silence has far-reaching implications. Yahweh does what Abraham and Sarah fail to do, namely to enter into conversation with Hagar. Westermann suggests that "by the greeting and inquiry, the messenger takes part in Hagar's lot; he accepts her into the realm of *Shalom*. He enables her to make a trustful response and show herself ready to accept the word of this stranger. That this unknown one speaks her name indicates that he is an 'other,' one who knows; his friendly attention to Hagar evokes her trustful reply" (p. 244).

The questioning by the messenger of Yahweh reveals that Hagar has an identity, but it is tied to Sarah. It is true as Trible remarks that the questions by the messenger "embody origin and destiny" (p. 15). Yet Hagar's answer suggests that there is no place of origin, but a slave owner from whom she is fleeing; and there is no certainty of destination and her presence in the wilderness testifies to this. Hagar the slave-woman has become a refugee, fleeing injustice and finding herself in a purgatorial world. The messenger recognizes that Hagar's destiny is tied to Sarah—as painful as it is, that is the reality. Thus, the issue at stake is one of restoration and reconciliation in the midst of inequities, injustice and power struggles. When Yahweh orders Hagar to return and submit to Sarah, one might be led to conclude that Yahweh is acting on the side of the powerful and seeking to uphold the status quo. At one level it does not appear to make much sense, particularly given the overall direction of the biblical material which places God unquestionably on the side of the poor. The irony is that the poor and powerless, arguably more than any other group need a voice, and they are the ones who are made voiceless. While Hagar is not allowed to participate in the decision making by the angel of Yahweh, the decision and promise regarding her future, she is in fact in dialogue with the angel. One cannot read of Hagar's situation and not think of those who live among us who are oppressed and voiceless. Who will provoke on their behalf? Both Hagar and Rekekah are given promises about their offsprings who will provoke the system and the dwellers of the center and will indeed in the contemporary sense of the word become provocateurs.

It is not difficult to draw parallels between the sending back of Hagar to Sarah and the plight of modern-day refugees. Common to our existence is the presence of political and economic refugees, huddled together in boats and warehouses, held in barracks and foreign lands, only to be told after having spent time in this "in-between" world, that they must return to their place of origin. There appears to be no justice when humans are forced by other humans, shaped by power structures, to remain in bondage. So what does the encounter between Hagar and Yahweh establish? The future of Hagar which includes a son and many descendants, will be forged out of a life of submission and slavery. In the face of hostility, Hagar will not only survive, but live, and be destined for a future, albeit through her son. The description of Ishmael's nature demonstrates that he will in fact not live like his mother as a slave. As Ishmael grew in the household of Sarah and Abraham, he must have been aware of the oppression which he and his mother faced. One cannot help but conclude that this kind of oppression and affliction are intrinsic in shaping children as they grow into adulthood. As is so often the case, the one who is the recipient of oppression learns that this is the way to live and survive. The conflict which will come to characterize the life of Ishmael can be explained through the experience in the Sarah/Abraham household. The return of Hagar to Sarah is not a return to the status quo. While the messenger's words might appear to be a reconstruction of an identical slave-mistress relationship as existed before, in fact Hagar is now aligned with a different source of power. Hagar now has the confidence of Yahweh, and while Sarah and Abram are covenanted with Yahweh, Yahweh's "preferential option" for the poor is evident here.

While Rebekah is never told not to discuss Yahweh's words to her, that is essentially what happens, and so de facto, she too is voiceless, though because of circumstances, self-imposed. Part of the critical role of voicelessness by the outsider is the reality that societal norm dictates such be the case. It is not that Rebekah is afraid or weak. Indeed there is evidence right from the start, that in many respects Rebekah is more forthright than Isaac, and certainly more adept at executing cleverly her plans. It is Rebekah who is concerned about her pregnancy, and she does not speak with Isaac about it but rather goes directly to Yahweh. Janzen observes, "Rebekah inquires of Yahweh who announces a destiny that has it roots already in her womb....Is this destiny fore-ordained by God? Do the twins struggle already in the womb because God has set them and their futures against each other?" (p. 95) Rebekah also must confront and deal with her internal conflict. One could surmise that there is a tearing apart of her maternal feelings for both sons and her loy-alty to the promise, versus her sense of loyalty to share what she knows with Isaac. Rebekah has the power of knowledge for she knows that God has selected Jacob and she is the one chosen to bear that knowledge and this by itself has the potential for conflict. Not all knowledge brings freedom. Some knowledge brings pain and anxiety. Since her knowledge will lead to the challenging of the conventions, Rebekah will have to find a means of carrying out the task. To some, Rebekah's actions might be seen to be nothing short of treachery and disloyalty, yet, of course there is no chastise-ment or condemnation or curse by God. Rebekah is God's deputy and she does what in her view is the thing to do.

Ishmael and Jacob while offsprings of the parallel promises and the principal architects to challenge the conventions, including the role of the primogeniture, they will proceed in very different directions. Ishmael is described as one who will be fearless and combative and not only against the enemy but against his own kin. Jacob is not described thus. Whether it is his encounter with Laban or Esau, he seeks to use trickery and deceit rather than force. This is not to say that he is reticent; we would recall the encounter in the

night where he refuses to allow the being to de-part without bestowing on him a blessing. "Jacob is fleeing from the consequences of his (and Rebecca's) hoax, and in that flight he does receive the first fruit of his usurpation. Yahweh stands next to him and speaks to him as familiarly as he spoke to Abram." (Rosenberg and Bloom, p. 214)

Jacob's all-night encounter with the nameless divine being is symbolic at different levels. It would be easy to say somewhat reductionistically that this was a harmless struggle. The one who has usurped and undermined the convention will be confirmed with a name change, but it will happen in the dark of the night where the divine being ap-pears and disappears anonymously. Even though not in the same way, Ishmael is also named by God, indeed the only person in Genesis who is named by God, and this naming is also revealed away from the routine of everyday life. It is given in the wilderness. It is clear that both the future of Ishmael and Jacob through the promises received will be marked by conflict, one in the wilderness and the other confirmed in the dark of night while wrestling. Indeed for the promise to proceed con-flict will become the prime feature which must be employed and then resolved. Brueggemann captures the reality of the conflict with Jacob succinctly and clearly when he concludes, "The conflict with Jacob is a conflict not with 'spiritual' realities, but with the ways in which human life has been institutionalized. Primogeniture is not simply one rule among many. It is the linchpin of an entire social and legal system which defines rights and privileges and provides a way around internecine disputes. But that same practice which protects the order of society is also a way of destining some to advantage and others to disadvantage." (p. 209)

The conflict which will characterize the life and legacy of Ishmael is not spelled out but in a somewhat casual and general way it is mentioned. It is as if to suggest that this is simply the way it is for the one who will have to function from the outside. We are told that Ishmael will be "a wild ass of a man" and Jacob, as we discover will be at great odds with his brother and his uncle Laban. These are two scenarios of conflict singled out for Jacob, and so like Ishmael, he too will function from the vantage point of conflict. One is left to wonder whether in both of these cases we have an accurate prediction by God that Ishmael and Jacob will prevail through their own resources and strength, which might very well include conflict. Even though conflict will be the primary mode of being in the case of both Ishmael and Jacob, both of their mothers to whom the specific promises are given, dialogue with the divine. Those who function on the margin are not simply relegated to the state of the voiceless by the divine.

The election of Jacob overturns the role of the primogeniture and in so doing, discards the notion, both ancient and contemporary, that the good is rewarded and the evil is punished. Not only is this thrown out but God in fact establishes what the convention might regard as evil. Both of these stories clearly establish that God expects human convention to be challenged and provides divine initiatives to ensure that this is done and conflict is one of the means of doing so. We the readers are left to draw conclusions about which of the promises are good and which are evil. The fact is that the text does not lead us to any absolute conclusion, though convention dictates that we think in a certain way. Conflict and strife are almost universally seen as evil. Not surprising many who read and study these texts have continued to posit this notion. These parallels suggest otherwise.

Sources Cited

Brueggemann, Walter. *Genesis.* INTERPRETATION (Atlanta: John Knox Press, 1982).

Janzen, J. Gerald. *Genesis 12-50: Abraham and All the Families of the Earth.* (Grand Rapids, MI: W.B. Eerdmans Publishing Co., 1993).

Mukherjee, Bharati. "Genesis (Hagar)" in *Communion: Contemporary Writers Reveal The Bible in Their Lives.* Ed. David Rosenberg. (New York: Anchor Books, 1996), 89-102.

Pitzele, Peter. *Our Fathers' Wells: A Personal Encounter with the Myths of Genesis.* (San Francisco: HarperCollins, 1995).

Rosenberg, David (translator) and Harold Bloom (interpreter), *The Book of J* (New York: Grove Weidenfeld, 1990).

Rosenblatt, Naomi H. and Joshua Horwitz. *Wrestling With Angels: What the First Family of Genesis Teaches us about our Spiritual Identity, Sexuality, and Personal Relationships.* (New York: Delacorte Press, 1995).

Trible, Phyllis. *Texts of Terror: Literary-Feminist Readings of Biblical Narratives.* OBT (Philadelphia: Fortress Press, 1984).

Visotzky, Burton L. *The Genesis of Ethics: How the Tormented Family of Genesis Leads us to Moral Development.* (New York: Crown Publishers, Inc. 1996).

Westermann, Claus. *Genesis 12-36.* trans. John J. Scullion (Minneapolis: Augsburg Publishing House, 1985).

Section 6

Peace and War

Religion, War, and Peace

Anjana Narayan and Bandana Purkayastha

On June 2, 1979, only eight months after his elevation to the papacy, John Paul II delivered a carefully worded sermon before a vast audience of nearly one million Catholic faithful who jammed into Warsaw's Victory Square and the surrounding streets. In advance of this open-air Mass and his first visit to his native land as the Roman Catholic pontiff, John Paul pored carefully over the wording of his message in a conscious effort to inspire a peaceful, religiously centred toppling of the communist government in Poland.

During his sermon, the pope offered a prayer for his homeland: "Come down, Holy Spirit, come down and renew the face of the land—this land." In response, his enthusiastic audience began to chant, "We want God! We want God!" Leveling a subtle but unmistakable jab at the throat of the atheist communist government of Poland, the pope declared:

> Christ cannot be kept out of the history of man in any part of the globe, at any longitude or latitude of geography. The exclusion of Christ from the history of man is an act against man. Without Christ it is impossible to understand the history of Poland.

At this point the crowd punctuated his discourse with even more thunderous chanting: "We want God! We want God in the family! We want God in the schools! We want God in books! We want God!"[1]

Pope John Paul's role in the demise of Soviet communism only a decade after his visit to Poland was significant. Following the collapse of the Iron Curtain, the former Soviet premier, Mikhail Gorbachev, remarked that "Everything that happened in Eastern Europe in these last few years would have been impossible without the presence of this pope and without the important role—including the political one—that he played on the world stage."[2] Gorbachev's breathtaking declaration may actually be overstated, but the statement suggests that the Church and papacy played at least an important inspirational role in the organization of the Solidarity movement and

Anjana Narayan & Bandana Purkayastha, "Religion, War and Peace," *Religion in World History*, pp. 99-113. Copyright © 2006 by Taylor & Francis Group LLC. Reprinted with permission.

the collapse of communism in Poland and, eventually, the rest of Central and Eastern Europe.

As long as human beings occupy the planet, religious values will influence actions that lead to war and peace. Some social scientists may still wish to ignore this reality, but increasingly scholars and policy-makers are convinced that religion is essential to the calculus of war and peace. There is little doubt of the relationship between religion, violence, and war, and recent history only confirms the arguments of the previous two chapters. Al Qaeda's protracted conflict with the West, which erupted with renewed clarity in New York City on September 11, 2001, the Middle Eastern conflict between Israel and the Palestinians, fighting among Christians and Muslims in Nigeria and the Sudan, and the seemingly endless violence in Kashmir and Kosovo, represent only a few examples of how religious ideologies actually militate against world peace on a day-to-day basis. Indeed, the seeds of discord are sown in the official teachings of most religions.

The establishment of genuine peace often hinges on issues of economic justice and the protection of fundamental human rights. Despite the widespread acknowledgment of this reality, the doctrines of some religions, as interpreted by many of their adherents, permit or even encourage the marginalization of certain groups. The Western religious traditions of Christianity, Judaism, and Islam, for example, discriminate significantly on many issues pertaining to gender, and Islamic teachings on the role of the state make it extremely difficult for Muslim societies to afford the full scope of civil liberties to those who adhere to other religious traditions.

This reading of the past implies that religions themselves often comprise a craggy seedbed for the cultivation of peace initiatives. Because they are internally divided, Islam, Judaism, Christianity, Hinduism, and other religions are frequently at war with themselves and others. Radical Islam has received the most notoriety in recent years, and has now influenced the opinions of many otherwise liberal thinkers in the West toward all Muslims, literally (and incorrectly) pitting the majority of moderate Muslims against people of other faiths. In 2004, Bruno Guiderdoni, perhaps the foremost Qur'an scholar in France, deeply lamented the demise of the moderate European style of Islam, a casualty of the crossfire between radical Muslims and an increasingly impatient Christian West. Guiderdoni remarked:

> The radical Islamists accuse us of treason, while Christians and others see us as wolves in sheep's clothing. They distrust us now. They are more and more convinced that all we are trying to do is to lull Westerners into believing that Islam is harmless.[3]

Internal bickering and strife are by no means unique to Islam. Within every religion, subgroups are frequently at odds and find it difficult to maintain peaceful discourse with one another. Hasidic Jews who differ even on minute points with dominant religious leaders have, they report, become targets of physical and mental abuse within their own communities. The recent rise in the number of black church burnings in the U.S. South verify that Christians with different perspectives or skin colors have yet to find ways to peacefully coexist with others in their own communities.

Religious leaders who are highly critical of politicians' inability to make peace often exhibit the same dogmatic and inflexible qualities they condemn in politicians. For example, the Vatican apparently wasted an unprecedented opportunity to improve deeply strained relations with the Russian Orthodox Church in January 2002 when Metropolitan Pitirim of Volokolamsk agreed to meet with John Paul II to consider mending what he and his delegation described as the Russian

Church's "utterly unsatisfactory" relationship with Rome. The situation between the two churches appeared hopeful when, only a few weeks later, the pope elevated four apostolic administrations in Russia to diocesan status, creating a new ecclesiastic province of Moscow, an act which the Vatican fully recognized at the time would obliterate what little good will it had established with the Russian Church in January. Whether the Roman Church's decision was calculated or simply a matter of poor timing, the incident demonstrates that religious leaders, like politicians, often fail to practice the peacemaking they preach.

Unfortunately, the precise causes of human conflict are usually very difficult to trace even long after the battles have ended. The issues that precipitate armed conflicts spring from ideologies charged by politics and economics. The seemingly ubiquitous religious dimension tends only to cloud the picture. Combatants are usually drawn from the common ranks of societies, and the rank and file often holds religious convictions that influence their comportment in war. Religion provides the mythological frameworks upon which combatants are able to justify killing those outside their own religion and, when circumstances warrant, even those who may share identical religious convictions. Reflecting on an interview with a former American soldier, one Christian author graphically illustrates how, during human conflict, otherwise deeply religious men and women may forfeit all of their normal transcendent values.

World War II was at its height. Forces were engaged in what was known as, "The Battle of the Bulge"—or "The Christmas War of 1944." The fighting was fierce in the bitter cold and snow.

The Allied Forces bombed and established control of a strategic area. The commanding officer turned to several of his men and said, "Sweep across that field, and kill all German soldiers still entrenched in the snow. I want no prisoners. Absolutely none!"

One of the American soldiers selected gives his account of what happened next. "As I walked, I immediately shot and killed two wounded and suffering soldiers." He continues, "Then, suddenly I approached a tall, young guy. . . .

"He was leaning against a tree. He wasn't wounded—simply exhausted. He had no food, no water, no comrades in sight, no ammunition. Fear, fatigue, defeat, and loneliness overwhelmed him. He spoke English with a beautiful . . . accent.

"When I noticed a little black Bible in his shirt pocket," he reminisces, "we started to talk about Jesus and salvation.

"Wouldn't you know it, that lanky German soldier turned out to be a born-again Christian who deeply loved the Lord.

I gave him water from my canteen; I even gave him crackers. Then, we prayed and read God's Word together. And we wept together too."

His voice began to tremble, as tears splashed down his cheeks. His face began to reflect anguish.

"It seems like only yesterday. We stood a foot or so apart, as he read a Psalm from his German Bible. Then, I read Romans 12 from my King James translation. He showed me a black-and-white picture of his wife and daughter."

The soldier took a deep breath. "You see, in those days, I was a young man in my early twenties. I had just graduated from a Christian college in Illinois and hadn't had time to sort out my thoughts on the war.

"Maybe that's why I did what I did.

"I bid my German brother farewell, took several steps away, then returned to the soldier. Romans 13, the "thou shalt not kill" commandment, the promises of eternal life, the Prince of Peace, the Sunday school distinction between killing and murder, the irrationality of war—all swirled in my mind.

"When the German soldier saw me returning, he bowed his head and closed his eyes in that classic prayer posture.

"Then it happened. I said three crisp sentences that I still repeat once or twice a week when I have nightmares about the war, "You're a Christian. I am too. See you later."

"In less than a second, I transformed that defenseless Christian soldier into a corpse."[4]

The endless stream of haunting stories like this one that are part and parcel of every war demonstrate that religious men and women are as capable of killing their enemy as anyone else. If the deeply religious are often incapable of controlling their urge to kill, it is easy to understand why religions are so frequently at the very heart of skirmishes and wars.

Yet despite religion's protracted history of fomenting and abetting political discord, nearly every religion harbors a peace tradition that emphasizes the importance of conflict resolution and the avoidance of bloodshed whenever possible. If one is willing to approach religions *qua* religion that is to say in the understanding that religions are potentially beneficial frameworks of meaning for entire cultures and societies and not utilitarian tools to be exploited or somehow "adjusted" to leave off their deeply held orthodox

teachings—then they can help achieve peace. If peacemakers recognize and appreciate the many textures of faith lying within each religion, they will be far better equipped to utilize religious resources that ordinarily may be overlooked. With few exceptions, each religion offers sacred stories and teachings that address the importance of social harmony and, consequently, each tenders a viable tradition that, when fully apprehended, can offer a major tool for those who have invested in the peace process.

Christianity: just war, just peace

In its origins, Christianity abhorred every form of violence. Jesus taught his followers not only to "turn the other cheek" when enemies attacked but required that they "love your enemies, do good to those who hate you, and pray for those who abuse you." While Jesus may have resorted to the use of (or threat of using) corporal discipline when he fashioned a whip and drove moneychangers and disreputable merchants from the Jewish temple, there is no evidence that he approved of Christian participation in warfare. There is also no evidence that Jesus ever issued an explicit command forbidding involvement in police or military actions.

We know that early Christians served in the Roman military, but their numbers apparently remained small. While most Christian writers of the second and third centuries weighed in against Christian participation in the military, it is difficult to determine whether their anti-military outlook reflected a rejection of violence or a refusal to worship the emperor, something the Christians considered idolatrous.

By the end of the third century many Christians served in the military. In 312, Constantine recognized the potential utility that Christians in his military and throughout society represented just as he prepared to go into battle against his arch-nemesis and rival for the title of Roman emperor, Maxentius. A pagan sun worshiper, Constantine invoked assistance from the supreme God and then claimed to see a sign "IHS" (the first letters of Jesus' name) in the sky along with the words "conquer by this." Later that evening he claimed to encounter Jesus, who told him to use the sign "as a safeguard in all battles." Constantine defeated Maxentius, and shortly thereafter legalized Christianity. Within the same century, Christianity shifted from its position as a legally recognized Roman religion to achieving status as the official state religion. Consequently, it had to come to terms with its involvement in war.

St. Augustine, the fifth-century Bishop of Hippo who is usually credited with setting the framework for a Christian just war theory, actually expressed his opposition to the concept of self-defense. Individual Christians, he argued, have no authority to resort to violence when they or their property are threatened, yet they are compelled by the calculus of love to defend innocent others who are being attacked, even if it costs them their very lives. Drawing his just war teachings from the old Roman legal tradition, Augustine taught that right authority is vested in the state, which is obligated to bear the sword in defense of all citizens who fall under its care. He qualified this justification for going to war by placing certain strict limits on how wars may be fought.

During the Middle Ages, the Augustinian teachings on Christian involvement in war dovetailed with other philosophies and became what we now recognize as the Western just war tradition. In the twelfth and thirteenth centuries, the ideas of various theologians led by Thomas Aquinas and numerous relatively unknown canon lawyers began to emerge as a coherent system. Deriving many aspects of their just war ideas from Muslim jurists who were developing similar policies on the conduct of war, medieval Christians refined the Augustinian categories into their current form of *jus ad bellum* (categories of determining under what circumstances it is justifiable to go to war) and the *jus in bello* (just conduct during the war). Christian theologians and ecclesiastical officials played a significant role in the creation of the *jus ad bellum* category, while the knightly class (those who actually fought the church and empire's battles) helped frame the just conduct positions.

After 1500, Protestant thinkers including Hugo Grotius and Martin Luther helped refine the Christian theory of just war, although Augustine's two major categories remained valid.

Jus ad bellum
1. Just cause: the cause must be morally justifiable (e.g., defense of innocent civilians or self defense)
2. Right authority: only proper authorities (usually the state) may decide to go to war.
3. Right intent: combatants and their leaders enter wars with the intention to bring about a greater good.
4. Proportionality: given the fact that all wars create their own negative results, decision-makers must never enter a conflict when the end results are worse than would be the case if conflict were avoided.
5. Peaceful conclusion: to be a just war, the end must be a just peace.
6. Last resort: all other possible means of settling major disputes must be explored before war is entered.

Jus in Bello
1. Proportionality: even at the tactical level, combatants must not generate more evil than the evil they seek to stop.
2. Discrimination: The lives of non-combatants must be protected whenever possible.

Although the categories of the Christian just war theory present useful guidelines, each bears its own set of problems and ambiguities. All wars, even just ones, tend quickly to deteriorate into to- tal wars wherein it becomes difficult to determine which side is actually promoting the good. For example, while few objective observers question U.S. involvement in the fight against Germany and Japan in World War II, many Americans, including some veterans of the war, continue to question the morality of America's use of the atomic bomb in Japan, which led to the deaths of hundreds of thousands of civilians and only a small number of combatants.

Both Protestant and Catholic groups have recognized the difficulties inherent in maintain- ing a genuinely just war tradition, and have stated their interest in returning to the pacifistic teach- ings of the primitive Christian Church. During the Reformation period, the followers of Menno Simons established their Anabaptist tradition largely on the basis that all acts of violence are prohibited. Simons and his Mennonite followers applied a literal interpretation to the words of Jesus in the Beatitudes: "Blessed are the peace- makers, for they shall be called children of God" (Matthew 5:9), and assumed that anyone who promoted war under any circumstance could not be truly Christian.

Later, in sixteenth-century Britain, George Fox's pietistic group, the Society of Friends, or the Quakers, determined that all men and women have within them the goodness of their Creator and therefore should not be physically harmed under any circumstance. In contrast, the Roman Catholic Church, so instrumental in creating the just war tradition, has historically upheld the doctrine, allowing, and at times encouraging, Catholics to participate as combatants.

While all recent popes have upheld the concept of a defensive just war, since the mid-twentieth century a shift toward a strong peace ethic has emerged in the Catholic Church that has cap- tured the imaginations of laity and clerics alike. Following World War II, a largely lay pacifist group calling itself *Pax Christi* was organized in war-torn Europe. The movement eventually spread to more than thirty countries and today enjoys consultation status within the United Nations. *Pax Christi* eschews all forms of violence, including warfare and preparation for war. Many Christians argue that their faith requires that they respond passively and actively to violence. They must avoid bloodshed at all times, or at least whenever possible, and they must become actively involved in the peace-building process if wars develop.

War is only one form of injustice, as the African-American struggle for civil rights in the U.S. demonstrates. Before the American Civil War, Denmark Vesey of South Carolina, Nat Turner of Virginia, and other southern U.S. blacks drew upon their fundamental religious convictions as they planned armed rebellions, or in the case of Turner in 1831, actually car- ried out a bloody slave uprising against whites who denied them the most basic civil liberties. After the war, blacks faced a steep uphill fight on the road to gaining their civil rights. In the 1950s and 1960s, an extraordinary Baptist minister, Martin Luther King, Jr., led the black Civil Rights movement in the United States. While some historians concede that, given the conditions under which blacks lived in the United States, King would have been justified in resorting to an armed rebellion, he determined that a more effective weapon in the hands of the oppressed was non-violent resistance. Guided almost entirely by their faith, King, Andrew Young, and their closest associates in the Civil Rights movement never wavered in their determination to resist white oppression through protest. Their commitment to non- violent protest continues to serve as one of the most important models for peacemaking in the new millennium. King's question to his fellow protesters—"Are you able to accept blows without retaliating?"—demanded an ethic they believed could only be realized in the context of an abiding faith in God.[5]

Islamic ways of peace

The Prophet Muhammad readily used military force in his efforts to establish what he envisioned as a more just economic and social order. Like the Hebrew scriptures of Judaism and Christianity, the Qur'an describes the providential hand of God in the lives of those who fight on his side:

> An example has been set for you by the two armies who clashed—one army was fighting in the cause of God, while the other was disbelieving. They saw with their own eyes that they were twice as many. God supports with His victory whomever He wills. This should provide an assurance for those who possess vision.
>
> (Qur'an 3: 12)

"Jihad" is the principal means by which Islam is spread throughout the world. In common Western parlance, jihad has become synonymous with holy war, which is only one facet of its meaning. The word literally means "striving" to do the will of God through inner transformation.

Throughout much of its history—and based upon the Qur'anic call to restore humanity to its pristine, pre-adamic state—Islam asserted that it should conquer all territory in the world in order to establish universal Muslim rule. When the West checked Islamic expansion in France and the East halted its advance in India, the majority of Muslims gave up the concept of a universal Muslim rule on earth and, consequently, turned to the more irenic aspects of jihad such as the personal battle against sinfulness and striving to

act justly. It would not be an overgeneralization to argue that whereas Christianity was founded on pacifist convictions and eventually learned to press its agenda at the point of a sword, Islam was founded partially on military principles, and eventually discovered that it could coexist with other religious groups in peace.

Despite its confrontational foundations, Islamic teachings on the importance of discourse and arbitration provide important tools for peacemaking that should be recognized and respected. The Qur'an teaches the importance of settling disputes through polemics and, when necessary, through divinely inspired arbitration. In the seventh century, Muhammad himself relied on arbitration to settle a dispute he had with a Jewish tribe, and the fourth Caliph, Ali, agreed to resolve a quarrel with the Syrians, avoiding what might have developed into horrible internecine violence.

Much of the problem of misunderstanding the current place of Islam in world affairs revolves around Western attempts to characterize the Muslim "mind," which of course does not exist anymore than does a Christian, Jewish, or Hindu mind. The radical fringe of any group or society should never serve as the bellwether of its core. Highly influential Islamic peace organizations such as the International Islamic Forum for Dialogue have worked tirelessly to restore the voice of moderate Islam on the world stage. For example, in 2004 the organization helped develop a communiqué issued jointly with the Vatican that appealed to Christians and Muslims for ongoing prayers for peace, and "an immediate end to all conflicts, including all forms of armed conflict, as well as forms of aggression against the security and stability of peoples." Moreover, the joint communique affirmed "the rights of peoples to self-determination, so that human life be spared, especially that of innocent people, children, women, the elderly and the disabled."[6]

As other religions approach their Islamic neighbors they must grapple with the very genuine threat posed by the terrorist networks that claim Muslim connections. They will fall short in the peace process, however, if they fail to recognize the complexity of Islamic societies and elect instead to apply facile stereotypes based upon the latest headlines. Unfortunately, few news organizations expend the effort needed to comprehend and describe the lives of rank-and-file Muslims who, like their Christian, Jewish, and Hindu neighbors, yearn for a world where they and their children may dwell together in peace.

The way of ahimsa: religion in India

Like Christianity, Hinduism has, over its long history, developed a just war tradition. Hinduism's universalism, or the belief that the paths to the one truth are many, has tended over time to reduce the level of religious tension that many Hindu faithful experience with those outside their tradition. This openness to the teachings of other traditions has made it possible for many Hindu leaders to assimilate different religious perspectives into their belief systems.

The Hindu traditions of justice and peace have deep roots. The ancient writings of Hinduism provide the foundations for the peaceful intentions expressed by most Hindu adherents. While the *Bhagavad Gita* describes war as a caste duty, it establishes certain strict rules for combatants involved in war. For example, the *Gita* teaches that non-combatants and prisoners who have been wounded must be protected and afforded dignified treatment by their enemies. It is true that the *Vedas*, *Bhagavad Gita*, and *Upanishads* do not instruct their readers at much length about systematic peace-building activities, yet they extol the social and spiritual values of *ahimsa* (non-violence), *kshama* (forgiveness), and *shanti* (peace),

all essential building blocks of conflict resolution. In a passage that resembles the teaching of Jesus, the scriptural epic poem *Ramayana* teaches that one "should not retaliate when another does you injury. Even if those who do wrong deserve to be killed, the noble ones should be compassionate since there is no one who does not transgress."[7]

The epic poem *Mahabharata*, which, along with the *Ramayana*, continues to exert social and religious influence throughout Southeast Asia, maintains a fascinating dialectic between condemnation and forgiveness, the brutality of war and the wiser paths of peace. While the epic tale is primarily dominated by examples of the horrors of war and revenge, within the text there remains a message about the value of peace. Perhaps no call for peace is more striking than the one which the *Mahabharata* conveys on behalf of an old woman whose son has been killed. After she is informed that "Killing an enemy brings merit," the grieving mother replies, "Forgiving an enemy brings greater merit."[8]

The ancient texts found life in Mahatma Gandhi. Under him, the way of ahimsa grew in stature and became a prominent ethic within much of Hinduism as the religion began to support resistance against British colonialism. Gandhi's teachings have been and remain highly influential in the lives of other great religious leaders, including Martin Luther King, Jr., and like other advocates of non-violent resistance, Gandhi's vigorous support for the non-violent ethic was guided by his abiding faith in the principle of absolute truth that he described as "God." The non-violent Hindu recognizes that God is present in every thing and every person and understands that he or she must respect all people, including one's enemies.

Jainism, like its cousin Hinduism, finds its ethical roots in the non-violent principle of ahimsa, which the Jains uphold as the first of their five great vows. The Jain approach to ahimsa may be rightly described as the most radical in the world. The Jains forbid nearly all forms of killing or violence and enjoin compassion toward every living creature. A Jain sacred text, the *Ayaramgasutta*, declares that, "One may not kill, ill-use, insult, torment, or persecute any kind of living being, any kind of creature, any kind of thing having a soul, any kind of being." Consequently, devout Jains refuse to hunt or consume animal products and many, especially those who adhere to the monastic tradition, are careful to avoid stepping on any living thing, including insects. For the Jain, all acts of selfishness or cruelty bind the individual to the material world, whereas unselfish acts that lead to self-deprivation or personal suffering hasten escape from this coarse existence.

Jains are passionately committed to the cause of world peace and actively participate in all major peace-building initiatives. Some Jain leaders publicly demonstrate their support for world peace efforts by praying, fasting, and participating in other acts of asceticism. In 1998, a Jain ascetic leader, Sri Sahaj Muni Maharaj, successfully completed a 365-day fast (he consumed only two glasses of warm water per day) on behalf of world peace. Many other Jains encourage a more systematic approach to building world peace. Bawa Jain, a deep admirer of Gandhi who immigrated to the United States from India as a child, currently directs the International and United Nations affairs of the Interfaith Center of New York and serves as Secretary General for the Millennium World Peace Summit of Religious and Spiritual Leaders. Organized under the auspices of the United Nations, the Summit continues to identify and promote coordinated efforts among the world's great religious traditions in support of UN peace and social initiatives.

Tribal conflicts and the paths of peace

Models of peacemaking are also found in smaller religious communities. Among the tribal groups of the world, the Mountain Arapesh of New Guinea provide perhaps the most stunning example of peace-building skills among a people. Even before the period of German and Australian colonialization that quelled internecine warfare in the region, the Arapesh radically censured all forms of violent behavior, or even acts that might provoke others to become violent. From an early age, Arapesh children participate in many community events with their parents so that they may learn the art of non-violent living. The Arapesh firmly uphold principles of social justice, but in its most extreme form, conflict resolution entails isolating the offending party from other members of society. The Arapesh teach that violent behavior can be traced to sorcery and bad magic that displeases the ancestor spirits who guide their clans.

Native American societies learned first hand what it meant to fall victim to the perpetrators of unjust warfare. Americans of European descent were generally unwilling to consider peaceful means of coexisting with the native population. U.S. President Thomas Jefferson expressed the sentiment shared by most white Americans when he wrote to his Secretary of War Henry Dearborn that whenever the U.S. Military deemed it necessary to use force against an Indian tribe, it would never lay down its weapons "till that tribe is exterminated, or is driven beyond the Mississippi." Jefferson took this to the next step when he declared "in war, they will kill some of us; we shall destroy all of them".[9] In such a tough political environment, anyone who expressed openness to genuine peace-building activities with the native cultures was almost certainly fated with anonymity and a lacklustre career.

Many Native American groups attempted to overcome the hostility and enter into a lasting peace with the European settlers. As the forced migration stories of the Wyandotte, Cherokee, and other tribes attest, their diplomatic gestures were frequently repaid with extermination methods shrouded in the more publicly acceptable "Indian Removal" policies. Perhaps the majority of Native American groups had developed advanced peace-building skills long before Europeans arrived in the Americas. Some tribes divided leadership into warriors and peacemakers. Those who made peace walked the white path, whereas those who fought walked the path of blood, the red path. Among some tribes, the peace chiefs remained absolutely faithful to their ethic of peace. Many groups such as the Cheyenne placed high premium on peace-building based on a sort of religious *jus ad bellum* principle. Each generation, they taught, is spiritually connected to preceding and future generations. Every decision the tribe makes, especially those leading to war and peace, touches the lives of children to the seventh generation. Ideas of the sacred bind tribal leaders to policies that honor their children and those yet born. For American Indians and others, transcendent values that recognize the interconnectedness of all life provide a strong framework upon which to structure the establishment and maintenance of justice and peace.

The recent past demonstrates that religious peacemakers can successfully take theology from the seminary to the battlefield. In war-torn Nicaragua of the 1980s, the Conciliation Commission, led by mainly Protestant ministers, shaped the truce that ended armed conflict between the Sandinistas and the East Coast Indian tribes. Their success was made possible partly because many Nicaraguans held their clergy in higher regard than they did their politicians.

This same behavior of popular deference toward religious leaders helped secure peace in Northern Ireland, where Catholic priests and a committed minority of Protestant leaders opened an ecumenical dialogue that created enough common ground to bring about a cessation of violence. It enabled the collapse of Apartheid policies in South Africa, where a pacifist African bishop, Desmond Tutu, captured the imaginations of millions, both white and black, while Dutch Reformed Church officials guided predominantly white Christians away from their hostilities with black neighbors. Deep popular respect for Hindu leaders like Gandhi helped bring a peaceful end to Western colonialism in India. And similar deference toward their ministers inspired black Americans to organize themselves in churches following the U.S. Civil War, when they empowered themselves to resist the racist policies of whites.

Recent thinking

Modern social and political theory continues to grapple with the religion, war, and peace nexus. As in the past, consensus does not exist. What appears certain is that statecraft cannot succeed unless it recognizes the legitimacy of religious concerns. While economic and social justice will always remain critical elements in peacemaking, diplomats must recognize that increasing wealth and the establishment or retention of liberties alone may not end conflict. Turmoil emerges in liberated societies and often does so because religious adherents believe their deeply held transcendent values are threatened by forces they may or may not comprehend.

There is a growing recognition among several groups charged with the task of securing peaceful coexistence that religions are not always detrimental to the peace process. The Center for Strategic and International Studies in Washington, D.C., among other groups has developed recognition of religion's vitality to the peace-building enterprise.

The Center's Post-Conflict Reconstruction Project leaders have recognized that without the infusion of a spiritual dimension that promotes an attitude of forgiveness for acts already committed the vicious cycle of revenge in most cultures may be impossible to break.

Peacemakers may not share these same values, but their failure to respectfully address different religious traditions and experiences can precipitate the collapse of an otherwise earnest effort to establish a just peace. Policy-makers reared in a consumer-driven society and who operate under the assumption that everyone, including non-Westerners, are motivated by similar values will probably remain frustrated in their work. In perhaps the majority of cases, religious leaders are not easily influenced by economic incentives, though the ill-informed social scientist and politician may fail to understand why. Some religiously motivated leaders may react angrily to what they interpret as an attempt to buy them off when, in fact, their highest values relate to that which is beyond time and space and are not subject to an earthly purchase.

Unfortunately, Western attitudes that are often paternalistic and even derisive toward religions and religious values continue to wreak havoc. Recently, one scholar, J. Harold Ellens, declared with a certitude that approaches conceit: "Now we understand Fundamentalism is a psychological pathology." Ellens reduces not just fundamentalism but all sorts of firmly held orthodoxies to the level of psychological phenomena. Of course, within a positivist construct, it is impossible to verify or dismiss the claims he makes. Ellens correctly argues that "most Fundamentalisms have resorted to gross violence at some point in their histories,"[10] yet he fails to mention that most non-fundamentalist factions have also resorted to the same sorts of violent activity. Non-believers have perpetrated violence from Russia to Cambodia, from Canada to Argentina. What Ellens and many other Western scholars fail to comprehend is that violence is endemic in humanity as a whole; it is not an exclusive product of the religious.

Ellens prescribes something of a containment policy for those who suffer from orthodoxy or fundamentalism: "It is imperative, therefore, that we identify Fundamentalism where it may be found, define and name it as the psychopathology that it is, engage it, contain its violent potentials, and reduce its influences as much as possible."[11] Although this rather chilling prescription may provide succor to many secular-minded Westerners, such a perspective—which in several respects actually mirrors the fundamentalism it challenges—cannot possibly help facilitate peace among groups that, for better or worse, honor deeply held religious values. Until scholars and diplomats are committed to the difficult task of engaging with religions as they actually are and not as they may wish them to be, their efforts to achieve genuine peace will bear little fruit.

If peace negotiators hope to achieve any measure of success with their assignments, they must invest considerable time and energy into learning about the religions of those with whom they collaborate. They will also do well to listen carefully to what each group perceives as threats to its existence. Whether fundamentalism and other orthodoxies are pathological or not really does not address the point that men and women throughout the world always have been willing to die for transcendent values that mean little to those who fall outside their traditions. Such attitudes are potentially dangerous, but one should never underestimate the power of religion in people's lives. Despite its capacity for great good, religion is and will remain a dangerous force. It is even more dangerous when dismissed as a sickness and relegated to the backwaters of intellectual discourse. One need only look as far as Eastern Europe to see how containment policies under communism have failed.

Perhaps the "white path" of peace unfolds best when scholars and diplomats take time to understand religion, its meanings, and values for those whose beliefs may at first come across as exotic or even futile. This willingness to engage requires considerable humility and recognition that our own beliefs and convictions may seem equally mysterious to those we engage.

The next chapter continues this discussion by concentrating on some of the social questions that have influenced world history and religion's role in them. As in previous chapters, it demonstrates the extensive reach of imperial communion.

Notes

1. See, for example, J. Williams, "Earthquake in Rome", *The Tablet,* December 10, 2002. Online. Available HTTP: <http://www.thetablet.co.uk/cgi-bin/archive_ db.cgi?tablet-00673> (accessed April 24, 2004).

2. B. Keeler, "A Giant Among Popes," *Newsday.com,* October 12, 2003. Online. Available HTTP:<http://www.newsday.com/news/nationworld/world/ny-pope main1012,0,4614240.story> (accessed February 8, 2004).

3. Uwe Siemon-Netto, "Analysis: Beheadings Cause Muslims Grief', *Washington Times,* Online. Available HTTP: <http://www.washingtontimes.com/upi-break ing/20040621-115445-7143r.htm> (accessed July 6, 2004).

4. Suhail Hanna, "Piecemeal Peace," *Eternity,* December 1981, 32, p. 30.

5. M.L. King, Jr., "Letter From Birmingham City Jail," in *Why We Can't Wait,* New York: Penguin, 1964, pp. 77-100.

6. "Islamic-Catholic committee calls for peace prayers" (2004) *Independent Catholic News.* Online. Available HTTP: <http://www.indcatholicnews.com/ismco.html> (accessed August 23, 2004).

7. Quoted in John Ferguson, *War and Peace in the World's Religions,* New York: Oxford University Press, 1978, 29.

8. Quoted in Rajmohan Gandhi, "Hinduism and Peacebuilding," in Harold Coward and Gordon S. Smith (eds), *Religion and Peacebuilding,* 2004, Albany: State University Press of New York, p. 57.

9. David E. Stannard, *American Holocaust.* New York: Oxford University Press, 1992, p. 119.

10. 10 J.H. Ellens, "Fundamentalism, Orthodoxy, and Violence" in J.H. Ellens (ed.), *Destructive Power of Religion: Violence in Judaism, Christianity and Islam,* Westport, CT: Praeger Publishers, 2004, pp. 139-140. For a balanced appraisal of fundamentalism that examines the complexity of its involvement in conflict and peace, see R. Scott Appleby, *The Ambivalence of the Sacred: Religion, Violence, and Reconciliation,* Lanham, MD: Rowman and Littlefield Publishers, 2000, pp. 95-104.

11. J.H. Ellens, "Fundamentalism, Orthodoxy, and Violence" in J.H. Ellens (ed.), *Destructive Power of Religion: Violence in Judaism, Christianity and Islam,* Westport, CT: Praeger Publishers, 2004, p. 140.

Holy War Over Ground Zero

Joseph Bottum

There, the sign that says "Sharia," the hand-drawn letters dribbling down in streaks as though they were bleeding. And there, another sign—this one reading "No Mosque at Ground Zero" in patriotic red, white, and blue.

And there, the off-duty policemen come to join in, and there, the bikers up from Pennsylvania, and there, the microphoned speakers crying out "This is our cemetery"—"This is sacred ground." And there, the film crews watching like hawks for violence, and there, the *on*-duty policemen, also watching like hawks for violence, and there ... and there ...

Flags and shouts and placards and confusion. The whole messy, strange, inspiring, disturbing thing—an August 22 rally against the building of a mosque near the site in New York where the World Trade Center once stood. Organized by the Coalition to Honor Ground Zero, the rally brought a few thousand people out to protest Imam Feisal Abdul Rauf's Cordoba Initiative: a plan to build a $100 million Islamic mosque and community center, thirteen-stories high, in glass and steel, where a building damaged in the attacks of September 11 once stood.

Nearly everyone in America seems to have opined on this situation already. Cheering it, fearing it, sneering at those who object, mocking those who favor the building of the mosque. President Obama was for it, before he was against it: first giving a speech about religion and our constitutional system so high-minded that it was audible only to bats—and then, as criticism mounted, hurriedly explaining that he wasn't actually lending his support to the project. *That is not what he meant at all. That is not it, at all.* The man is turning into J. Alfred Prufrock, here before our eyes.

Perhaps New York Mayor Michael Bloomberg deserves credit, then, for saying straight out, and sticking to his position, that the mosque "is as important a test" of "the separation of church and state as we may see in our lifetime." Indeed, he added, "We would be untrue to the best part of ourselves—and who we are as New Yorkers and Americans—if we said 'no' to a mosque in Lower Manhattan."

And yet, there's something in that Bloombergian line that puts one's back up. Something condescending, superior, and hectoring. Something of the school marm and, more to the point, something of the 1950s high-liberal technocrat who just doesn't like the messiness of human interaction. And if we could reach down to the root of the mayor's error, we would have some understanding of how religion actually works in a constitutional democracy.

Of course, the first thing that has to be said about the building of an enormous Muslim center so close to the destroyed towers is that it's *wildly offensive*. And the second thing to be said is that it's wildly constitutional.

The offensiveness looks like this: Regardless of how it is intended, it will be perceived by radical Muslims around the world as a giant monument, in the heart of the beast itself, to their success in attacking America. Indeed, it will be perceived by many Americans that way. The funereal and memorial emotion that embraces one on a visit to the Ground Zero site will be weakened—poisoned, just a little—by the presence of this new, grand construction.

Yes, there have been other mosques in the vicinity for years, but they are small, ordinary things, not this grand statement. And yes, the organizers of the project insist that they are moderates, with a history of intra-religious cooperation. So what? Muslim institutions do not have a good track record for preventing themselves from being taken over by radicals, and moderation relative to the rest of Islam (as Ross Douthat has pointed out) isn't moderation relative to the rest of America. People died here in the name of Islam, and we're not really eased all that much merely because the people behind the Cordoba Initiative insist they hold a different kind of Islam.

Meanwhile, the constitutionality looks like this: The government really shouldn't be in the business of regulating the ways in which the sheer existence of a religious building offends the public sensibility. "This is America," President Obama intoned, "and our commitment to religious freedom must be unshakeable."

Yes, the New York City government is still refusing permission for the Greek Orthodox church destroyed in the attacks of September 11 to rebuild. And yes, one wishes that the unshakeable commitment to religious freedom didn't get shaken so much when the topic is, say, forcing pro-life pharmacists to issue morning-after pills or requiring Catholic hospitals to perform abortions.

But the principle remains sound, even when it is violated or honored only in the breach. It isn't simply that religious institution have a right to be treated no worse than other institutions. They have, in fact, a right to be treated *better*, with *more deference*, by the government under our constitutional scheme. If such an institution wishes to be offensively bloody minded, there isn't—or, at least, there shouldn't be—much that an American government can do about it.

Which is almost what Mayor Bloomberg and President Obama (initially) said. Almost. They rightly insisted on the constitutional principle that government could not intervene, but then they drew the conclusion that the discussion should thus be over—and that only bigots and un-American theocrats would continue agitating against an Islamic center near Ground Zero.

The self-congratulation in all this is a little hard to take—a kind of belief that, unfolded in full, would betray a vast sense of superiority to both those culturally backward Muslims who must be offered such tolerance and to those culturally backward Americans who must be lectured on tolerance.

The deeper problem with this line, however, is that it assumes government is the only actor: the only power, the only arbiter, the only law in America. If the government can do nothing, than nothing can be done.

The *New York Times* columnist Maureen Dowd wrote a column that might be the model for this kind of thinking about public affairs—this way of *feeling* about public affairs. Curiously calling for ex-President Bush to enter the debate and calm the people current-President Obama was incapable of soothing, the column was profoundly bothered by the mere existence of criticism. The failure to build the mosque, Dowd perversely declared, would be a triumph for those who hate America: "the ultimate victory for Osama and the 9/11 hijackers is the moral timidity that would ban a mosque."

Real democracy is messy. It's got protestors and agitators and banners and manners and morals and financial pressures and gossip and policemen on horses keeping an eye out to make sure it doesn't turn violent. Oh, yes, it's also got government, but apart from paying for those policemen, government ought not to be too deeply involved as these things sort themselves out. If what the Muslims want to do is not illegal, than government should have nothing more to say.

That does not mean, however, that everyone else should also have nothing more to say. The attempt to build a large, new mosque and Islamic center anywhere near the site of the World Trade Center is so offensive, so bizarre, and so deliberate that it should be stopped.

And stopped it will be, through the offered mediation of New York's Archbishop Dolan, or the skittishness of the financial community, or the disturbance of the neighbors, or the anger of the protestors, or the refusal of the building contractors. It will be messy, and it will be sharp. Inspiring and disturbing, with loud shouts on the streets and a few quiet words in the back rooms.

But that's democracy—it's how things get done when you accept that government shouldn't do everything. The churches and the synagogues have long experience with this kind of democratic negotiation. Time for the mosques to learn how to do it, too.

Challenging the Empire

The Conscience of the Prophet and Prophetic Dissent

Hemchand Gossai

Arguably it is the case that biblical scholarship over the last 400 years or so has been shaped principally by the Reformation/Counter-Reformation and the Enlightenment. In large part what this has done is to emphasize the centrality of rationalistic thinking and somewhat later, historical criticism. Indeed for a prolonged time these methods have been granted a privileged status, and in all of this time, while surrounded by the presence and influence of imperialism and colonialism, biblical scholars have been remarkably reluctant to employ other methods in shaping the trajectories of biblical hermeneutics.

> There are two greater dangers within the field. One is an uncritical acceptance of the principal tenets of the discipline, and the other, its failure to relate it to the society in which it word is done. Biblical studies is still seduced by the modernistic notion of using the rational as a key to open the text and fails to accept intuition, sentiment and emotion as a way into the text. By and large the world of biblical interpretation is detached from the problems of the contemporary world and has become ineffectual because it has failed to challenge the status quo or work for any sort of social change…. Western theologians have yet to offer a sustained theological analysis of the impact of colonialism. [For example] colonialism has not received anything like as much attention as the Holocaust in recent theological reflection on the West. (Sugirtharajah, 18-19)

I propose that a "hermeneutic of prophetic dissent" is essential for challenging and countering any such positioning. Let me illustrate with a contemporary example.

On April 19th 1985, Elie Wiesel, Holocaust Survivor and Nobel Peace Laureate received the Congressional Medal of Achievement at the White House; Ronald Reagan was the President of the United States. In the days surrounding the ceremony President Reagan found himself in a conflicted situation as to whether he should proceed on a planned trip to Bitburg cemetery particularly after it was discovered that SS soldiers were buried there. President Reagan decided to proceed with his trip as planned. Wiesel on this public occasion at the White House spoke directly to President Reagan.

> Allow me Mr. President to touch on a matter which is sensitive. I belong to a traumatized generation; to us symbols are important. Following our ancient tradition which commands us to 'speak truth to power,' may I speak to you of the recent events that have caused so much pain and anguish?
>
> We have met four or five times. I know of your commitment to humanity. I am convinced that you were not aware of the presence of SS graves in the Bitburg cemetery. But now we all are aware of that presence. I therefore implore you Mr. President in the spirit of this moment that…you will not go there. That place is not your place. (p. 176)

Like Wiesel, Micaiah is not with the king for an informal conversation; in fact the agenda is formal and precise. What is spoken will not be "behind closed doors." This is public. To further intensify the formal occasion, the physical setting with all the grandeur in I Kgs 22 is described at great length. Like the White House, the King's Court is a place of power and authority. Micaiah is put to the test. There are moments when one might speak the truth in a neutral or private setting but not here, for Elie Wiesel chose not to speak privately with the President. When truth is to be told that challenges the State and the considerable power of the Office, it cannot be a private transaction but a public pronouncement.

Analogues are hardly perfect and surely the one used here is no exception, but we witness a quality of courage to speak the truth in the face of daunting possibilities. Howsoever one views this, finally there is a palpable element of vulnerability by the one who challenges the source of power.

As a world we should not be surprised that the moments of war, some of which have lingered on for a hundred years have punctuated the landscape of world history. It is a tragic commentary that often, though by no means always have we come to think of war as giving identity and definition to many generations. Presently, several countries in the world are involved in wars and still others employ the rhetoric of war in political discourse and engagement. We have had recent evidence in the United States where wondering and questioning are viewed by some as undermining the direction of the State; some even view these fundamental human principles as subversive. Yet, in such extraordinary circumstances how can there not be questions. Biblical narratives and histories remind us that one is propelled into war for a variety of reasons, and in fact a leader of the State might even seek to determine divine assent to justify. In this paper I propose that we reflect on 1 Kgs 22 a narrative that remains remarkably relevant and pointed in its implications.

As one example of the fundamental nature of the relationship between the Hebrew Prophets and the various political, religious and judicial institutions of their day, this paper explores the interface of two seemingly unequal powers, that of the prophet as a solitary figure over against the power of the State, most notably 1 Kgs 22 vested in the person of the King Ahab. An essential component of this is understood principally through the military and the voice of the majority who subscribe to a broad imperial role of government. The challenge by a prophet outside the circle of "assenters" seeks to redefine "power" and reassert an indispensable role for the "voice of conscience."

The paper engages the particularity of this biblical text with contemporary neo-imperial powers and their approaches to nations and peoples who differ based on political and religious ideologies

In matters of truth and the moral conscience of the prophet, there is no retreat. Punishment in the form of imprisonment and the meager rations will be meted out to Micaiah, but the prophet is unflinching in his commitment. In speaking the truth Micaiah will do so at considerable cost, like every other prophet who speaks the truth as was the case also with Amos and Jeremiah among others. The prophetic truth must be spoken and once spoken there is going back.

Self evident in the reading of the Hebrew Prophets are the wide-ranging issues and occurrences against which the prophets spoke. The invectives they pronounced have variations that are not only present today, but in many circumstances, either tolerated or for that matter embraced or woven into the fabric of our society. There are different layers of conflict that permeate 1 Kgs 22: nation against nation; prophet against prophet; monarchical power against divine power, among others. There is no doubt that there is a conflict of interest. The voices of power resounding out of the halls of power do not necessarily echo the voice of God. Each of these tensions exists independently and yet each intersects in significant ways. Additionally and worthy of singular note is that of the pervasive tension between truth and lies. There are numerous surprising revelations regarding those who seek the truth and those who tell the truth and those involved in deceit and lies. Micaiah insists that he must speak the truth (v. 14) and then immediately proceeds to do otherwise. (v. 15) Ahab does not want to hear the truth, but rather he want to hear *his* truth; truth based on what he has already determined. Part of the complexity here is that Ahab, the king insists on the truth—but in fact he really only want confirmation for his decision to enter into war. Thus what he insists on publicly is not what he wants to hear. The king wants the truth—in the public—this is what the public must hear and believe. But this drama is doubly disingenuous for not only is the king finally not interested in the truth, but he sees the truth as a mere tool to be navigated around, negotiated away, and finally a casualty. The king simply cannot have a prophetic challenge to his authority. Even the "propping up" of Ahab at the end of the narrative is a deception in order to perpetuate the truth of the power of the State. To the degree Ahab is the principal representative of State power, then the power is sustained only by a lie, before the truth is known for even the State can only feign death for so long. Ahab's war is ill conceived and unwise, and yet, God will use it to destroy the king.

When the king of Israel is asked to inquire of God, the immediate response is to ask those who are employed by the king. The guild of prophets is clearly in the king's employment, and it evident that their role is not to speak on behalf of God, but on behalf of the king. The manner in which the question is asked makes it clear where the focus is. Not unlike poll questions, this one too is designed to elicit a particular answer. They assure the king, unanimously, in one voice that this is a good idea and that indeed God will deliver Ramoth-gilead into his hands. They are no qualifications; no stipulations. Go to war, and the city will be yours. Such is the immediate and uncritical response. They do not ponder; they do not take it to God and wonder, they simply apply the answer that the king is seeking, and thus it is the case that in this instance, it seems that the prophetic voice is collapsed under the force of imperial power. Four hundred advocated in the war room in unison, "go up; go up; go up." Ahab intentionally determines what he will do and places restrictions on a future divinely shaped and guided. Listening to the report of the four hundred voices of Ahab's prophets, Jehoshaphat knows instinctively that all is not well. Certainly this kind of hasty unanimity cannot be the voice of God and thus he asks for another prophet who might be available. What he seeks is one who does not appear to be a surrogate of the State. There is an ongoing intrigue/tension/conflict between "truth" and "the labyrinth of lies" in this story.

This is the point at which Micaiah ben Imlah enters the scenario. The king of Israel knows Micaiah, and it is clear that he intentionally seeks to keep his voice silent. If there is a something to be said about the king of Israel, he does not finally seek to hide Micaiah, nor his deep disdain for the prophet. Even Jehoshaphat chastises him for ridiculing Micaiah in this manner. He knows that his history is such that Micaiah is fearless in telling of the truth and thus he hides him. The imperial power seeks to hide the prophetic power.

One should certainly not confuse Micaiah the prophet as the "enemy of the State" as perhaps Ahab would like to identify him. In fact Ahab deems him to be so even before Micaiah makes any pronouncements. This prophecy regarding Ahab's fate does not in any way reflect a condemnation of the people. It is true that as the king, Ahab is a "corporate personality", but in this case the king's punishment is not a reflection of the people but as Nelson suggests the "fate of the people is separate from that of the monarch, the leader." (p. 150) Indeed from the beginning we are told by Ahab that he hates Micaiah. Whatever the earlier prophecies might have been the hatred appears to be personal, and thus intentionally distinguishes himself from the people. Even though there is no biblical record, it is indisputably clear that Ahab and Micaiah had a prior relationship, a tempestuous one from all accounts that existed before the recorded encounter in 1 Kgs 22. In fact given the nature of the reference it seems that there must have been several encounters and the animosity has heightened. Had it not been for Jehoshaphat's inquiry, Ahab would not

have mentioned Micaiah. In fact if Jehoshaphat is unaware of Micaiah, one is left to wonder why Ahab would have mentioned him. Here again Ahab's interest in "truth" surfaces and the question as to what this means for him emerges. The issue as to why Ahab would make this known is something of a mystery. Ahab might have felt compelled to speak the truth despite his personal disinclination. The prophet's pronouncements will not be determined on the basis of whether he is liked or disliked by Ahab or whether believed that he would not prophesy good. Indeed by whose standard is *bwef* defined? What does it mean for the prophet to prophesy "good?" From Ahab's perspective "good" is equated with agreement with him. "Good" for Ahab is the sustaining and sanctioning of monarchical power. The king's personal inclination, disinclination or for that matter his personal animosity cannot be the ultimate guiding principles on which the decisions are made.

Ahab cannot claim by any measure that he does not know the truth, for in fact he *does* know the truth; he insists on being told the truth, but really has no discernible interest in the truth. It is instructive that Ahab does not insists on the truth by the four hundred prophets, and when Micaiah tells him the truth he nonetheless proceeds as if he had not heard anything new or different from the four hundred prophets.

Ahab wants a war and a war he will have, but as in all wars there are vagaries over which a leader might not have any control. It is true that the declaration of war is the prerogative of the leader of a nation; advisory or legislative bodies may suggest or opine; debate or vote, but finally the leader decides. A nation or a people may be given particular or general reasons for a war or talk of war, but in the case of Ahab there is no reason given and it is his decision entirely, and he anticipates the outcome. In this instance the singular unknown element is that of Yahweh's plan to use the war for Ahab's final demise. No war comes without a price, and if the only casualty in the military undertaking would be the life of Ahab, then perhaps one might argue that this is justifiable. However the death of Ahab would not be the only cost, but the often overlooked or neglected cost of the peace that existed between the countries. Certainly given the history between Aram and Israel one might be led to believe that this was a tenuous peace, but a three year old peace it was nonetheless.

How important is this Ramoth-Gilead that peace between the nations must be sacrificed? The narrator of this text deems it significant enough to mention that these nations coexisted peaceably for a duration of three years. This, I would argue is more than passing in importance, and certainly not to be construed as incidental. Assuming that the narrative only has material relevant for the story then it is incumbent upon readers to ponder on the significance of such a reference. Ahab's insistence in regaining the disputed territory is such that peace is sacrificed and becomes a casualty. This is not a trifling feat as Israel and Aram (Syria) seemed to be constantly at war. This lengthy narrative follows on the heels of an alliance between Aram and Israel, as together they held off the powerful imperial army of Assyria.

One might legitimately argue that the very act of war, particularly when there is peace between the nations, creates fear, pain and suffering for the citizens of the respective nations. Whatever has been the history between Aram and Israel what we know is that the people were in a peaceful existence with each other when Ahab made his decision to go to war. There is no textual indication or inference that there is a royal envoy, conversations or negotiations from Ahab to the King of Aram. When nations are adversaries, diplomacy and conversations are important; here peace exists, and this would arguably be the principal reason for diplomacy. But none of

these principles appear to matter to Ahab and perhaps the unsuspecting attack seems to be his guiding principle. What precipitated the change from a peaceful relationship to one of war was the decision by King Ahab to recapture the disputed territory of Ramoth-Gilead, and indeed the value of Ramoth-Gilead has not been determined in the scheme of national identity. Moberly suggests that the juxtaposition of Ramoth-Gilead and Naboth's Vineyard, both involving Ahab and land acquisition might indicate an abuse of power (p. 4). The pursuit and conquest of territory in both instances do not suggest any particular benefit, except the building of political power and capital. This disputed territory has precipitated a call to war, and Israelite, Judahite, and Aramean blood will all stain the land before it is all over.

Ahab seeks a partnership between with Judah and its king, Jehoshaphat. As new alliances between Judah and Israel are made, old ones disintegrate, and a former peace partner becomes the adversary. Jehoshaphat immediately, indeed without any intervening question establishes that his military force is at the disposal of Ahab. Ahab's coalition with Jehoshaphat certainly brings about the desired alliance though it meets with an unexpected and compelling request by the latter. Jehoshaphat does not engage with the king of Israel as to the reason for the sudden interest in, or arguments for war, but rather the matter hinges on the issue as to whether this might be God's intent. "Inquire first for the word of the Lord" insists Jehoshaphat. The fact that YHWH is the covenanted God of Israel and Judah, is not enough to enter into war against an enemy. Jehoshaphat does not trust the "truth" of Ahab's 400 prophets; God will not simply sanction State power for its own sake. Jehoshaphat knows that in matters of truth neither the voice of the majority nor the voice of power will suffice.

While imperial power has structural support, prophetic power is invariably embodied in a voice beyond the center. Jehoshaphat seeks to do the right thing, and ascertain what God desires, for he knows that in both national and international matters, God is the central player and it is God's word which will constitute the ultimate dictate. What is the divine purpose at this point, and importantly, who might speak on behalf of God? Can the voice of the imperial power also be the voice of God? Can the political establishment speak on behalf of God? Is the voice of God simply meant to sanction what has already been decided? Then and now, discerning and determining who speaks on behalf of God has been a point of dissention.

Ahab is not only willing to go to war, but there seems to be an urgency to do so. The pace is only slowed down through the engagement of the prophet and the ensuing conflict. We have a seemingly promethean struggle between the king, the imperial force with the support of the structure of government, and the prophet who functions without structure or institution. The one who initially caused the pace to be slowed down is the one coalition partner, Jehoshaphat, and when he receives the truth that he too seeks and perhaps might even have believed, it still does not matter, and follows Ahab anyway. As devastating as the call to war is, the narrative renders it as a critical point of departure for something greater and more urgently challenging. Among other trajectories within the text, a tension of great magnitude looms between imperial power and prophetic power.

While the kings sit on their thrones arrayed in their royal robes, with the guild of prophets telling the kings what he wishes to hear, a messenger is set to Micaiah to seek his prophecy regarding the war that is about to be waged. But the reality is that the messenger has no intention on eliciting a genuinely prophetic word from Micaiah. Zedekiah, clearly a "yes man" for the king even symbolically displays a horn to gore Aram. The imperial power seeks unanimous approval, but prophetic power cannot be collapsed under such pressure. The imperial prophets have spoken with one accord, and this is the pressure that is levied against Micaiah. The messenger does not even formally ask Micaiah to seek God's word; he is simply told what the imperial majority has pronounced and what he should likewise do. When Zedekiah approaches Micaiah there is clearly an unabashed "arm twisting" and the message is perfectly scripted.

Preparations for war, in both theatre and rhetoric are well underway as the machinery of the State has been effected. It is a shocking realization that the king has no intention of hearing what the word of God is, for he has already determined what he will do. Moberly suggests: "To challenge the complacencies and self deceptions of the human heart and mind with the searching truth of God will regularly provoke a hostility whose consequences may be devastating. To try to avoid this by being more accommodating risks becoming a prophet whose message is ultimately self serving." (p. 15) Micaiah's initial response is exactly as one would expect. "As the Lord lives, whatever the Lord says to me, that I will speak."

Yet when Micaiah comes before the king, his word is exactly as the other prophets have spoken. We have this peculiar situation of knowing that Micaiah will speak the truth, and yet, in the face of imperial power he says what the king wishes to hear. To simply agree as he did initially is immediately seen for its transparency, even by Ahab who seeks such approval.

Contrary to his imperial trappings, the king of Israel knows that Micaiah's initial word is not true, and he seeks "the truth" despite himself. But Micaiah's response is instructive. Even Micaiah shrinks in the face of imperial power, and one should not imagine that prophetic testimony is oblivious of the power of the State for Micaiah is aware of the danger, and his initial response demonstrates self-preservation. The narrative leading to this point has made it altogether clear that Ahab and the Queen Jezebel are utterly unscrupulous and violent. Micaiah's initial response is understandable.

The history of the Crown's actions when it is challenged and confronted even in the name of God, is to resort to violence. Micaiah has good reason to be reluctant and yet he must speak the truth. There is nothing that Micaiah is able to say that will align him with the Crown. The voice of the prophet is not the voice of the State, and Ahab feels vindicated that indeed Micaiah turns out to an enemy of the State. Yet, the enemy of the State as Ahab sees him is the one who speaks on behalf of God.

So the quest for truth is made public, but when the truth comes, the one who bears it must be silenced. Micaiah will be placed in detention. (22:26-28) Micaiah is imprisoned; he is given "prisoner food" and the idea is that in the imprisonment and demoralizing of Micaiah, the word that he speaks will be discounted or even likely silenced. The larger issue of course is not simply the feud between the Prophet and the State; the mouthpiece of the King and God's prophet Micaiah, but in reality the silencing of God. The belief is that in silencing the prophet, the prophetic oracle will also recede if not disappear. One thinks of Solzhenitsyn and Havel, both of whom have written so remarkably poignantly about such silencing. Moreover, as we see in contemporary society, when there is disagreement with those who bring a prophetic voice, then the powers that be, vilify and ostracize them and often call them "crazy." Perhaps in doing so, the general public will believe that the prophetic word has been weakened. Here too, one is reminded that Elisha is called "mad" also by the establishment because of his prophetic words.

When he outlines his vision which speaks of a scattering, a people without a king and a society that will collapse into chaos, he is imprisoned and physically weakened. Despite what Micaiah

pronounces, Jehoshaphat maintains his alliance with Ahab and follows him into war. But we know that Jehoshaphat does have a vision that contains a striking and dramatic component that God in fact will use the war for the death of Ahab. Not only will the policy of Ahab not succeed, indeed death will come to Ahab because of an unwise act. What we have is a clash of two designs of foreign policy, Ahab's and God's. Shalom is beyond Ahab, and ultimately his warring intent will lead to his death, for he has been enticed, seduced and finally blinded by his own military machinations. His justification is not predicated on any kind of genuine discussion or listening, but rather territorial dispute has expanded itself into the realm of certitude regarding ownership and belonging.

Given what Micaiah has spoken we are not surprised given the track record of Ahab that Micaiah is imprisoned for his words. The Crown has the power to silence, in the hopes of undermining, even unraveling the truth. In the face of challenges, the State seeks to silence the voice of the critics and those who pose an alternative. Thus even as Micaiah is silenced the vision not only lives on, but it is directed by God. In a striking juxtaposition of two powers, both State and God prepare for war and while Ahab imagines and anticipates God already knows the outcome. This war will ultimately not be about the disputed land of Ramoth-Gilead, or Israel versus Aram, but about Ahab; he realizes this as he disguises himself as a peasant soldier. But external changes and disguises will not do, for this war is out of his hands and is guided by God. His fate has been sealed. The war which he himself initiated would lead to his death, and there is nothing to stem the tide of his demise.

In the United States patriotism is narrowly construed and understood as that which lends support to the State sanctioned position and voices that challenge are deemed unpatriotic, often silenced and frequently demonized. Micaiah's pronouncement establishes with unencumbered clarity that State ideology as powerful as it may be and as widely as it is embraced by operatives of the State, must not be confused with divine affirmation.

We know that with all of the State planning, the military alliances, the political maneuvering, and the rhetoric of peace through war, ultimately this is neither the only word nor the final word. As this narrative comes at an end there is an enduring message. The destiny of a people which is often viewed as tied to its leader is not necessarily so. In the case of Israel the leader dies and the people return home in peace. The alignment of God with the goals of the State cannot be assumed and there are moments when God will protect the people from their leaders. The people will survive in peace despite an ideology of war.

At the end as Ahab is wounded by accident, and he dies in the process of a "lie" as he is being propped up in his Chariot. The irony is that he is being overlooked as the king and yet he is killed. The tensions and layers in the narrative are multiple; certainly among them is the ever present question: "who will speak for God"?

The four hundred prophets claim to speak for God, but in reality in this instance they represent a thinly veiled collective mouthpiece for the crown even as they are used by God. The voice of the prophet on God's behalf need not be measured quantitatively or by decibels, but by truth, even quiet and devastating truth. This is the measure. God will use whatever measures, whether a truth speaking prophet or lying Spirits to bring about the demise of Ahab. God's "lying spirits" work; Ahab's "lying" through his disguise does not. He dies, despite himself. In both "truth" and "lie" Ahab is outdone.

Sources Cited

Berlin, Adele. "A Rejoiner to John A Miles with some Observations on the Nature of Prophecy." *The Jewish Quarterly Review*. N.S. Volume 66, No. 4 (April 1976) pp. 227-237.

Bodner, Keith. "The Locutions of I Kings 22:28: A New Proposal." *Journal of Biblical Literature*. 122/3 (2203), 533-46.

Brueggemann, Walter. *1 & 2 Kings*. Smyth & Helwys Bible Commentary. Macon, Georgia. 2000.

Crenshaw, James L. *Prophetic Conflict* (BZAW 24; Berlin/New York: de Gruyter, 1971).

DeVries, S. J. *Prophet Against Prophet: The Role of the Micaiah Narrative (I Kings 22) in the Development of Early Prophetic Tradition*. Grand Rapids: Eerdmans, 1978.

Hamilton, Jefferies M. "Caught in the Nets of Prophecy? The Death of King Ahab and the Character of God." *CBQ* October 1994, volume 56, Issue 4, pp.1-9.

Lash, Nicholas. "The Church in the State we're in" in *Spirituality and Social Embodiment* (Ed. L. Gregory Jones and James J. Buckley; Oxford: Blackwell, 1997) pp. 121-137.

Mowberly, R.W.L. "Does God Lie to His Prophets? The Story of Micaiah ben Imlah as a Test Case." *HTR* 96:1 (2003), pp. 1-23.

Nelson, Richard. *First and Second Kings*. INTERPRETATION. John Knox Press, 1987.

Roberts, J.J.M. "Does God Lie? Divine Deceit as a Theological Problem in Israelite Prophetic Literature." In *Congress Volume: Jerusalem 1986* (Ed. J.A. Emerton; VT Sup 40; Leiden: Brill, 1988), 211-220.

Robertson, D. "Micaiah ben Imlah: A Literary View" in *The Biblical Mosaic: Changing Perspectives* (Ed. R. Polzin and E. Rothman. Philadelphia: Fortress; Chico, CA: Scholars Press, 1982), 139-146.

Sugirtharajah, R.S. *The Postcolonial Biblical Reader*. Oxford: Blackwell Publishing. 2006.

Walsh, Jerome T. *I Kings* (Berit Olam; Collegeville: Liturgical Press), 1996.

Wiesel, Elie. *From the Kingdom of Memory*. Summit Books, 1990.

Section 7

Religion: Suffering and Hope

Tragedy Versus Hope?

A theological response

Eduardo R. Cruz

Let us face the facts: whichever universe is available for us, we are still in an existential situation of estrangement from it. This also means that our consciousness is alienated from the possibility of a comprehensive and permanent understanding of the cosmos. It follows that some dissonance is to be expected, not only within scientific discourse itself, but especially when different disciplines are invoked. In other words, in the dialogue between science and religion we must acknowledge that discourses from different approaches may pass through each other, leading to misunderstanding perhaps, but also to opportunity for further inquiry.

The chapter by Arnold Benz, 'Tragedy versus hope: what future in an open universe?', is a good example, first, of an acknowledgment of the differences in approach, and, second, of such an unintended dissonance. In fact, while the scientific side of his theses is expounded with ease and precision, something to be expected from a leading expert in the field of cosmology, the exposition of crucial terms such as 'tragedy' and 'hope' is marred by some distortion of meaning.

The purpose of the present response is not so much to face the challenge of an open future in full-blown theological terms, but rather to give more precision to these two non-scientific terms, tragedy and hope. We will also show that the 'tragedy versus hope' framing of the situation is inadequate, pointing rather to a 'hope through tragedy' approach.

On tragedy and the tragic

It is a common phenomenon in any language that a word, with time and usage, may acquire a new, transposed meaning, alongside the original one. That is the case with 'tragedy.' In common usage, it means '2a: disastrous event: CALAMITY b: MISFORTUNE' (*Webster's Ninth New Collegiate Dictionary*), whereas the original meaning is closer to '1b: a serious drama typically describing a conflict between the protagonist and a superior force (as destiny) and having a sorrowful or disastrous conclusion that excites pity or terror' (*idem*). The stories of Prometheus and Sisyphus come readily to mind when we try to grasp the breadth of cosmic and biological evolution.

By reading Benz's essay we are led to the common usage meaning, which is likely to impoverish the argument. The Earth being burned by the sun in 10^9 years, and 'heat death' coming in 10^{100} years, are surely misfortunes, albeit only from our petty, anthropomorphic perspective. But any other scenario for the distant future would also be gloomy: 'big crunch,' eternal rearrangement of the universe, fleeing through worm holes, even the scientifically impossible eternal continuity of the present state of the universe. Steven Weinberg (1977: 154) is more precise at this point, speaking of 'the grace of tragedy.'[1] We have to take seriously the words of the psalmist about our lot:

> Thou turnest man back into dust; 'Turn back,' thou sayest, 'you sons of men'; for in thy sight a thousand years are as yesterday; a night-watch passes, and thou cast them off; they are like a dream at daybreak, they fade like grass which springs up with the morning but when evening comes is parched and withered. So we are brought to an end by thy anger and silenced by thy wrath. Thou dost lay bare our iniquities before thee and our lusts in the full light of thy presence. All our days go by under the shadow of thy wrath; our years die away like a murmur. Seventy years is the span of our life, eighty if our strength holds; the hurrying years are labour and sorrow, so quickly they pass and are forgotten.
> (Psalm 90:3-10 in the *New English Bible*)

We are latecomers in the universe, and soon will pass away. We experience fate and indifference in the cosmos, and the absence and wrath of God. The Judaeo-Christian tradition, indeed, is filled with 'flirtations with the tragic' (to use the apt expression of Lee Humphreys—see Humphreys 1985: 73), and the message is harsh and straightforward: whatever hope we can expect from the universe that science is able to describe, it comes in a strange yet graceful manner. No Disney-like dream-come-true expectations here! To be fair, Benz does point out that for the Christian tradition 'hope lies not in protection from crisis, but rather in the formation of newness.' We will explore the nuances of his argument in the section on hope below.

Elsewhere we have explored in some detail the convergences and divergences between the form and spirit of the tragedies of ancient Greece and our religious heritage (Cruz 1996: 72-80, 94-7, 101-3, 143-6, 156-62). In doing so, we relied almost entirely on other sources, which means that using 'tragedy' without referring to sources such as these may introduce even more misunderstandings in academic discourse. To be fair to Benz, even sophisticated theologians and philosophers may think that it is not necessary to work out the meaning of 'tragedy' (e.g. Haught 2000: chapter 7; Rolston 2003). The tragic must be distinguished from the farcical, the unfortunate, the sorrowful, the pitiful, and the pathetic. Only where there is greatness and nobility is the tragic present. Is there any nobility in the universe?

'Hope contrary to all reason'

As opposed to 'tragedy,' Benz's essay has several references to 'hope,' all of them being beyond any serious questioning. As his starting point for religious experience is the Christian tradition, he rightly takes the paschal event as the pivotal element that grounds hope for the future (see also Benz 2000: 119-22). Hope is no wishful thinking, insofar as it is grounded on reliable witnesses. Moreover, Christian religious experience has as its main content the ever-presence of this unique event, the resurrection of Jesus Christ. But, within the conditions of existence, the cross is also ever present. As Jürgen Moltmann once said, 'the Cross of Christ modifies the resurrection of Christ under the conditions of the suffering world so that it changes from being a purely future event to being an event of liberating love' (Moltmann 1974: 185).

Because of the very nature of the paschal event, it is possible to say that tragedy is not opposed to (versus) hope, but there is an intimate relationship between them. Reinhold Niebuhr, for example, acknowledged this relationship long ago: 'The second Adam is crucified by the first Adam, particularly by the first Adam who is trying to be good and is seeking to build up government and churches and standards of conduct which will hold sin in check' (Niebuhr [1937] 1965: 182). He then continues in the same vein: 'The modern church ... has forgotten that the Kingdom of God enters the world in tragic terms. The "prince of glory" dies on the cross.' He combines the two assertions by saying: 'The Kingdom of God must still enter the world by the way of crucifixion.' The connection between tragedy and the cross, however, would not be fully established if God's plan and will were not in some way involved in it. Therefore, Niebuhr concludes by saying: 'In the very crucifixion God has absorbed the contradictions of historic existence into Himself. Thus Christianity transmutes the tragedy of history into something which is not tragedy' (*ibid.*, 184, 185, 193). This 'something which is not tragedy' is hope.

What is valid for human history is also valid, *mutatis mutandis*, for cosmic history. Benz himself hints at this dialectical process, indicating in the explication of his fourth thesis what it is possible to ascertain by the sciences. 'Similarly, the extreme order constituting living beings cannot last. Death is unavoidable for several reasons ranging from chemical decay to physiological deterioration. It is, on the other hand, a *necessary* ingredient of evolution' (Benz 2002; my emphasis). For the Christian this assertion, warranted by the sciences, has a clear resonance in John 12:24: 'In truth, in very truth I tell you, a grain of wheat remains a solitary grain unless it falls into the ground and dies; but if it dies, it bears a rich harvest.' Further exploration of this life-through-death theme may be found in several contemporary authors (e.g. Rolston 1987). The tricky point here, however, is how to understand the meaning of 'life *ever*lasting' in the scientific picture. But let us move first to some epistemological considerations.

Where is this opposition, tragedy versus hope, to be located in Benz's view? Perhaps we have to look for a possible double standard in his epistemology. Indeed, when he works within his field, cosmology, he clearly adopts 'the present world-view of science.' This includes novelty within chaotic and quantum-mechanical systems, implying that: a) science seeks suitable explanations for unique events also, starting with the Big Bang itself; b) this explanation goes beyond the standard, causal form. For example, explanations for the increase in entropy and for self-organizing processes may take a teleological form; scientific explanations also involve pattern recognition (eighth thesis).

But when it comes to the foundations of Christian hope, Benz seems to retreat to a more strict, instrumentalist epistemology. He thus resorts to sober statements such as: 'Scientific measurements and observations must be reproducible and objective'; 'It is worth recalling that no objectively certain facts are available concerning the Easter event'; and 'It [hope] cannot even be made plausible to scientific reason'. By drawing such a sharp borderline between scientific measurement and religious experience or faith, the author seems to borrow from logical empiricism the dichotomy between the context of discovery and the context of justification, and to completely disregard theology as a cognitive enterprise.

Well, precisely because of the peculiar nature of this 'hope contrary to all reason,' the latter being understood as Niebuhr understood it (i.e. as the practical, commonsensical reason which seeks 'to build up government and churches'), this hope can be made plausible to scientific reason. It is true that the 'wisdom of the cross' is a 'stumbling-block to Jews and folly to Greeks' (1 Corinthians 1:23), but on the other hand it is true that science too bursts through commonsense (science has a 'heretical nature'—see Cromer 1993, Ridley 1996), robbing wishful thinking of its illusory hope. Theology, on the other hand, cannot stop short of any standards of rationality in its efforts to submit its arguments on the cross and resurrection to public scrutiny.

Does this mean that the future depicted by science matches the hope of Christians based on the paschal event? Not quite so, if we seriously take into account our own introductory remarks. Yet, the literal (and preferably mathematical) language of science, as Benz himself recognizes, does not rule out the symbolic language of religious experience. It is true that in the latter case there is some measure of circularity we do not know the referent of the symbol outside of its own enacting in myth and ritual but symbols such as 'eternal life' and the 'Kingdom of God' are not opposed to the tentative depiction of the ultimate fate of the universe in terms of 'photons, positrons and electrons.' Science does know the future of the universe (unavoidable decay), and at the same time does not know it (uncertainties in the physical theories). Likewise, the Christian symbol does know the future (reversal of decay into a qualitatively different stage called 'resurrection'), and at the same time does not know it—religious sensibility can only hope (*sperare*) for the future in faith and love, based on a unique event in the history of the cosmos and humankind alike, the death and resurrection of Jesus Christ.[2]

This unique event bestows meaning on the 'grace of tragedy' of Weinberg. Rolston also reminds us that Weinberg was not the first to be astonished by this ambivalent nature of the universe:

> Suffering through to something higher is always messianic. Transfigured sorrow is ever the divine glory. That was never more true than at Calvary, but it has always been true ever since the capacity for sorrow emerged in the primeval evolutionary process. The creatures 'were always carrying in the body the dying of Jesus' even before he came. J.B.S. Haldane found the marks of evolution to be 'beauty,' 'tragedy,' and 'inexhaustible queerness.' But beauty, tragedy, and unfathomable strangeness are equally the marks of the story of this Jesus of Nazareth. It is a fantastic story, but then, again, to recall the conclusion of a puzzled astronomer, Fred Hoyle, the universe itself is a fantastic story.
>
> (Rolston 1987: 328; see also Rolston 2003)

We are not sure, however, that it is possible to go along with Rolston all the way. Without a sustained treatment of God's freedom and transcendence, on the one hand, and the grounds for hope in christological and eschatological terms, on the other, it is difficult to assert the Goodness of Creation. Philip Hefner's position seems to be more consistent at this point (Hefner 2003).

Conclusion

Our earth is 'the third rock from the Sun,' a speck of dust in the immensity of the cosmos. Yet, in this tiny corner of ours the universe became self-conscious, was ennobled and gracefully vested with beauty, truth and love. It does not matter whether it has happened before, or will happen again in the future. We do not know, and perhaps never will know. What is important is that, in the long life of the universe, in our fleeting passage on earth, a flash of awareness is taking place. Dust has become 'vital,' capable of foresight and expectation. I agree entirely with Benz when he uses the following metaphor: 'Despite decay and death something new will arise out of this existence, just as our planet formed from cosmic dust, the ashes of former stars.' Dare we say something more, to avoid falling into wishful thinking? I think so: as hope is both a theological virtue and embodied in symbols, this 'something new' may be experienced now in fragmentary anticipation and confidence (see Cruz 2003). 'When I look up at thy heavens, the work of thy fingers, the moon and the stars set in their place by thee, what is man that thou shouldst remember him, mortal man that thou shouldst care for him? Yet thou hast made him little less than a god, crowning him with glory and honour' (Psalm 8:3-5). Only a being crowned with glory and honour can withstand tragedy and wait diligently for a new creation to be formed out of mere ashes, but also out of the side of the pierced one. Through this witness of ours, the universe itself becomes the 'ecological niche' of tragedy and hope, holding in check any assignment of the equally anthropomorphic idea of 'fate' to its everlasting future.

Notes

1. In his book Benz also mentions the often-cited phrase by Steven Weinberg: 'The more the universe seems comprehensible, the more it also seems pointless' (Benz 2000: 169, n.24). It is a pity that he, together with many other commentators, does not quote Weinberg to the very end: 'But if there is no solace in the fruits of our research, there is at least some consolation in the research itself. ... The effort to understand the universe is one of the very few things that lift human life a little above the level of farce, and gives it some of the grace of tragedy' (Weinberg 1977: 154). Granting that cosmology can be discussed at the crossroads of astrophysics, metaphysics and theology, to speak of 'the grace of tragedy' is a nice way to give much food for thought and amazement.
2. It may be argued that such sensibility leads to quietism. Our response, however, deliberately excludes the realm of human action—we are restricting ourselves to natural processes.

References

Benz, A. (2000) *The Future of the Universe: Chance, Chaos, God?* New York: Continuum.

—(2003) 'Tragedy versus Hope: What Future in an Open Universe?', in W.B. Drees (ed.), *Is Nature Ever Evil? Religion, Science and Value*, London: Routledge.

Cromer, A. (1993) *Uncommon Sense: The Heretical Nature of Science*, Oxford: Oxford University Press.

Cruz, E.R. (1996) *A Theological Study Informed by the Thought of Paul Tillich and the Latin American Experience: The Ambivalence of Science*, Lewiston, NY: Mellen University Press.

—(2003) 'The Quest for Perfection: Insights from Paul Tillich', in W.B. Drees (ed.) *Is Nature Ever Evil? Religion, Science and Value,* London: Routledge.

Haught, J.F. (2000) *God after Darwin: A Theology of Evolution*, Boulder, CO: Westview Press.

Hefner, P. (2003) 'Nature Good and Evil: A Theological Palette', in Willem B. Drees (ed.) *Is Nature Ever Evil? Religion, Science and Value*, London: Routledge.

Humphreys, W.L. (1985) *The Tragic Vision and the Hebrew Tradition*, Philadelphia: Fortress Press.

Moltmann, J. (1974) *The Crucified God: The Cross of Christ as the Foundation and Criticism of Christian Theology*, New York: Harper & Row.

Niebuhr, R. ([1937] 1965) *Beyond Tragedy: Essays on the Christian Interpretation of History*, New York: Charles Scribner's Sons.

Ridley, M. (1996) *The Origins of Virtue*, New York: Penguin.

Rolston, H., III (1987) *Science and Religion: A Critical Survey*, New York: Random House.

—(2003) 'Naturalizing and Systematizing Evil', in Willem B. Drees (ed.), *Is Nature Ever Evil? Religion, Science and Value*, London: Routledge.

Weinberg, S. (1977) *The First Three Minutes*, New York: Basic Books.

Tragedy Versus Hope

What future in an open universe?

Arnold Benz

Recent evidence from astronomical observations suggests that the universe will expand forever. Nevertheless, all cosmic structures from galaxies to planets and even the matter of the universe itself are bound for decay and destruction. Life cannot continue forever, as the planet Earth will become uninhabitable, the Sun will burn out, and the galaxy will contract to a black hole. The history of all things ends intrinsically in tragedy.

On the other hand, the past history of the universe is full of spontaneous appearances of new phenomena. Not only have new stars and living beings been formed, and still are, but new dimensions for development have also opened up that did not exist in the beginning.

Will this cosmic creativity continue in the decaying universe, and is there any hope for this universe? Hope for something new is an emotion based on existential sensations. Religious hope expects the new from beyond this space and time. Science and faith thus will and must remain in dispute concerning the future. The outlook into the future is a crucial test for the significance of propagated values and of the dialogue between science and religion, which so far has been constricted to the issues of past evolution.

Observations of distant supernovae have shown that their parent galaxies move more slowly than would be expected in a uniformly expanding universe (Riess *et al.* 1999; Perlmutter *et al.* 1999). As the light that reaches our telescopes today was emitted a long time ago, the result means that the universe used to be expanding more slowly than it is today. In other words, the expansion of the universe is accelerating and will probably continue forever. Does that mean that the universe will exist forever? Maybe, but certainly not in its present form.

Most ethical thinking and acting are oriented towards the future and based on certain expectations. The future is the primary nexus of ethics, science and religion (Benz 2000). The past development of the universe makes it clear that the evolution of the universe is very innovative and impossible to predict. We will have to distinguish between various forms of perception leading to different prognoses and expectations.

Thesis 1. All things in the universe decay.

Predictions have always played an important role in astronomy. Old Egyptian astronomers were able to predict the yearly flooding of the River Nile, and Babylonians could predict lunar and solar eclipses. The goal of today's astrophysics is the understanding of the formation of cosmic structures, and their evolution and decay.

The planet Earth is bombarded by meteorites, and occasionally such impacts have led to major catastrophes. Their influence on biological evolution has been profound, but life on Earth has continued. This will not be the case forever. The Sun has already fused a few per cent of its hydrogen fuel into helium. The pressure in the centre has increased and the fusion rate is increasing. Since its formation, the Sun's luminosity has grown by 40 per cent. Our star will enter the red giant phase in 5.5 billion (10^9) years. The surface temperature will sink to 3000 °C, and the diameter will increase by a factor of one hundred. For this reason the temperature on Earth will rise beyond a thousand degrees, too hot for any life. Our planet will no longer be habitable.

After the red giant phase, the Sun will contract to a white dwarf and will cool over 10^{15} years. Since the size of the Sun will then be only about that of the Earth, it will not be able to radiate enough heat to warm the Earth significantly. The temperature on Earth will approach the frigidity of space at minus 270 degrees.

Perhaps life will migrate to other stars and planetary systems. However, this is not possible for infinite time. New stars still form, but the hydrogen in our galaxy will last for only some 100 million future stars. The last stars will develop at the edge of the Milky Way, possibly triggered by a collision with another galaxy. Some time in 10^{13} years the epoch of star light will end. The last white dwarfs will cool and no star will shine any more.

Galaxies lose energy through the very rare encounters between stars. Gravitational waves carry off energy, and some stars may be slingshot out of the galaxy. The orbits of the remaining stars contract and the diameter of the galaxy shrinks. The remains of stars will eventually disappear in the central black hole of the Milky Way, where gravity is so large that even the emitted light falls back. The central black hole currently contains 2.7 million solar masses and is located 25,000 light years from here.

The matter outside black holes does not live infinitely, as even protons, the most stable nucleons, will decay radioactively. According to the prevalent but still speculative theories, protons (and with them all other matter) will decay in about 10^{33} years. Their decay produces positrons and photons.

Even black holes do not live forever. They probably emit a weak thermal radiation at their horizon and thus are losing energy. After some 10^{100} years the massive black holes in the centre of galaxies will evaporate in this way and disappear. The universe will finally consist only of photons, positrons and electrons. Although the very distant future is still speculative, due to uncertainties in the physical theories, it seems unavoidable that all cosmic objects and even the universe itself will decay.

Is the universe a tragedy, where innocent individuals are bound for destruction? Is the existence of heavenly bodies, animals and human beings an absurdity without purpose or meaning?

> Thesis 2. The evolution of the universe has been extremely creative. The very possibilities for the formation of matter, galaxies, stars, planets and life have developed only in the course of time. Even today new things are forming.

In our Milky Way, a regular galaxy of a few hundred billion stars, about ten new stars are born every year. The formation of stars takes roughly ten million years. Some hundred million stars thus are forming today in our astronomical neighbourhood. The cosmos overflows with fertility.

Stars evolve from interstellar molecular clouds, well known for their beautiful, fluffy, dark structures. In places where the gas is denser, gravity attracts more gas. The fluctuation gets denser and attracts even more, so the process reinforces itself. The interstellar matter concentrates gradually into cloud cores until these collapse under their own gravity. The gas then falls freely towards the centre of the core, where the remaining angular momentum forms it to a rotating disk.

After ten million years the temperature and density in the centre become large enough to start the fusion of hydrogen to helium. Nuclear energy of stupendous proportions is unleashed and the additional gas pressure stops further contraction. In the innermost part of the vortice equilibrium between gravity and pressure forms: the star is born.

The cosmos as it appears today to the observer did not emerge in the Big Bang. Even the simple hydrogen atoms formed half a million years after the beginning. The Sun's age is only one third of that of the current universe, about 14 billion (10^9) years. Human consciousness has existed only for a few hundred thousand years, one hundred thousandth of the age of the universe, i.e. in the cosmological present.

When we look up at the starry sky on a clear night and believe that at least the stars are the same as always, this impression arises from the fact that our timescale is too small. In reality, the universe displays amazing dynamics; the origin of stars and formation of planets only represent one segment of processes that build upon earlier cosmic events such as the formation of matter out of elementary particles in the early universe or the origin of galaxies. Qualitative development is a fundamental characteristic of the cosmos, and time plays a crucial role.

The cosmos materialized not as in a theatre when the curtain rises, the stage is set, and the play begins. The universe formed much more dramatically, as if in the beginning there was only a glowing magma that solidified to stone, from which a building was made. Therein a workshop for stage design and an actors' school appeared, a stage and the auditorium were built, everything collapsed, was rebuilt etc., and finally our play started.

> Thesis 3. The notion 'God' does not appear in astrophysics. When scientists communicate their observations and theories they do not use this term.

Is a creator involved in this dynamic creativity? For more than two hundred years scientists have pointed out again and again that this hypothesis is not needed (e.g. Laplace 1799). Obviously, much remains unexplained scientifically, yet there are already models of how even the universe may have formed from a vacuum according to physical laws. In this sense there are no gaps in the rational understanding of the universe from the Big Bang to the evolution of humans that could be interpreted only as a result of the action of a supernatural being. Existing gaps are the working fields of scientists, who have the great goal to diminish or to close them.

For philosophers one essential question remains: why did something form and not nothing? The question addresses the fundamental issue of a principle behind the laws of nature. That all things have formed is indisputable, and considerations similar to those of the Greek philosophers in the fifth century BCE on the 'foundation of being' are appropriate. Its modern analogue in a dynamic universe would be a principle of structure formation. Appealing here to God's creative will, however, may introduce a mere metaphysical entity without direct relation to science or to the questioner.

> Thesis 4. The new does not emerge from nothing, but is a new organization of existing or decaying entities.

Physical theories describing the formation of the universe are still very speculative and unproven. Nevertheless, it is imaginable that the universe could have formed from a vacuum containing zero energy but obeying all physical laws known today. It could have 'borrowed' energy against gravitation during a fluctuation in the primary vacuum. It would follow from this vacuum hypothesis that the universe did not originate from nothing, but from a physical entity, the vacuum, and according to pre-existing rules.

Star formation is an example of how new structures are created even today. Nonetheless, it is not an eternal circle. When the energy is exhausted, stars shrink to white dwarf stars or explode as supernovae and heave a part of their matter and ashes into interstellar space. There, new stars form again and in addition completely new structures, planets, emerge from the cinders of previous generations of stars.

Similarly, the extreme order constituting living beings cannot last. Death is unavoidable for several reasons ranging from chemical decay to physiological deterioration. It is, on the other hand, a necessary ingredient of evolution. Animal species can persist only by selective adaptation in a sequence of generations. Through the death of individuals, a species survives when conditions for life change. In special circumstances, possibly produced by unusual environmental stress, extremely rapid evolution may lead to a new species.

> Thesis 5. Within the frame given by the conservation laws, the future is

open. The universe is not a clockwork mechanism.

Today's technology is based on conservation laws, such as the constant energy in a closed system. There are other physical parameters conserved in processes of nature. The conservation laws make it possible to predict the future of a system, as for example our solar system, including the nine planets, but only to a certain extent. The view into the future is limited for almost all natural systems because they are only weakly stable. This means that a small deviation from the initial orbit will bring the system into an orbit that deviates increasingly at an exponential rate. Such systems are called chaotic. Although the systems behave causally, their development cannot be predicted after a certain interval, called the Lyapunov time. This time horizon depends on the system and can be milliseconds in microscopic structures up to millions of years in planetary systems. The motion of the Earth, for example, cannot be predicted for more than 100 million years.

Chaos limits qualitatively the description of nature by mathematical precision, and thus the applications of science to technology. The chaotic character of nature also lowers certain expectations raised by the age of Enlightenment, when the cosmos was pictured as a machine in which individual parts fitted together like the gears of a clock, according to its given design. If a gear turns at a certain angle, another one rotates the predetermined amount. If the first gear turns at double the angle's size, the angle of rotation of the second gear doubles also. This view of the universe was, without a doubt, linear and does not describe the present world-view of science.

Another limit of the scientific knowing of the future is the uncertainty of quantum mechanical systems. As position and velocity cannot be known simultaneously and with infinite precision, the future development is given only by probabilities. In quantum mechanics, the very basis of today's physics, reality materializes when an irreversible interaction occurs, such as an observation. What lies ahead is not yet determined and will be decided only later.

The chaotic behaviour of most systems in the universe and quantum mechanical uncertainty limit the prognostic capabilities of science.

Whether this openness is intrinsic or follows necessarily from the everlimited accuracy of measurement makes no difference in practice. The future is neither fully predictable nor determined. It is open.

> Thesis 6. It is quite imaginable that something unexpected could arise in the future that would be as new as life on Earth was four billion years ago. This kind of newness certainly cannot be foretold, for such evolutions are chaotic.

The reliability of scientific predictions is very good concerning, for example, the exhaustion of an energy supply. The remaining lifetime of the Sun, some 6 billion years, is well known. Its decay is certain. All scientific prognoses of the future —whether for living creatures, planets, stars, galaxies or the universe itself—thus can only foresee decay at the last. The Sun will become cold, the Earth will lose itself in space, and even the matter in the universe will decay into radiation.

For systems with many interacting parts, like the planetary system or terrestrial weather, this is different. Their development is unpredictable after a certain time, and thus chaotic. Although the system may be in the process of decay, new structures can form spontaneously in a state of non-equilibrium at certain locations. There is an intriguing asymmetry between the decay of all objects in the universe, which we can predict quite accurately, and chaotic systems that cannot be predicted and that may even form new structures.

Most structures astronomy has detected in the universe have a touch of surprise. Most would not have been predicted if humans had been around at the time of formation. Afterwards causal laws and chance may explain them.

> Thesis 7. The universe and its development appear to be optimal for human beings. However, there is no scientifically provable hope for new beneficial development.

The universe has properties that are necessary for the developments that have led finally to the evolution of living beings. The basic physical parameters are precisely such that life could arise. The properties of the carbon nucleus, for instance, are favourable for its easy forming in nucleosynthesis, but this is not so for oxygen, the element that would have depleted carbon otherwise. The evolution time to intelligent life is about half the lifetime of a solar-like star, but not orders of magnitude longer. There are many more such fine tunings of the universe that are necessary for our existence.

The anthropic principle states that the observed cosmic and biological developments are the a priori condition for the possibility of cognition: 'What we can expect to observe must be restricted by the conditions necessary for our presence as observers' (Carter 1974). To put it more simply, to make it possible that we can wonder at all why the universe is as it is, the universe must be exactly as it is, for otherwise we would not be there to wonder. This principle proceeds from the tenet that the human being is part of the universe and has originated according to natural laws. It reminds us that, as for any observation, the limits of the measurement apparatus (in this case the observer himself) must be taken into consideration.

Historically, the anthropic principle was formulated just at the time when it became clear to astrophysicists that the universe had a beginning and that evolution began with the Big Bang. The observed coincidences are a priori conditions for the possibility of biological evolution. They must have been given before we could perceive the world at all. Certain physical, chemical and biological characteristics are required. Yet the anthropic principle is no explanation of the cosmological coincidences. As established fact that must be fulfilled by any acceptable model of the universe, it is a triviality. The anthropic principle, however, makes one conscious of how strongly human existence is grounded in the whole of the cosmos and what consequences follow as a result of this participation for our theoretical cognition.

To explain coincidences on the level of the whole universe, there appear to be three possibilities:

1. There are physical reasons, which we still do not understand, why the universe must be exactly as it is (a causal explanation).
2. There are many universes. We inhabit one that has the correct characteristics for evolution and for life (a selective explanation).
3. The universe is given a direction, the goal of which is to create life (a teleological or purpose-oriented explanation).

The usual methodology of modern science proceeds from what is observed, and seeks a causal explanation. With the selective explanation, the anthropic principle becomes a selection criterion among many universes with random characteristics. Each of these universes would have other basic constants and other conditions at the beginning. Their totality would perhaps be an infinite ensemble of universes. According to the definition of the term 'universe', we could, however, observe no other except our own. The extension of the sciences beyond our reality into other, unobservable universes is therefore a step in the metaphysical direction, from which a number of experts turn away on principle.

The teleological explanation (*telos*, Greek for 'end, goal, purpose') introduces a structure of finality into science. It has been taken into serious consideration, even though it is largely rejected, and has unleashed much emotion in the camp of rationalistic scholarship. The new law would ascribe a tendency to the cosmos that enables life to come about, similar to the characteristic of constant energy. Unlike energy conservation, for which no scientifically proven exception is known apart from temporary quantum effects, this character of finality would only guarantee the necessary conditions for life and would not be compelling. It seems unlikely that this view will ever find the kind of consensus other natural laws enjoy in physics. Nevertheless, finality is not a stranger to the analytical structure of otherwise causal physics. The second law of thermodynamics contains finality with an assertion pointing to the future—the increase in entropy—without citing a causal basis. Self-organizing processes have an attractor or a goal towards which they independently set a course. It gives them a direction towards which the causal micro-processes line up. Finality does not contradict causality and does not exonerate science from the task of finding the individual causal events.

The anthropic principle explains at least partially why the universe appears 'good' for us and made to the benefit of humanity. To sustain a development that led to conscious beings in which the universe can think about itself, the universe must have certain conditions. The anthropic principle cannot explain why there is such a development at all.

From the above discussion it must be concluded that the anthropic principle cannot be applied to the future. Some developments are predictable from conservation laws with great certainty, but they may not be 'good' for us. Some new structures are conceivable, but newness remains speculation.

> Thesis 8. Pattern recognition is an important way to perceive. We cannot mathematically predict the future, but recognize patterns in the 'signs of the times'.

Because there are these two counter-streaming, unpredictable developments of decay and formation, recognition of patterns plays an important role. Pattern recognition is a significant way of human apprehension and is distinct from pure measurement. Here we make an important step from the exact sciences to other sciences and finally in the direction of religion. Pattern recognition means that we can interpret perceptions and construct their meaning. Two steps are required.

First, out of countless perceptions and experiences human reason selects facts that are considered typical. This selection may occur unconsciously, without reflection or even by computer. Concerning the future, we search for and select the 'signs of the times'. The second step in construction is the recognition of a pattern. Patterns are derived from previous perceptions and experiences constituting mental prototypes. A pattern is recognized by its similarity to the new situation, if the probe and the example agree within a certain margin. Errors can occur when a pattern is not recognized or a pattern is erroneously found to fit. The two-step interpretation by selection and pattern recognition constitutes a successful method for solving certain problems and has important applications in technology, such as robotics.

The way we anticipate the future depends on how we interpret the present. There is a choice of various patterns: it is getting better; it remains as it has always been; it gets worse and worse; something new will appear. The fourth pattern is central for Christian hope, where the events of Good Friday and Easter are the archetype. The four patterns are diametrically different. Independent interpretations of the same present may thus contradict each other. Only later experiences will confirm or refute an interpretation.

Interpreting the present is important as the coming future may require preparation, initiative or defence. Human beings are masters of interpretation, very likely because reliable pattern recognition was a selective advantage in the evolution of the *Hominidae*. Those who interpreted well had more chances to survive and have descendants. The future punishes those who interpret wrongly.

> Thesis 9. Hope is not a scientific term. It can only grow in a trusting relationship. Such trust involves a certain foreknowledge with which a person faces the future.

Scientific predictions can be objectively justified. Hope, however, is not independent of a subject. It touches on the relationship between the subject and the world. On the basis of this relationship, reality is perceived in a different way than on the basis of the scientific method. Hopes are based upon promises, ideals or the perception of the world as creation. Hope cannot be brought about by dogmas or metaphysical constructions but must accord with one's own perceptions.

The Christian tradition does not postulate the sort of optimism in which the development of the world is seen as a straightforward progression towards the good and the reasonable. Its hope lies not in protection from crisis, but rather in the formation of newness. The last book of the Bible, the Revelation of John, expresses this perspective in apocalyptic visions. Hope is established within a divine dimension of time, namely its creativity. The crisis will be overcome, though it is not specified how this will occur in concrete terms. It is not easy for scientifically minded people to accept a hope for which there is no causal justification. The scientific pattern for 'the formation of newness' cannot establish Christian hope, but can make hope understandable by supplying relevant metaphors. As with the concept of creation, the scientific 'how' must recede into the background, where hope for the future is concerned.

The apostle Paul expressly describes the resurrection of Christ as the basis for Christian hope (1 Corinthians 15: 12-19). What took place on Good Friday followed by Easter, says hope, will occur again in some comparable fashion. The experience-pattern of crisis and redemption has this precedent by which hope can be gauged at any time. It is not surprising if Christians always come back to Good Friday and Easter. Moreover, the transcendent basis for hope becomes obvious in this prototype, since the resurrection appeared as a part of the new to come from beyond space and time. Christians hope for nothing less than newness in the realm of death and in a world of merciless decay; in religious language, they hope for a new creation.

> Thesis 10. Many of our perceptions, in particular relating to religion and expectations of the future, cannot be objective as the human being participates in and is part of the process.

Scientific measurements and observations must be reproducible and objective. The researcher is exchangeable and the result independent. In religious perceptions, on the other hand, a human being is always strongly involved. I would not say that such participating perceptions are purely subjective, as they are often reported as a relation to an outside entity. Such perceptions are universally human and change the life of many people in a visible and often very positive way. If 'reality' denotes what has a lasting effect in real life, these changes testify to the experienced reality. The human being directly takes part in the process of perception and is the observing instrument. Thus the observer is not interchangeable, as in the case of experiences of art. It follows that seminal perceptions are the very starting points of both science and religion. However, they are fundamentally different. The two fields of experiencing reality consequently span two different planes of methodology and language.

It leads to misunderstandings and false expectations in the present discourse between science and theology, when the two planes of perceptions are not clearly separated. This difference is the reason why science can neither prove the existence of God nor deny it. It is as hopeless to find a compelling trace of God in scientific results as to find a palm tree in a Canadian forest. There is no direct path from scientific measurements to religious experience.

The path can only be indirect and through the human consciousness. For example, the apparent fine-tuning of the universe to the benefit of evolution is certainly amazing. If a person on the basis of other experiences believes in God, he or she can apprehend in cosmic evolution the work of God. Only then the fact that something has formed and not nothing (the Principle of Formation) becomes what is meant by the biblical concept of divine creation. Without participating perceptions it remains an abstract principle.

It is worth recalling that no objectively certain facts are available concerning the Easter event. The Good Friday-Easter pattern makes sense only on this other level of perception—the participatory level, where subject and object meet in an interactive relationship and form a whole. So neither the pattern nor the hope can be regarded as objectified facts. Christian hope does not follow from an interpretation of nature independent of the observing person and cannot be objectively confirmed.

It cannot even be made plausible to scientific reason. Like love, hope is not compulsive, but is rather something like a gift that one can accept or not. Hope is no abstract idea, for ultimately hope becomes integral to one's humanity and changes nothing less than the condition of human life.

If we speak of 'hope contrary to all reason', we acknowledge that the factual appearances as observed in science do not define the whole of reality.

> Thesis 11. Hope is based on participating perceptions.

How does one arrive at such hope? In hope, religious experience expresses itself on the level of faith. Such experience formed originally from elements of existential sensory perception, particularly in everyday life. It also includes relational, 'interior' perceptions of wholeness, dream-like visions, and sudden insights while completely conscious. The traditional pattern helps to identify and to integrate these perceptions. Living with hope, I do not perceive time only as a sequence of causal processes or chance occurrences, and as an infinitesimally brief present. Once the hoped-for future enters the picture, time embraces duration. It is the duration of waiting until newness forms. Through attentive waiting, we may occasionally discover foreshadowings and intimations of the future newness. But this kind of perception requires patience, and a willingness to develop a reciprocal relationship to reality.

The tension between science and religion concerning the expectation of the future cannot be fully harmonized and must remain. It is the tension between practical knowledge and visionary hope. This tension is within ourselves, not between fields of inquiry, and it is an important part of reality and of our life.

> Thesis 12. Nature has always been a source of metaphors for experiences on

the level of participating perceptions. Today science has partially and unconsciously taken over this role.

The two planes come into constructive contact when a pattern of one plane serves as an image in the other. This comes about when a religious experience is expressed by a metaphor (Greek for 'transfer') from science. A metaphor transfers a well-known pattern (e.g. 'formation of new structure') into the other plane of concepts. The notion of 'hope' could thus be communicated by the following metaphor:

> Despite decay and death something new will arise out of this existence, just as our planet formed from cosmic dust, the ashes of former stars.

The hope that is expressed here cannot be deduced from the physics of planet formation, but must originate in the plane of religious perceptions where this boundless confidence is experienced.

Hope for new is one of several patterns for the interpretation of the signs of the times. If we live with this pattern, the past development of the universe may become a metaphor for the future of our existence. And more, by interpreting scientific results they are evaluated on the basis of other, additional experiences. The scientific facts then appear in another perspective and in a different light: the universe is revealed as a continuous creation not a horrible tragedy, and there is hope for creation also in the future.

References

Benz, A. (2000) *The Future of the Universe: Chance, Chaos, God?*, New York: Continuum.

Carter, B. (1974) 'Large Number Coincidences and the Anthropic Principle in Cosmology', in M.S. Longair (ed.), *Confrontation of Cosmological Theory with Observational Data*, Dordrecht: Reidel. Laplace, P.S. (1799) *Traite de la mecanique celeste*.

Perlmutter, S. *et al.* (1999) 'Measurements of Omega and Lambda from 42 High-Redshift Supernovae', *Astrophysical Journal* 517: 565-86. Riess A. *et al.* (1999) 'BVRI Light Curves for 22 Type I A Supernovae', *Astronomical Journal* 177: 707-24.

Judaism, Christianity, Islam

Hope or Fear of Our Times

Mustafa Ceric

"The evil we are talking about here was not committed by Christians, but by those who have broken all the teachings of Jesus. Those who have raped women and killed innocent people have no religion. They are simply murderers."[1] I wish Alija Izetbegovic was able to come personally to this conference and read you this and many other of his statements concerning his understanding of religion and morality in the context of world affairs of today.

Unfortunately his age and health did not allow him to be with you today in Los Angeles. He has asked me to represent him and to convey to you his warm salams, or greetings, and sincere thanks for giving him the Omar Ibn Al Khattab Distinguished Pathfinders Award for his contribution to "visionary leadership and magnificently distinguished service to Bosnia, Islam, and humanity" and for your interest in his ideas about the role of religion in today's world.

I am sure you are familiar with his work *Islam between East and West,* in which he tried to explain the role of religious morality in the context of the time of communism, hoping for Islam to be an avant-garde in promoting the morality in politics that would lead to a moral as well as political reform of society.

In the meantime, President Izetbegovic, has published other works[2] that are more autobiographical than religious in their form and content, but certainly they express his moral and political opinions concerning both national and international issues of our times. Having experienced the time of totalitarianism, President Izetbegovic is a strong advocate of fair and balanced democracy, free thought and speech, for he believed that only free men can assume moral responsibility. This, in turn, led him to the belief that only free and democratic Muslim societies can be morally strong and politically wise. In addition to that, Izetbegovic believes that a good education on all levels is the best way for Muslims to earn the rightly deserved respect of the global community.

Needless to say, I hold the same views, but I must admit that I am not able to present to you fully what Alija Izetbegovic really is in the richness of his Islamic morality and in the greatness of his political thought. However, I have humbly accepted his request and your kind invitation to come to this honorable conference with a sincere desire to share with you our Bosnian experience, which is both painful and hopeful in our search for truth, justice, peace, and reconciliation. Therefore, I am pleased and honored by Izetbegovic's choice to represent him here today and by the kind invitation of my dear brother Dr. Mahmoud M. Dakhil to witness your goodwill that is represented in such highly esteemed religious dignitaries and scholars.

The United States of America is the mightiest nation in the world today. It has a historic chance to become the greatest nation in modern history as well. Hence, it is worthy of mention here that for someone to be big and mighty does not necessary imply that he is equally great and always right. He will, however, be both great and right by promoting truth, justice, and freedom, the values that are dear to each person and every nation on our planet regardless of his or her or its religion, nationality, race, or color. This is what we, the small nations, hope for: that the big nation does not fail to be great and that the mighty does not forget to stand right. And this is exactly what I am pleased about here because I see Omar Ibn Al Khattab Foundation, the University of Southern California, Hebrew Union College-Jewish Institute of Religion, and the Institute for Advanced Catholic Studies coming together to discuss the ways that will lead all of us to the greatness of our faith in One God who created us out of a single substance and made our world rich in the diversity of our physical and spiritual being.

It is with that idea in mind that I have chosen for my presentation on this occasion the title *Judaism, Christianity; Islam: Hope or Fear of Our Times*, hoping that I will be able to highlight a long-felt need for the children of Adam and Eve and the spiritual offspring of Nuh, Ibrahim, Musa, Isa, and Muhammad (peace be upon all of them) to recognize the fact of their common spiritual

roots, so much so that there is no religious source of their own that can be properly understood without referring to the source of the other. While reading the Holy Qur'an, a Muslim cannot but feel in almost every page of it the presence of the People of Book (*Ahlu-l-kitab*). By the same token the Jews and Christians cannot read any relevant book of the world history without recognition of the Muslim presence in all fields of human life.

Sure, the Qur'an criticizes some Jews and Christians, but it does the same with some Muslims as well. It is the Muslim moral responsibility not to take advantage of the critique of others in the Holy Qur'an in order to cover the Muslims' own shortcomings. If nothing else, because the Qur'an, as the word of God, is almost unique in appreciating the goodness of people of other religions, especially of the *Yahud* and *Nasara*, the Muslims have a duty to carry out the spirit of tolerance in the midst of religious pluralism. Here is one of many verses of the Holy Qur'an that clearly indicates that fact: "Verily, those who have attained to faith (in this divine writ), as well as those who follow the Jewish faith, and the Christians, and Sabians[3]—all who believe in God and the Last Day and do righteous deeds shall have their reward with their Sustainer; and no fear need they have, and neither shall they grieve" (2:62).

Of course, it would be naive to conclude that there are no differences between Islam and other religions and, more specifically, between Islam on the one hand and Judaism and Christianity on the other. The point here is not a vague notion of poor flattering or cheap religious propaganda, but a sincere conviction based on the most important Islamic source that teaches Muslims how to cope with religious pluralism of their own and how to appreciate the fact that this world is not made up of one religion or one nation. For if God wanted the world to be so, He could make it so. Rather, He wanted the people of this world to be multiple in their religions and nations so that they may compete with each other in good deeds.

This idea of the competition in good deeds applies, especially, to these three world religions of the Book—Judaism, Christianity, and Islam—not only because of their claim to the similar heritage of the Book, but also because of their heritage of a unique historical interaction that could not be avoided in the past and their historical responsibility that cannot be ignored in the future. It is precisely in this historical unavoidability of Judaism, Christianity, and Islam that I see hope, but also, I must say, I sense a kind of fear. My hope is based on the good heart of the majority, though very often silent in its goodness, of sincere Jews, Christians, and Muslims who seek their own peace in the similarity of these religions rather than in conflict among them.

Unfortunately, there is a very loud minority in all three religions who, in fact, see in the similarity of Judaism, Christianity, and Islam the very reason for conflict rather than peace. This kind of attitude leads us almost to the conclusion that the similarity, and not the difference, provokes the conflict while the difference brings the respect. We are familiar with the history of a severe debate among the similar, not different, religious groups, the debate that has often turned into a very violent conflict. I have in mind some historical conflicts between the Sunnites and the Shiites in the Muslim religion and the conflict between the Catholics and Protestants in the case of Christianity. I am sure that such examples exist in Judaism as well.

The logic of this kind of conflict among those who are similar, whatever it may be, lies in the false notion that in order for me to keep the purity of my religion, the deep difference must be seen of the other who is similar to me, but, at the same time, his difference is not tolerated. This is, I believe, the real issue of the relationship between Judaism, Christianity, and Islam today: their similarity, not the difference in their spiritual roots; their hope, not the fear from each other; their love, not the hate of each other; and their justice toward each other, and not the oppression of each other.

Of course, I can speak on behalf of Muslims and say that we have all the more reason to remind the Jews and Christians of our similarities because we are told over and over again in the Qur'an and the Sunnah that Moses was a great prophet, while Jesus was the prophet of God who was raised up to heaven almost at the beginning of his mission (Muslims believe that Jesus was not crucified). The Muslims may disagree with Jews and Christians, but they should not show disrespect for the prophets of *Tawrat* and *Injil*.

Unfortunately, as Stephen Schwartz has observed, Muhammad has an evil reputation among Westerners that sets him apart from Moses and Jesus. Jews and Christians reject Muhammad as the apostle of a religion they fear. Jews deny that Jesus was Messiah, but many among them have come to recognize him as a great religious teacher. Little such respect has been accorded to Muhammad. Rather, the Arabian prophet has been treated with contempt, both by Jews, who have tended to ignore him, and by Christians, who load his name with insults. Islam is considered by most Westerners a hideous, bloodthirsty, intolerant, and aggressive cult, and Muhammad himself has been widely portrayed by non-Muslims as devious, brutal, and perverted. Jews carried away by outrage have fostered bestial images of Muslims. Equally biased Christians have denied that the God worshipped by Muhammad and his followers is the same as the God of Jews and Christians.[4]

I have cited this statement of Schwartz in order to show, once again, that the difficulty in our relations is not the difference, but similarity. You will notice, for example, that the above-mentioned attitudes toward the Prophet of Islam would be almost impossible to hold toward Confucius or

Buddha, because they are different and it is not difficult for us to respect their way of religion. In the spirit of our similarity, then, I would like to proceed and to remind you that the Bible says, "In the beginning, was the Word";[5] that the Qur'an asserts, "In the end will be the Word of God";[6] and that in the middle is man, hopeful to know the beginnings and fearful to meet the ends.

Would man's knowledge about the beginning improve his behavior in the middle and would his prophecies about the end make him responsible for what he says and does in the middle of all things around him? Will a common road from cosmogony to eschatology of Judaism, Christianity, and Islam lead humanity to a middle path of decent ethics and morality?

One thing is for sure: man is not eligible to know the beginning of the first creation, simply because he was not witness to the creation of the heavens and the earth, nor of the creation of his own self (Qur'an, 18:51). The same goes to his prophecies: man is not entrusted to tell when and how the end of the world should be because he is too selfish to afford the continuity of the creation after his personal departure (Qur'an, 79:42).

Instead, man is invited to have faith in the word of God and remember that the moment Adam and Eve had tasted the apple, the human story of disobedience and courage began. Their disobedience has been condemned and their courage glorified. Those who see Adam and Eve's disobedience only increase human guilt; and those who see their courage only increase human arrogance. Adam and Eve are guilty because they had broken the law; they are arrogant because they had tasted the knowledge.

Consequently Adam and Eve had to leave the peaceful garden and come to the turbulent Earth that is full of hope for their success, but also contingent with fear from their failure. Only, now they realized the significance of law and the risk of knowledge. Their repentance for disobedience

has been accepted, and their courageous adventure has been inherited. It became too late for them to go back to the garden by their knowledge alone. They had been told that they ought to earn the garden back by faith in God Almighty and by trust in the Law of His Word.

The Adam—man—and the Eve—woman— have been constantly reminded by Nuh (Noah), Ibrahim (Abraham), Musa (Moses), Isa (Jesus), and by Muhammad (peace be upon all of them) that God is with them as long as they listen to Gods guidance. They have been told not to listen to the whispering of Iblis (Satan) because he is among their worst enemies.

By Noah they were supposed to learn the necessity of building the Ark for human salvation; by Abraham they have been taught how to distinguish true God from false gods; by Moses they should have appreciated the power of law in the face of injustice; by Jesus they might have discovered the love in suffering. And by Muhammad (peace be upon all the prophets) they have been told that the secret of success in this world is in truth and justice.

Of course, man and woman have never entirely denied God's guidance. Yet they have never fully accepted it. They often wanted to lead their lives as if there were no God. Yet again they thought themselves to be like God. They liked the idea of human beings as the image of God, as if there had been no other creatures as beautiful as him or her, if God needs any image at all. It is man's desire to see himself like the image of God or to deny God altogether that led him to "taste the apple" once again. This time, his falling from the heat of the image of God to the cold reality of animal was, indeed, a big event; almost like Adam and Eve's fall from the Garden of Eden. Man was happy by the new knowledge of his beginning. He thought that he had finally freed himself from the heavy lightning of the image of God to the enlightenment of the image of his own mind. He has celebrated his new time and looked to his bright future on his own. He felt no need to apologize to anyone for taking the image of an animal, not even to monkeys, which might wonder how is it that humans want to be like monkeys. But sadly we can see that it is less probable that some monkeys become men than for some men to become monkeys in the sense of their lack of decent and responsible behavior.

However, the more man stayed in the cold reality of the world of animals, the sooner he realized how difficult it is to be like an animal. Why? It is because man is neither like God, nor is he like an animal. Man is simply like man. He is comparable only with himself. God is not comparable with anything, the least with man who likes to be like an animal. Man cannot be an image of God because he cannot be God to judge the man as God's creature. Man is too ignorant to be allowed to carry out God's final inquisition; he is too meek to hold God's power; and he is too selfish to maintain God's full justice. And man cannot be an image of an animal because he has his heart and mind. Man is too precious to God to be an object of holocaust; he is too proud to be ethnically cleansed; and he is too intelligent to allow the law of the jungle to prevail.

Hence, both according to the Bible and the Qur'an, two things we can learn from the story of Adam and Eve: first, the man's desire for eternity and his longing for a kingdom that never decays; and, second, his fear to meet the end of the things he has made to stay beyond the termination of his life on the Earth. We have plenty of examples of their desires: from the ancient time of the pyramids to the modern time of huge towers in major cities around the world.

It is, then, in his desire to be remembered and in his fear to be forgotten, that man is impatient to regain the lost eternity of Adam and is unhappy to see the end of his garden of influence on the Earth. But once again, here and now in the garden

of Earth, something like a ghost is whispering to man: "Atomic weapons and the weapons of mass destruction shall lead thee to the tree of eternity and to a kingdom that never decays."

Can Adam and Eve this time avoid the seduction of the evil voice of Satan, or are they ever destined to make the same mistakes? Is there any place left for Adam and Eve to run away from the garden of Earth with their sins? Can Adam and Eve win over the fear and fulfill the desire of humanity for eternity that is beyond the end of our temporal stay? Is humanity at the end of its history that promises a new beginning, or is it at the beginning of the end of its ever-hoped-for liberty, equality, and fraternity?

To the historian Ibn Kathir al-Qurashi al-Dimashqi (d. 1373) the history had the beginning and the end during his lifetime, so he wrote the book of *al-Bidayah wa el-Nihayah* (The Beginning and the End).[7] No, Ibn Kathir did not mean to inform us about the end of history, but rather to indicate that as far as he is concerned, history ends at his departure from the garden of Earth; the rest of it he leaves to God.

It is not unusual that some religious men who have been deeply concerned about the destiny of humanity announce from time to time the end of the world because of their impatience against the temporal imperfections. In fact, it was considered that religion is the only source for such announcements as the end of the world. Perhaps, in order to remove this kind of unpleasant reminder, Dom Aelred Graham came with an idea in 1971 to tell us about *The End of Religion*.[8] He explains how it has been thought by some that science will take the place of religion and that we will then feel safe from the fear of any kind of ends, at least the one that religion is frightening us from.

To his disappointment, however, John Horgan tells us that we are at *The End of Science*[9] and that because we face the limits of our knowledge in the twilight of the scientific age, we have to go back to some kind of religion, reminding us of the prediction of almost forgotten German philosopher Spengler, who observed in *The Decline of the West*, "As scientists become more arrogant and less tolerant of other belief systems, notably religious ones, society will rebel against science and embrace religious fundamentalism and other irrational systems of belief." Spengler predicted that "the decline of science and the resurgence of irrationality would begin at the end of millennium."[10]

After the assumed end of religion and the suspected end of science, what else can one expect from Francis Fukuyama than for him to declare *The End of History and the Last Man*?[11] Fukuyama is not afflicted with the religious pessimism of the medieval sort. This is the scholarly sophisticated mind of the modern man who sees the end of history because he cannot comprehend the world beyond his scholarly possessed ideas, as if he really possesses them for himself and for his own lifetime only. Fortunately, man does not possess the ideas. He only chooses them as they fit his particular needs or beliefs.

The same goes with the new "prophet" of the modern time Samuel Huntington, who sees the new world in the context of *The Clash of Civilizations and the Remaking of World Order*. It is not only that these two cannot go together—the clash of civilizations and the world order—but that these ideas cannot go with a sound mind of any order whatsoever.

Therefore, I tend to agree with John Lukacs that we are *At the End of an Age*[12] of scientific shortcomings and historical untruths. We are entering, or we are supposed to be entering, a new area in search for a new meaning of religion and culture, of science and history—indeed of a world order that will not end with an atomic blast or with weapons of mass destruction, but will begin with moral must and human trust that will enable

our children to remember us and not to forget us forever.

If dreaming is free of charge, without which dreaming there is no change, then let us have a dream that the wise man from the East, if he still exists, and the rational man of the West, if he still thinks, hail the moral man of the Earth, who can bear the moral must and hold fast to the human trust in the future of our world that is made to be for many tribes and nations so that they may know each other better. Why? Because I believe that neither the meek nor the aggressive will inherit the Earth, but only those who cooperate in truth, justice, peace, and reconciliation among people and nations.

Therefore, we should not allow that the already passed road of humanity be reverted from freedom to slavery, nor allow that bright science be swallowed by dark mythology, nor that the noble might be replaced by the ugly might. The future of humanity lies in our trust in God and our belief that this world is the best possible world that we could have inherited from our ancestors. Let us believe that we should not destroy it for the sake of those who will come after us, because God only knows the ends of all things and the beginnings of all springs.

All of us should stand firm in the belief that we know neither the beginning nor the end of the world. Ours is the middle of the road from the eternity (*ezel*) that is out of our touch and to the eternity (*ebed*) that is out of our reach. By the mercy of our Lord, we are not left alone in the middle of our journey from the eternity to the eternity—we have the Word of God that was in the beginning and that will be in the end. We claim that we are committed to strive for hope, love, and justice. But whose hope, whose love, and whose justice? Don't we realize that love and justice must temper the Jewish hope? Don't we, equally, see that hope and justice must follow the Christian love for a neighbor? And finally, don't we agree that hope and love must come out with the Muslim justice for all?

It is in the context of the Muslim commitment to justice for all that I would like to offer you two doctrinal and historical Islamic principles that everyone can share. First, it is the clear statement of the Holy Qur'an, "la ikraha fil-din," "Let there be no compulsion in religion,"[13] a statement that brought the idea of freedom of religion, or freedom of conscience, that is considered today to be one of the most fundamental values of our globe. Should I remind you that as recently as September 27, 1480, the Spanish sovereigns Ferdinand and Isabella issued an order to establish in their kingdoms tribunals to judge cases of "heretical depravity," to become known as the Spanish Inquisition. This fact of history Professor Benzion Netanyahu brings to our attention in this way: "The royal decree explicitly stated that the Inquisition was instituted to search out and punish converts from Judaism who transgressed against Christianity by secretly adhering to Jewish beliefs and performing rites and ceremonies of the Jews."[14]

My intention here is not to embarrass any person or religion, but to show the significance of the testimony of Stanford Shaw, the Jewish author, who has this to say about an interesting political as well as moral legacy of Islam:

> Neither the people of the Republic of Turkey nor those of Europe and America fully realize the extent to which Turkey, and the Ottoman Empire which preceded it, over the centuries served as major places of refuge for people suffering from persecution, Muslims and non-Muslims alike, from the fourteenth century to the present. In many ways, the Turks historically fulfilled the role subsequently taken up by the United States of America beginning in the late nineteenth century.[15]

I have quoted this witness not because I think that one can justify all the historical actions of the Ottoman sultans, but to demonstrate that it was due to the above-mentioned short but very powerful Qur'anic statement of the seventh century that the Muslim scholars developed the concept of the protection of five fundamental rights, what we call today "human rights," of each and every person regardless of his or her religion or nationality: the right to life (*nafs*), the right to religion (*din*), the right to freedom (*'aql*), the right to property (*mal*), and the right to dignity (*'ird*).

It is quite regrettable that the modern Muslim intelligentsia has failed to pick up on this doctrinal and historical foundation of an Islamic avant-garde for human rights to build up social, political, and moral institutions in the Muslim world that would guarantee the development of a genuine democratic system. What more is needed for the modern Muslim intelligentsia to know about the intellectual legacy of Islam after the testimony of the prominent historian Arnold Toynbee (1889-1975), who wrote concerning the work of the great Muslim intellectual Ibn Khaldun (1332-1406): "He conceived and formulated a philosophy of history which is undoubtedly the greatest work of its kind that has ever yet been produced by any mind in any time or place."[16] There is nothing to be added to this testimony, except to affirm that the failure to advance culture further lies not in Islam, but in the cultural insecurity of the modern Muslim intelligentsia that has failed to collect the delicious intellectual fruits, such as that of Ibn Khaldul and many other Muslim intellectuals.

One of the reasons that I am here in full capacity as a Muslim of the European origin is the universal declaration of equal rights that the Prophet Muhammad (peace be upon him) had delivered at one of his ceremonies on the hill of Arafat when he said: "Kullukum min adam wa'adam min turab, la fadl li'arabi 'ala 'ajami, wala li'ajami 'ala 'arabi, wala li'abyad 'ala aswad, wala li'aswad 'ala abyad ilia bitaqwa." ("You are all children of Adam, and Adam is from clay. Let there be no superiority of an Arab over a non-Arab, nor a non-Arab over an Arab, and neither shall be a superiority of a white over a black, nor a black over a white person, except by good character.")[17]

I don't know whether the American Baptist minister and leader of the civil rights movement from 1963, the most honorable Martin Luther King Jr., was aware of the above-mentioned universal declaration of the Prophet Muhammad (peace be upon him), but I do know that we are all in a desperate need today to listen to those divinely inspired messages. Of course, I am aware that my power is too frail to be Kings voice, but my heart is full of hope to have Martin Luther King's dreams today as his were yesterday that my three children will one day live in a world where they will not be judged by the faith of their heart but by the content of their character. And, I am equally enthusiastic to tell you that I believe in Martin Luther King's insight that "the choice today is not between violence or nonviolence; it is either nonviolence or nonexistence."

We should have understood by now that no one has the monopoly on righteousness, no one has the monopoly on retaliation, and no one has the monopoly on pain. On the contrary, we are all entitled to do right things and to be recognized thereby. We are all designated to strive and protect our freedoms, and we are all vulnerable to the pain, whether it comes from the democratically elected government or from voluntary suicidal individuals or groups.

In light of these thoughts I invite you to have hope, love, and justice for all that Jews, Christians, and Muslims can deliver to the world, which needs to be freed from fear and poverty now more than ever before, and I call you to join me in a Bosnian prayer:

Our Lord
Do not let success deceive us
Nor failure take us to despair!
Always remind us that failure is a temptation
That precedes success!
Our Lord
Teach us that tolerance is the highest degree of power
And the desire for revenge
The first sign of weakness!
Our Lord
If you deprive us of our property,
Give us hope!
If you grant us with success,
Give us also the will to overcome defeat!
If you take from us the blessings of health,
Provide us with the blessing of faith!
Our Lord
If we sin against people,
Give us the strength of apology
And if people sin against us,
Give us the strength of forgiveness!
Our Lord
If we forget Thee,
Do not forget us!

Notes

1. Alija Izetbegovic, "Mir je spasio Bosnu (Peace Saved Bosnia)," in *Godisnjak 2002 BZK Preporod*, Sarajevo, 2002, 20.

2. Alija Izetbegovic, *Notes from Prison, 1983-1988* (Westport, Conn.: Praeger, 2002); *Inescapable Questions (Autobiographic Notes)* (Leicester: The Islamic Foundation, 2003).

3. "The Sabians seem to have been a monotheistic religious group intermediate between Judaism and Christianity." See *The Message of the Qur'an*, translated and explained by Muhammad Asad (Gibraltar: Dar alAndalus, 1984), 14 n 49.

4. Stephen Schwartz, *The Two Faces of Islam* (New York: Doubleday, 2002), 2.

5. "The New Testament by John," in the *Holy Bible, New International Version* (Zondervan, 1993), 505.

6. "About what do they (most often) ask one another? About the great word (*al-Nabe'u-l-azim*) on which they disagree. Nay, but at the end they will come to understand it" (Qur'an, 78:1-4).

7. 'Imad el-Din ibn Kathir al-Qurashi al-Dimashqi, *el-Bidajetu we elNihajetu,* uredio 'Abdullah el-Turki (Dar el-Hidzrah, 1996).

8. Dom Aelred Graham, *The End of Religion* (New York: Harcourt Brace Jovanovich, 1971).

9. John Horgan, *The End of Science* (London: Abacus, 1998).

10. Ibid., 23-24.

11. Francis Fukuyama, *The End of History and the Last Man* (New York: Free Press, 1992).

12. John Lukacs, *At the End of an Age* (New Haven Yale University Press, 2002).

13. See *The Holy Qur'an,* translation and commentary by A.Yusif Ali (Lahore, 1934), 103.

14. See B. Netanyahu, *The Origins of the Inquisition in Fifteenth-Century Spain* (New York: Random House, 1995), 3.

15. See Standford J. Shaw, *Turkey and the Holocaust* (London: Ipswich Books, 1993), 1.

16. See Arnold Toynbee, *A Study of History* (London: Oxford University Press, 1934), vol. 3, 322.

17. See A. J. Wensinck and J. P. Mensing, *Concordance et Indicies de la Tradition Musulmane* (Leiden, 1969), vol. 7, 300.

Section 8

Religion and Science

Religion and Science

Mikael Stenmark

One issue of concern for philosophy of religion is the relationship between science and religion. In what way should we understand the relationship between two of the most influential achievements of human culture?

Philosophers have for a long time been interested in this topic, but the broader academic scene within which this discussion has taken place has drastically changed within a few decades. What once was a specialized conversation between small numbers of scholars has now become a topic for scholars from a variety of academic disciplines. This discussion has also burst on to the public scene in ways which would have been almost unthinkable in the 1970s or 1980s. There has been a veritable explosion of books, papers and conferences on science and religion, new courses on science and religion added to the curriculum, and a number of centers (e.g., the Zygon Center for Religion and Science, the Ian Ramsey Centre) and societies (e.g., the European Society for the Study of Science and Theology and the International Society for Science and Religion) have also sprung up. New journals specifically focusing on the science and religion encounter have been released such as *Zygon: Journal of Religion and Science* and *Theology and Science,* and websites launched such as *Metanexus* and *Counterbalance.*

Philosophers have, surprisingly enough, played a minor role in this new emergent interdisciplinary study of science and religion, which has instead been dominated by theologians and natural scientists. Nevertheless, the science-religion debate raises a host of interesting philosophical questions.

How to relate science and religion

One issue of interest concerns precisely how science and religion can be related. How could we, in an illuminating and unbiased way, characterize the main possible ways of relating science and religion?

A first possibility is to maintain that science and religion are rivals. They compete on the same turf and in the end one will emerge as the winner. This *conflict view* has been defended by

Mikael Stenmark, "Religion and Science," *The Routledge Companion to the Philosophy of Religion*, pp. 692-701. Copyright © 2007 by Taylor & Francis Group LLC. Reprinted with permission.

both philosophers and scientists. John Worrall maintains: 'Science and religion are in irreconcilable conflict. . . . There is no way in which you can be *both* properly scientifically minded *and* a true religious believer' (2004: 60). Edward O. Wilson writes that science will eventually be able 'to explain traditional religion . . . as a wholly material phenomenon' (1978: 192).

Conflicts between science and religion can be avoided if they are taken to be inquiries in separate domains. The *independence view* maintains that science and religion are not rivals at all because they have no turf in common. In *Rocks of Ages*, Stephen Jay Gould claims that the idea that there has been and still is a war going on between science and religion is wrong. Instead he maintains that each inquiry frames its own questions and criteria of assessment. Gould writes that 'the net, or magisterium, of science covers the empirical realm. . . . The magisterium of religion extends over questions of ultimate meaning and moral value. These two magisteria do not overlap, nor do they encompass all inquiry' (Gould 1999: 6).

Any view in between the conflict view and the independence view would have to presuppose an overlap between science and religion, that is, some area of contact. Hence, the *contact view* says that there is an intersection between science and religion. They are different practices, but science and religion overlap in some respect.

Claiming that there is a *conflict* between science and religion is not, however, a sufficient condition for being a defender of the conflict view. This is so because conflict between science and religion is compatible with both the conflict view and the contact view. Although a necessary condition for being a proponent of the conflict view is to claim that there exists a conflict between the two practices, more is needed, since this is something a spokesperson for the contact view could maintain as well. The additional requirement would, it seems, consist of the idea that religion can never be reconciled with science. One and only one of the two will stand as the winner in the end.

But here we run into problems because when scholars call certain persons advocates of the 'conflict view,' it is because they believe there is a serious and comprehensive clash between religion and science, not necessarily that there is no area of compatibility whatsoever. Ian Barbour (1997) and John Haught (1995), for instance, count not only scientific naturalists or materialists but also religious literalists as advocates of the conflict view. But even if Christian fundamentalists, for instance, see a serious and profound conflict between science and religion, they surely would deny that religion can never be reconciled with science: once scientists get their theories right, they claim, most of the conflict will disappear.

If we accept this description, then we can say that someone maintaining that there is conflict at many intersecting points between science and religion would count as a spokesperson for the conflict view rather than for the contact view. This would mean that a defender of the contact view basically believes that science and religion have different aims, means, and subject matter but that there is nevertheless some area of overlap. What this implies is that probably the most fruitful way of understanding these three science-religion views is to see them as three positions on a scale where the conflict view is located on one end and the independence view on the other with the contact view in the middle, though its boundaries are a bit fuzzy.

Different kinds of contact views

Many who are engaged in the science-religion dialogue today seem to defend some kind of contact view. Even if Barbour's 'theology of nature' entails that the main source of theology lies outside science, scientific theories may nevertheless affect the reformulation of certain religious doctrines, particularly the doctrines of creation and human nature. On these issues there is an overlap between science and religion. Richard Swinburne (1996) and probably most defenders of natural theology would think the traffic goes the other way around. The existence of God is made probable by evidence discovered by science such as the 'fine-tuned' character of the universe, namely that the fundamental parameters of the early universe seem to be fine-tuned for the conditions required for the emergence of life and intelligence.

Others have pointed to the similarities between the methodological structures of science and religion (or theology). Philip Clayton and Steven Knapp (1996) maintain that both science and theology make truth claims about reality, which could be understood in terms of a similar explanatory model, namely inference to the best explanation. Moreover, Nancey Murphy (1990) thinks that Imre Lakatos's notion of a scientific research program, with a hard core and a surrounding protective belt of auxiliary hypothesis, could successfully be applied to theology.

Some of the thinkers who have been more skeptical toward religion can also be classified as proponents of the contact view. Michael Ruse (2001), for instance, believes that there is contact, sometimes tension, and even disagreement between science and religion (more exactly between Darwinism and Christianity), but that although it is not easy for a Darwinian to be a Christian, it is possible.

What is evident, however, is that some scholars think that the overlap between science and religion is fairly limited, and the reformulation of the content of these practices will seldom be called for, whereas others think, for instance, that significant doctrinal reformulation of religion is necessary. It might therefore be fruitful to distinguish between a *weak* and a *strong* contact view. How should one make such a distinction?

One idea is to suggest, as Barbour does, that someone who limits the area of contact to metaphysical presuppositions, methods of inquiry, conceptual tools or models and the like exemplifies the weak contact view, whereas the strong contact view adds to these the theoretical content of science (theories) and religion (beliefs and stories). But suppose that someone claims that the methods of the two practices are or should be the same in the sense that the only evidence that ought to be allowed in both science and religion is observational evidence of the kind that is used in the natural sciences. Such an overlap at the methodological level between science and religion might entail far more radical changes in religion than if we maintain that, for instance, the Christian doctrine of original sin must be modified because of changes in scientific theory. The same results would follow—when it comes to theories of language—if one embraced the positivist idea that the only cognitively meaningful statements are empirical propositions verifiable by sense data. Many religious statements would then lose their cognitive status, failing even to be true or false.

But perhaps we should instead focus on the need to reformulate religion in the light of the development of science. So, whether it has to do with the aims, the means, or the result of using these means to achieve these aims (which include the formation of beliefs, stories or theories), proponents of the weak contact view maintain that substantial reformulation of religion will seldom be called for. Proponents of the strong contact view, on the other hand, claim that substantial reformulation of religious aims, methods or beliefs /doctrines will fairly frequently be called for.

Notice, however, that if we do this, we presuppose that the traffic only goes in one direction, from science to religion. This reflects the general assumption of the science-religion debate, namely that contemporary science is all right as it is; it is religion that needs to change. But the problem is that there is a significant group of scholars who do not think that science is acceptable as it is and who in various ways argue for a science shaped by religion—people who believe that there is a need to develop a 'faith-informed science' (see the last section). We need a typology which also allows for this kind of view. The suggestion is therefore that we define the *weak contact view* as the view that merely minor reformulations or changes of either science or religion are called for in the area of contact and the *strong contact* view as the view that more substantial reformulations or changes of either science or religion are called for in the area of contact.

However, if we define the strong and weak contact view in this way, then both theological conservatives like Alvin Plantinga (1991; 1996) and liberals like Gordon Kaufman (2001) would be identified as defenders of a strong contact view, even though they have radically different views. Kaufman argues that changes in scientific theory make it necessary to reconstruct the conception of God that has traditionally been endorsed by Christians, Muslims, and Jews. There is a conflict between a personal conception of God and scientific theories about cosmic and biological evolution. Plantinga, on the other hand, is ready to question in the light of his Christian beliefs parts of evolutionary theory.

It might, in other words, be useful to add another element to the typology. By adding it, we can identify not merely strong and weak versions of the contact view, but also determine whether their advocates tend, when a conflict or tension arises in the area of contact, to give priority to science or to religion. The *science-priority contact view* states that when there is a conflict in the contact area of science and religion, then a reformulation or change of religion is called for unless there are very good reasons to believe otherwise. The *religion-priority contact view* states that when

there is a conflict in the contact area of science and religion, then a reformulation or change of science is called for unless there are very good reasons to believe otherwise. Hence, Kaufman has a strong tendency to think that it is something within the practice of religion we should change, whereas Plantinga believes instead that it is something within the practice of science that needs to be altered. When a conflict or tension arises, advocates of these different views place the burden of proof on opposite sides.

A possible objection to the type of typology developed here is that it is too ahistorical, universal, and static to provide a useful map of the relationship between science and religion that people throughout the ages have advocated. This could be avoided if we understand that the characterization of different ways that the science-religion relationship developed are compatible with the idea that they can—and indeed have—changed. If we accept that science and religion are social practices, then like all other social practices, they can change over time. As a result, it is possible that at time t_1 there is no overlap between science and religion; but owing to, say, scientific theory development at time t_2, there is an area of contact between these two practices and perhaps at time t_3 there will be a union between science and religion, or vice versa. Hence there is no immediate risk that the typology proposed would turn out to be too ahistorical and static to provide a useful map of the relationship between science and religion.

It would not be too universal either, because the typology is applicable to not merely variation over time but to different kinds of sciences and different kinds of religions. In other words, science could be explicated in terms of a particular discipline like physics or biology or in terms of all the natural sciences or the natural sciences and the social sciences, and so on. Religion could be explicated not merely in terms of different religions such as Christianity, Islam, and Buddhism, but also in terms of denominations within a religion such as Orthodox, Catholic, and Protestant Christians. Hence the relationship between the natural sciences and Christianity at time t_1 might look quite different from the relationship between the natural sciences and Buddhism at time t_1.

The methodological challenge to religion

Beliefs, theories, and the like are acquired, revised, or rejected in the actual life of both science and religion. These processes involve reasoning of some sort. Do practitioners in both fields endorse the same kinds of reasoning or if not, should they endorse the same kinds of reasoning? Many have seen this as a challenge to religion. All religions face the challenge posed by the successful methodology of science. Science seems to provide a reliable—perhaps even the only reliable—path to knowledge, whereas religion seems to be subjective, emotional, and based on traditions or authorities. This constitutes the *methodological challenge to religion*.

Is it legitimate critically to challenge the way beliefs are formed, rejected, and revised in religion by taking science as the paradigm example of rationality? In the broadest sense, any 'methodology' of science and religion refers to the means of different kinds that are developed in these practices to obtain the goals that characterize these activities in question. A subset of these means is the 'epistemic' one dealing with belief formation, justification, and revision. So first, when we have a good grasp of the goals of science and religion, it seems we are in a position to determine whether the means their practitioners have developed to achieve these goals are successful, interchangeable, or movable from one particular practice to another.

Practitioners of religion and science have some aims in mind when they do what they do; so what is it that they are trying to achieve by these activities? What is offered here is an outline of how one can think about the teleology of science and religion. Roughly, we could assume that the overall aim of religion is to help people theoretically understand and practically integrate the divine dimension of reality into their lives and thereby release its capacity or value for their lives and for their existential concerns. The practitioners of religion differ in their accounts of what the appropriate means are for bringing about this change, but they seem to agree that this is a primary aim of religion. We could say that religion has a *soteriological goal*. In Christianity this typically means that salvation lies in a personal relationship with God through Jesus of Nazareth. Science, on the other hand, is generally understood to lack this kind of concern.

Typically religion also has an epistemic goal (that is, it attempts to say something true about reality), but it is subordinated to the soteriological goal. This is true, at least, in the sense that many Christians do not merely affirm the truth of beliefs such as that there is a God, that God is love, or that God created the world. Instead their primary aim is to have an appropriate relationship with God so that they can implement the divine dimension of reality in their lives. For them it is sufficient to know what is necessary for them to live the life they must, in relation to God.

Scientists have the epistemic goal of contributing to the long-term community project of understanding the natural and social world. In a similar fashion, religious practitioners may have the aim of contributing to the religious community's long-term goal of understanding the divine, to the extent that this is understood to be possible for beings in our predicament. Note that even though this formulation parallels that of science, it is a more controversial and slightly misleading characterization in the religious case. This is because in religion, the emphasis is so much on *being* religious, on *living* a life in the presence of the divine. The epistemic goal of religion is shaped by the soteriological agenda. Therefore, it is perhaps more adequate to say that the epistemic goal of Christianity, for instance, is to promote as much knowledge of God as is necessary for people to live a religious life successfully (knowing that God is love, that God wants to redeem us, and how God redeems us, etc.).

A crucial difference between the epistemic goals of the two practices is then that in science the aim is to increase the *general body of knowledge* about the social and natural world, whereas in religion it is to increase the *knowledge of each of its practitioners* to such an extent that they can live a religious life successfully. To contribute to the epistemic goal of religion is first of all to increase, up to a certain level, the religious knowledge (say, at least to the level necessary for salvation) of as many people as possible (although Judaism is one exception to this rule). It is not, as in science, to move the frontiers of knowledge of nature and society forward as much as possible.

To achieve their epistemic goal, scientists work on different problems. They specialize and there is thus a division of labor. Moreover, scientists try to provide individuals belonging to different research groups with access to the data they discover and to the theories they develop. An integrated part of this process is not only cooperation, but also competition among scientists, allowing and encouraging the critical scrutiny of other people's work. In religion, on the other hand, the process of critical evaluation is done in quite a different and less systematic way. The key question in this practice is whether the means (or in scientific terminology, the methods) that have been developed by the previous generations of practitioners of Christianity, for example, to allow contact with God, to enable its practitioners to live a Christian life successfully and to help other people become Christians, are

still appropriate, or whether instead these means need to be improved or even radically changed in some way.

So whereas the mission of science is not to have all of us give up our old occupations and become scientists, the mission of many religions is something like that; it is to make all non-religious practitioners into religious practitioners and give people the religious knowledge they need to live such lives successfully. The social organization and the process and aim of critical evaluation will then look different if you are principally concerned with the question 'How could we improve our relationship to God and make the path to salvation understandable and compelling to people who are not yet practitioners?' rather than 'How could we improve our understanding of and control over events in the natural and social world?' Therefore, differences in the teleology of scientific and religious practice explain (at least to some extent) why different means are developed to attain the goals of these two practices, and it also shows that what has been a successful means in one practice could not automatically or straightforwardly be assumed to be also a successful means in the other.

The theoretical challenge to religion

For many in the science-religion dialogue, science raises a *theoretical challenge to religion*; that is to say, current scientific theories are understood to have implications for the content of religious beliefs and theological doctrines. It is assumed that at least there is an overlap here so that a reformulation of religious ideas about God, creation, human nature, and so forth might be called for. Some of the topics discussed concern all theistic religions (at least Judaism, Christianity, and Islam); others concern more specifically Christian beliefs and doctrines.

One set of issues focuses on *conceptions of God* and the scientific account of the world. Is a belief in a personal God compatible with scientific theories or must the divine be understood differently in an age of science? Religious skeptics such as Steven Weinberg (1994) maintain that the universe offers no evidence whatsoever that any divine personality underlies the universe and conclude that therefore we should not hold such a belief or any religious belief at all. Religious theists such as John Polkinghorne (1989) would claim such compatibility whereas religious naturalists such as Kaufman (2001) would agree with Weinberg but deny that his rejection of religion is justified. Instead, the divine needs to be reinterpreted as a profound immanent mystery, as serendipitous creativity. A discussion among religious theists in the science-religion debate is whether science supports or is more in consonance with a panentheist than a classic theist conception of God.

Another important question concerns how to understand divine action within a scientifically described universe. Some agree with Paul Davies (1992) that God designed the world as a many-leveled creative process of law and change in which he endowed matter with diverse potentialities and let the world create itself. Others, like George F. R. Ellis (2002), reject this kind of revised deism and maintain that quantum indeterminacy provides the 'gate' through which God can act on the physical universe. Polkinghorne suggests instead that we should see God's action as an input of pure information. In chaos theory an infinitesimally small energy input can produce a very large change in the system. God's selection among the possibilities present in chaotic processes could bring about novel structures, and in this way God could act in the universe.

Another set of issues centers on religious and scientific *conceptions of human nature* and our place in nature. The traditional Judeo-Christian view held that the first humans, Adam and Eve, were created in the Garden of Eden. But evolutionary theory entails that there never was a paradise without conflict, death, and suffering and that we are descendents of earlier pre-human beings. Not only does it seem as if the traditional doctrine of the Fall must go and the category of sin be reinterpreted, but the question must be asked: When and how did evolving hominids become beings created in the image of God? Different solutions have been proposed. For instance, Terence Penelhum (2000) suggests that Christians have to see the doctrine of *imago Dei* not as a statement of what human beings originally were, but as a statement of what they have the capacity to be. What about religious ideas concerning a free will and evolutionary accounts that we are determined by our genes, inherited from more primitive ancestors? How could Mother Teresa's behavior on the streets of Calcutta have been an expression of genuine altruism if, as Richard Dawkins (1989) and others have maintained, she and all of us are the survival machines of selfish genes?

Many biologists in particular seem to think that evolutionary theory implies both a meaningless universe and humanity's (*Homo sapiens*) being the result of a purposeless and natural process that did not have us in mind. This idea undermines the religious belief that there is a purpose or meaning to the existence of the universe and to human life in particular. A possible response is that even if we assume that God's knowledge is limited to everything that is or has been and what follows deterministically from it, it seems as though God's ability to predict with great accuracy the outcome of future natural causes and events is enormous (Stenmark 2001). We cannot, therefore, automatically assume that what is likely given such an amount of knowledge is the same as what is likely given the scientific knowledge that we happen to have. So if God planned to create us and if it is likely that we would actually come into existence, given what God can know about the future of the evolving creation, then we could reasonably claim that we are here for a reason, and that there is a purpose in this sense to our existence. To establish the opposite conclusion seems to require more than basing our calculation of probable outcomes on current scientific theories.

Neuroscientific studies of religious experience have also received a great deal of attention in the science-religion dialogue. Studies of brain activity during religious experiences at the least make it clear that religious experiences have correlates in brain functional states, and at the most that they (or many of them) are the result of abnormal neural activities in the temporal lobes and limbic system. As Jerome Gellman (2001) points out, even if some of these studies seem to be unjustifiably reductionistic, they have relevance for the possibility of an evidential case for the validity of mystical experiences of God.

The value / ideology challenge to science

The level of engagement described so far has typically been understood in terms of the relevance of the content of particular scientific theories for religious belief. If there is any traffic, it is assumed to be one-way: from science to religion. But this third challenge changes the flow of the traffic in an interesting way. Since at least the publication of Thomas Kuhn's *The Structure of Scientific Revolution* (1962), there has been a growing awareness within the philosophy of science, and perhaps even more significantly within the sociology of science, of the role of hidden ideologies and value-commitments within scientific knowledge production. These insights seem to undermine the received conception of science, the *value-free view*, and the self-understanding many scientists have of what they are doing as scientists. This is the *value/ideology challenge to*

contemporary science. These philosophers and sociologists have instead maintained that we need a new conception of science in which science and values are explicitly linked. We need a science that is infused with or guided by values, ideology, and by extension, religion. We must develop a *value-directed view* of science because it is excessively naive to think that science is an objective and universal enterprise which does not depend on any creed or ideology.

This opens up a way from religion to science; religion should shape science because realistically all we can have is a science which in fact is an androcentric science, a feminist science, a left-wing science, a faith-informed science, and so on. Science understood in this way will be explicit about the philosophical presuppositions, value commitments, and ideological elements that shape its practitioners and their activities. Plantinga's idea of an Augustinian science and Golshani's idea of an Islamic science would be examples of this way of thinking. Plantinga writes that 'in doing Augustinian science, you start by assuming the deliverances of the [Christian] faith, employing them along with anything else you know in dealing with a given scientific problem or project' (Plantinga 1996: 377). Golshani instead advocates an Islamic science by which he means 'a science that is framed within an Islamic worldview and whose main characteristics are that it considers Allah as the Creator and Sustainer of the universe; does not limit the universe to the material world; attributes a telos to the universe; and accepts a moral order for the universe' (Golshani 2000: 4).

On the one hand, it seems fairly clear that the value-free view is losing its credibility and many engaged in the science-religion debate seem to fail to take this into account. On the other hand, it might be possible to develop a plausible conception of science that is not an example of the value-free view but which nevertheless falls short of being an instance of an Augustinian or Islamic science (e.g., Stenmark 2004; response in Ratzsch 2004).

See also Creation and divine action (Chapter 30), The cosmological argument (Chapter 32), The teleological argument (Chapter 33), The sociobiological account of religious belief (Chapter 42), Miracles (Chapter 55), Religious naturalism (Chapter 62).

References

Barbour, I. (1997) *Religion and Science,* San Francisco, CA: Harper SanFrancisco.

Clayton, P. and S. Knapp (1996) 'Rationality and Christian self-conceptions,' in M. W. Richardson and W. J. Wildman (eds) *Religion and Science,* London: Routledge.

Davies, P. (1992) *The Mind of God,* New York: Simon & Schuster.

Dawkins, R. (1989) *The Selfish Gene,* Oxford: Oxford University Press.

Ellis, G. F. R. (ed.) (2002) *The Far-Future Universe,* Radnor, PA: Templeton Foundation.

Gellman, J. (2001) *Mystical Experience of God,* Aldershot: Ashgate.

Golshani, M. (2000) 'How to make sense of "Islamic Science"?,' *American Journal of Islamic Social Sciences* 17/3 (March): 1-21.

Gould, S. J. (1999) *Rocks of Ages: Science and Religion in the Fullness of Life,* New York: Ballantine.

Haught, J. F. (1995) *Science and Religion,* New York: Paulist Press.

Kaufman, G. (2001) 'On thinking of God as serendipitous creativity,' *Journal of the American Academy of Religion* 69: 409-25.

Murphy, N. (1990) *Theology in the Age of Scientific Reasoning,* Ithaca, NY: Cornell University Press.

Penelhum, T. (2000) *Christian Ethics and Human Nature,* Harrisburg, PA: Trinity Press. Plantinga, A.

(1991) 'When faith and reason clash: evolution and the Bible,' *Christian Scholar's Review* 21: 8-32.

—(1996) 'Science: Augustinian or Duhemian?' *Faith and Philosophy* 13: 368-94.

Polkinghorne, J. (1989) *Science and Providence,* London: SPCK.

Ratzsch, D. (2004) 'Stenmark, Plantinga, and scientific neutrality,' *Faith and Philosophy* 21: 353-64.

Ruse, M. (2001) *Can a Darwinian be a Christian?,* Cambridge: Cambridge University Press.

Stenmark, M. (2001) *Scientism: Science, Ethics and Religion,* Aldershot: Ashgate.

—(2004) 'Should religion shape science?,' *Faith and Philosophy* 21: 334-52.

Swinburne, R. (1996) *Is there a God?* Oxford: Oxford University Press.

Weinberg, S. (1994) *Dreams of a Final Theory,* reprint edn, New York: Vintage.

Wilson, E. O. (1978) *On Human Nature,* Cambridge, MA: Harvard University Press.

Worrall, J. (2004) 'Science discredits religion,' in M. L. Peterson and R. J. VanArragon (eds) *Contemporary Debates in Philosophy of Religion,* Oxford: Blackwell.

Further reading

Brooke, J. H. (1991) *Science and Religion,* Cambridge: Cambridge University Press. (A historical survey ofthe interaction between science and religion.)

Stenmark, M. (2004) *How to Relate Science and Religion,* Grand Rapids, MI: Eerdmans. (Explores different models of how to relate science and religion.)

Van Huyssteen, J. W. V. (2003) *Encyclopedia of Science and Religion,* vols 1-2, New York: Thomson / Gale. (Presents all the key concepts and issues in the science-religion debate.)

It's Bigger Than You Might Think

Broadening the Science vs. Religion Debate

Jefferson M. Fish

Skeptics sometimes frame the science versus religion debate as one of knowledge and enlightenment versus ignorance and superstition. This framing oversimplifies the problem in a number of ways. It leaves the impression that worldviews rejecting religion pose no danger to science. It also fails to make distinctions between religious approaches that are hostile to science and those that are not. Similar to the way this framing implicitly views religion as unitary, it implicitly views science as unitary—ignoring the varied disciplinary perspectives on the debate. Moreover, it often assumes that "science" refers to the physical and biological sciences, thereby omitting important evidence and logic-based contributions from the social and behavioral sciences. And by implicitly treating the debate as essentially a philosophical one, it often overlooks important cultural information.

Varieties of Skeptical Experience

A series of books in recent years, including a number of best-sellers, has made a compelling intellectual case for skepticism about religion. Reading them, one is struck not only by the force of their arguments, but by how little substantive overlap exists among them. Perhaps this is because, in addition to bringing strong academic credentials, the authors come from different disciplinary backgrounds: biology (Richard Dawkins, *The God Delusion*), journalism and literature (Christopher Hitchens, *God Is Not Great*), philosophy (Daniel Dennett, *Breaking the Spell*), neuroscience (Sam Harris, *The End of Faith*), and physics (Victor Stenger, *God: The Failed Hypothesis*).

Following the spread of Islamic fundamentalism abroad and the religious right at home, these authors and others have highlighted the conflict between science and religion. In its simplest terms, the conflict is between two ways of understanding the world: evidence and logic versus unquestioned authoritative texts and faith. But to understand the conflict and its implications better, the definition needs to be expanded—from science versus religion to science versus ideology, with some forms of religion (especially those fundamentalisms currently on the rise) being a subset of the ideologies that conflict with science.

Some have claimed that there is no conflict. Stephen Jay Gould, for example, referred to the non-overlapping magisteria of science and religion, with the former describing reality—what is—and the latter dealing with values—how we ought to act. It's true that you can't derive an "ought" from an "is," but critics of religion argue that knowledge of what the world is actually like better equips one to make moral judgments than do faith and dogma. On the other hand, theologians spend a lot of time considering issues of right and wrong and engaging in moral reasoning, and these must have the effect of sharpening their thinking. Still, reasoning from those faith-based premises which are at best unverifiable (e.g., God is everywhere) and at worst demonstrably false (e.g., the universe is only six-thousand years old), can only diminish the confidence we have in their conclusions.

Science does offer the possibility of experimental ethics—using controlled studies and cross-cultural evidence to understand the sociocultural, psychological, and biological processes involved in moral reasoning, and to evaluate the empirical consequences of different values or systems of values. It is true that the results of any such investigations would have to be considered with reference to some independent criteria, so that values (or meta-values) can't be kept out of the equation. However, nonbelievers would argue that our species evolved social tendencies—albeit *tempered by widely varying cultural circumstances*—that would prove adequate to the task, without added benefit from consulting religious authority. For example, the characteristically human traits of caring for children over many years and living with one another in social groups provide a sufficient explanation for viewing murder as wrong, without recourse to the Ten Commandments.

Insisting that the two magisteria are non-overlapping also would seem to imply that certain issues are off-limits for scientific investigation. This is a bad idea, since it's quite possible that future research will have strong implications for the religious domain—for example, turning religious experiences on and off through brain stimulation or drugs (psychedelics have been known to produce the latter effect, albeit unreliably), or making people more or less moral (the latter is known to result from certain brain injuries and toxic states).

Scientists as Skeptics

Comparative studies of the religious beliefs among Americans in the various natural and social sciences have produced some variability in results, related to differences in methodologies and samples. In one study, psychology and biology had the highest proportion of atheists and agnostics (over 60 percent), while in a larger study it was biologists and physicists (over 70 percent). Still, the pattern of results is clear. The percentage of nonbelievers and doubters is highest among scientists with the strongest intellectual credentials (members of the National Academy of Sciences; professors at elite research universities), and diminishes—while still remaining high— as the distance from this peak increases.

> Nonreligious and anti-religious political ideologies have also rejected scientific evidence when it conflicts with their tenets.

One might point to the differences in rates of disbelief among the sciences to ask whether the various disciplines differ in the degree to which they encourage an application of their professional skepticism to matters of religion. And since Americans are much more religious than Europeans, the percentage of atheists and agnostics among European scientists is probably significantly higher.

The different sciences provide differing reasons for skepticism about religion. For physicists, introducing God as a cause would interfere with or contradict their extremely powerful explanatory models that go all the way back to the Big Bang. The view of God as the cause of the Big Bang has many limitations in that it's unverifiable and merely raises the further question of what caused God. In a similar way, for biologists, introducing God as a cause would interfere with or contradict their extremely powerful explanatory model of Darwinian evolution—as has been widely discussed in recent years.

For psychologists, the evidence for religious belief comes from religious experience; and a pervasive finding from the scientific study of behavior is that subjective experience does not reliably correspond to reality. From perceptual illusions to false memories to socially influenced judgments, psychologists have learned to view people's experiences as phenomena to be explained, and not to be taken at face value. Thus, intense and even life-altering religious experiences are viewed as interesting psychological phenomena, rather than as telling us something new about reality. Among the explanations available for any particular instance are: expectancy (including cultural expectations and norms), the placebo effect, suggestibility, and hypnosis; stress; grief; sleep deprivation; sensory deprivation; toxic and drug-induced states; a variety of infectious diseases, metabolic disorders, and other medical conditions; various neurological conditions, including epilepsy; and a variety of psychiatric disorders. Furthermore, many scientists have experiences of religious intensity—of natural or human-made beauty—and may even produce works of art, music, or literature. Certainly they value such experiences deeply—they just aren't likely to attribute them to the existence of a reality that contradicts scientific evidence.

Given the general principle that extraordinary claims require extraordinary evidence, it's not surprising that scientists—from whatever discipline—find that religious claims fail to meet the tests that they and their colleagues use in their everyday work. Anthropologists have provided detailed descriptions of hundreds of faithfully held, wildly different, and mutually contradictory systems of religious belief. These can't all be true, and since they're based on faith there can be no basis for deciding among them. These ethnographic studies foster what might be called "disbelief by exhaustion." Furthermore, linguistic and other scientific analyses of religious texts, as well as comparative studies of religion, all point to the human origins of religious claims. For example, one study classified over 400 societies into six different types and examined their beliefs about God. A belief in a "Supreme Creator who is active and supports human morality" was found to be most characteristic of herding societies. One can easily see that herders who care for their flocks might view people as a flock under the care of a Supreme Herder. The ancient Hebrews were a Middle Eastern herding society, so their view that "The Lord is my shepherd" is more or less what one would expect.

Ideology versus Science

History shows that religions and their associated beliefs, like other cultural phenomena, change over time. The causes of such changes are diverse and often political (like military conquest or a ruler's fiat), but it is difficult to think of a better reason than persuasion by scientific evidence. In the words of the Dalai Lama, "If science proves some belief of Buddhism wrong, then Buddhism will have to change." In contrast to fundamentalists, many believers and theologians from a variety of religions would have no problem agreeing with such a statement—substituting their own religion for Buddhism in the sentence.

Like religious fundamentalism, nonreligious and antireligious political ideologies have also rejected scientific evidence when it conflicts with their tenets. Two prominent twentieth-century examples are Lysenkoism and the racist theories of Nazi Germany. Lysenkoism was a Soviet version of Lamarck's eighteenth-century theory of the inheritance of acquired characteristics; it rejected genetic findings that conflicted with the communist ideology of environmental determinism. The Nazi theory of Aryan superiority erroneously asserted biological reasons for group differences in culture and a biological justification for exterminating inferior cultures. Many scientists were imprisoned or perished under Stalin and Hitler, and many more buckled under pressure and committed acts of scientific dishonesty as the price of self-preservation.

> Seneca recognized this nearly two thousand years ago when he wrote, "Religion is regarded by the common people as true, by the wise as false, and by the rulers as useful."

More recently in the United States we have seen a rejection of Darwinian evolution and interference with stem cell research because of conflicts with some forms of Christianity, and distortions of and impediments to research on global climate change because they conflict with capitalist ideology and economic interests. While scientists haven't been imprisoned, their employment and research funding have been threatened and there has been a chilling effect on scientists' freedom of expression.

In other words, the key conflict is not between religion and science, but between ideology and science. As far as scientists are concerned, there are two key differences between religion, communism, fascism, capitalism, and other isms on the one hand, and science on the other. The first is that ideologies know the answer before you ask the question and require their adherents to agree; and the second, more problematic one is that they also require scientists to agree.

It is both fascinating and extremely difficult to try to understand the complex interactions of nature and nurture at the various levels of gene, organism, and ecosystem; of individual, society, and culture; of patterns at a given point in time and of changes over time on scales from nanoseconds to billions of years. It takes many years of hard work to gain the technical expertise to ask the relevant questions and chip away at finding answers. So it is easy to see that many scientists view it as hubris when religious people (many of whom lack the education or interest to inform themselves) dismiss their work out of hand because it conflicts with something in a book they consider holy.

Some claim that science itself is an ideology, dogma, or religion, and point to reigning scientific orthodoxies that have been and continue to be overturned. There is a big difference, however, between the use of evidence and logic to change scientific beliefs, and the use of power and unverifiable claims to change religious ones.

Scientists are human. They are products of their own society, culture, and epoch. They have their own strengths and weaknesses; ideals, foibles, and prejudices; and in their private lives may have strongly held religious or political beliefs. These may even influence the questions they investigate, or may create psychological blinders that lead them to misinterpret their findings. But science itself, with its emphasis on open discussion, skepticism, and testing alternative explanations, and its reliance on evidence and logic, contains a built-in corrective feedback mechanism that ideologies lack.

Religion, like other group identities, serves to create an us-versus-them division that can be used to further many ends. It unites a large group by convincing members that they share a common identity and interests, and disciplines wayward members. Ethnocentrism—viewing the world from the perspective of one's group—is a key element in holding groups together, whether united by religion, political ideology, or other social identities such as race, class, or gender (or some combination of any of those factors). And when a group is internally united by its ideology and ethnocentrically opposed to outsiders, it is easy to see how it might want to impose its ideology on others—including both potential members, and opponents such as scientists.

It is this coercive power of ideologies that constitutes the real problem for science.

And yet ideologies are extremely useful. Anyone who has tried to mobilize individuals to act knows how difficult it is; but governments need to do this on a massive scale. Dictatorships can use brute force, but democracies need ways to motivate the masses—to get people to want to do what their leaders want, without feeling that they are merely doing their bidding. Seneca recognized this nearly two thousand years ago when he wrote, "Religion is regarded by the common people as true, by the wise as false, and by the rulers as useful." During the Cold War, for example, when the Soviet Union suppressed religious expression, it was a useful tactic for the United States Government to contrast American religiosity with "godless Communism;" and the words "under God" were added to the Pledge of Allegiance. (Perhaps this tactic has outlived its usefulness. If we are now to be mobilized in a war against Islamic extremism, where religious conformity is forced on many people against their will, a secular state with individuals having the right to practice any religion or no religion would seem to have more appeal in the Muslim world than a Christian crusade pitting "our" religion against "theirs.")

Even so, it's understandable to ask, why now? Why are fundamentalist, anti-scientific ideologies spreading rather than declining?

The Contributions of Science to Anti-Science

During the nineteenth century, as the United States population advanced westward, displacing the indigenous peoples in its path, a religious movement known as the Ghost Dance spread among Native Americans of the Great Plains. In one version of the movement, the spiritual power of Ghost Shirts was said to protect their wearers from bullets—a claim demonstrated to be false when over 150 Lakota Sioux died at Wounded Knee.

Revitalization movements like the Ghost Dance occur during periods of great change, when old social forms no longer enable people to satisfy their needs. Such movements are usually transient and can be seen as rear-guard actions, bound to fail (though perhaps at catastrophic cost) before the inevitable adjustment to the new realities of the natural and social environment. Calls for Islam (or other fundamentalisms) to "accommodate to modernity" recognize that some cultural beliefs—no matter how widespread or useful they may have been in the past—are no longer adequate to functioning in the twenty-first century. It is noteworthy that these revitalization movements are occurring in the West—especially the United States—and not just in the less-developed Muslim world.

Meanwhile, the rate of change appears to be—if anything—accelerating. Whether we speak of technological innovation and economic globalization, or of the population explosion, environmental devastation, depletion of natural resources, and climate change, not only does change take place on a breathtaking scale, but it is often for the worse. Under conditions of pervasive and continuous change, the future is unpredictable. This means that, while the old ideologies may have to change or disappear, there will be no stable social or natural environment in the foreseeable future to which new social forms can adapt.

The best we can hope for is a world in which rapid and unpredictable change is understood to be normal, and cultural adaptation is seen as a rapidly evolving process, rather than the continuation of cherished traditions. Since cultural forms tend (almost by definition) toward self-perpetuation, one must be skeptical about this actually occurring. Furthermore, the fruits of science have helped people to live longer, and older people adapt to change less easily and often become more religious. Thus, both science-caused change and science-caused longevity may indirectly contribute to the rise in anti-science ideologies.

In summary, broadening the debate from science versus religion to science versus ideology, highlighting the differing contributions of the various sciences to the debate, and especially adding the knowledge and perspectives of the social and behavioral sciences to the mix create the context for a greater breadth and depth of understanding to the issues involved.

Jefferson M. Fish is a retired psychology professor and the author or editor of ten books dealing with social, cultural, and behavioral issues. His eleventh (in press) is titled *The Concept of Race and Psychotherapy.* He also writes a blog at *Psychology Today* (http://www.psychologytoday.com/blog/looking-in-the-cultural-nriirror).